For Sinners Only

For Sinners Only

The Book of the Oxford Groups

By

A. J. Russell

BottomoftheHillPublishing.com

ISBN: 978-1-4837-0455-5

Content

FOR SINNERS ONLY

Into the woods my Master went,
Clean for-spent, clean for-spent,
Into the woods my Master came,
For-spent with love and shame.
But the olives they were not blind to Him,
The little grey leaves were kind to Him;
The thorn-tree had a mind to Him
When into the woods He came.

Out of the woods my Master went,
And He was well content.
Out of the woods my Master came,
Content with death and shame.
When Death and Shame would woo Him last
From under the trees they drew Him last; '
Twas on a tree they slew Him -- last!
When out of the woods He came.
"A BALLAD Of THE TREES AND THE MASTER"
 quoted from the poems of the Sydney Lanier.

Chapter One

THE VOICE FROM THE BLUE

This is a book about sinners, for sinners, by quite a big sinner.

You may not like it. You may even hate it, as some are sure to do.

You may dislike the theme, for, though it introduces lovely people, it comes to grips with an unlovely subject. And solves its riddle.

You may dislike the characters as they are limned in print, but not in real life. As they are all living, you may encounter them yourself someday, and discover their excellence. At least one will live on as an historic figure when this generation has merged with the ages. Perhaps many.

Meanwhile, none can disprove the contents of this book or avoid its challenge. The story is true; the challenge is to you.

From the end of 1923 until the middle of 1926 I was Literary Editor of perhaps the most virile and progressive London daily newspaper. During that period certain events happened which drew me into the heart of the most astonishing group of people I shall ever meet. To-day groups of them are sprinkled about the earth changing the lives of those they encounter, giving all they possess and asking no return.

They are not an organization. None can tell their number. For in their own words: "You can't join; you can't resign; you are either in or out by the quality of the life you live."

They are probably the most extraordinary association of Christian adventurers since the first century. It is much too early yet to forecast their destiny. Their movement, in its sweep, may take one of two forms: it may become just another gem or facet of Christendom like those affectionately associated with Augustine, Francis, Luther, Wesley, Booth, and Moody; or it may speed up the re-union of Christendom, even Catholic and Protestant. It may revive first-century Christianity in every denomination, expel compromise from the lives of nominal Christians, make the church a true healer of broken homes, give purpose and direction to purposeless and misguided lives, set aloft to a fiery cross in every office, workshop, and institution, and really start the Christian millennium in this our twentieth-century.

As Literary Editor my job was to provide compelling newspaper features to engage the public interest and expand our circulation. In a surprising manner I stumbled on two unusual means of achieving my purpose, which I found were two cardinal practices of the amazing group I was subsequently to meet. I called these means Inspiration and Confession. They called them Guidance and Sharing.

It was Saturday, my free day, usually spent in my garden at Kent. Not that I enjoyed gardening, but it was a good exercise and kept me from the race-course, where I had spent many more exciting and expensive holidays.

I worked on, thinking of nothing in particular. Suddenly a strange experience came to me. There seemed to be a faint electrical crackling in the clear air about me. There was positively nobody else in the garden, but someone or something spoke to me: a voice that was audible and yet (paradoxically enough) quite soundless. That seems the only way to express what I shall always believe was a supernatural experience.

I felt a message impinge on my brain from the air. It alighted softly like the caress of a leaf or the touch of a gentle zephyr. It was accompanied by a sense of exaltation both pleasurable and unforgivable.

As to the message, there was nothing particularly striking about it, though when translated into action it produced phenomenal results. At this stage I do not clearly remember the exact phrase that came. I was just told to get twelve novelists to confess their religious beliefs in our newspaper. Apparently a good idea, but nothing to differentiate it from others that have come to me and thousands of other people. Only -- that queer feeling of its being implanted from without, perhaps for some specific purpose. And the pleasurable physical and spiritual reaction which attended it.

Almost immediately afterwards, both the idea and the incident tucked themselves away in the recesses of my mind and were completely forgotten for several months. Then one day, in early September 1924, I was asked to provide a good series for an autumn circulation-raising campaign on which a fairly large sum of money could be spent on publicity.

I went back to my room and began to think. Then the memory of that spring day in my garden returned. Intuitively I knew that here was the right subject already prepared. It was fortunate I had forgotten the message until now, the ideal period of the newspaper year to launch a new series. It would just catch the public returning from the holidays for the autumn.

Before then and since, when advocating other ideas on which large sums of money had to be risked, I may have felt trepidation. The arguments FOR were these; the arguments AGAINST were those. But this time I had a subtle confidence that some mysterious force supported the proposal and that nothing could prevent it succeeding. Naturally, psychiatrists would throw doubts on the supernatural origin of this series, and ascribe my experience to an emotional disturbance of the endocrine glands; or something thrown out by the subconscious. Let them. But I wish they could make those same glands work or that same subconscious self get busy whenever I am in need of help.

It is comparatively easy to get a good idea accepted, but far harder to get a company of famous novelists to come in on it, sensitive as they are to their own dignity and status, especially when it means disclosing their private life to the curious multitude. Ten writers of outstanding eminence, all well known in England and most of them well known in America, were intrigued by our extraordinary request and readily agreed to contribute. They were:

Arnold Bennett	Hugh Walpole
Sir Arthur Conan Doyle	Compton Mackenzie
Henry Arthur Jones	Rebecca West
Israel Zangwill	E. Philips Oppenheim
J. D. Beresford	H. de Vere Stacpoole

I forget why the number of novelist contributors was reduced from twelve to ten, the figure I had been given, but I remember this series ended far too soon, although we added one article from an anonymous correspondent, a second by Sir Arthur Conan Doyle, and two extra by the Bishop of London.

Giving "an unknown man" a chance to join up with some of the best writers in England was a happy idea (suggested by "The Unknown Warrior") which proved very popular. Of thousands essayed to air their religious views in conjunction with celebrated novelists, I selected the winning article. It contained an illuminating reference to a common failing of our readers and of myself, and because it was a clear statement of simple Christian faith that the masses would understand.

"The gambling instinct," said the Unknown Writer, "so often perverted and used for unworthy ends, is one of the most valuable instincts processed by man, and nowhere does it find a truer or more complete outlet and fulfillment than in religion. . . ." The writer continued: "Religion is betting your life and there is a God. I decided to bet my life there is a God, and more and more as the years go by I find that in so far as I yield up my will to God and open my heart to His indwelling, in so far as I try to live out my life in the Christ-spirit, the experiment works!"

Here, I thought, was something different for our friend the gambler: the man who was so consistently accused of being in the wrong -- praise from the quarter which usually attacked him. His praises could be used to prove Christianity. God wanted gamblers. Back God and watch Him win your own Derby. Perhaps an old idea to some in the Churches, but to the average gambler it was NEWS.

A born gambler myself, I had indulged a gambling instinct in the City, the casino, on the race-course. Like all gamblers, I had my successes. An occasional brief spell of victory, and then losses. Invariably I ended every gambling bout with a deficit balance, however "inside" the information. I was often right inside being "inside" -- however posh is the gamble, however long or short I went or held on. At last I came to believe that some little imp of misguidance had been specially delegated to perch himself at my ear and whisper the wrong advice whenever I gambled.

Curiously enough, I was shortly to find the gambling instinct strongly in evidence among the group of people I am about to describe. They are gamblers all; gambling recklessly with their own lives -- gambling on God.

As only "unknown men" had been asked to contribute the eleventh article, I was amused to hear a laughing feminine voice at the end of my telephone, announce that she was the author of the anonymous article we had just published. To make quite certain, I asked for a specimen of her handwriting. It corresponded with the written article. I asked her if she wanted money. She said "No." Further proof. And she called -- tall, thirtyish, and attractive, she seemed to me. I asked her who she was. She hesitated. She asked me to promise never to publish her name and I promised.

There are princesses in the movement dealt with in this book. But without her saying that she is a princess, I can state that her home is an English palace, though she was not living in it. At the time she was suffering from an apparently incurable disease, but had given her life to social work in a London slum. As her illness kept her indoors for a good part of the day, I advised her to drop her self-immolation in squalor and returned to the country and sunshine. She laughed at my lack of understanding, and went back to her social service. Some years after, she wrote me a letter appreciating the work of the people described in this book and reminding me of my bad advice. Instead of going to the country for a sunshine "cure," she had worked on in the slum for her Lord -- and been marvelously restored to health!

She told me she had written her manuscript for "My Religion" under what she believed to be "direct guidance," although not without trepidation, as she saw the invitation was only extended to men. But she had written a letter of explanation giving her full name, which somehow escaped my notice. Her article came to me interred in a high pile of manuscripts, written on both sides of the paper (sin of sins in journalism). The opinion was more than once expressed that her contribution, breathing as it did the spirit of confident faith and loving understanding of the prodigal mind, was the best of all. I am sure it did the most good.

Contributors to the "My Religion" series were not hampered by editorial restrictions. They could advocate whatever religious gain shows. If they had none, they could let their article explain why, provided there was no blasphemy. Judged by their writings, they were not a deeply spiritual company. Some were believing Christians; some were agnostics; all were honest. Compton McKenzie (a great writer) wrote a strong plea to Roman Catholicism, and the late Sir Arthur Conan Doyle for Spiritualism. I enjoyed the article by Hugh Walpole, who revealed himself as the typical son of a bishop. His article was well-liked, as was that Rebecca West, who wrote with her usual brilliance. Not one tried to define the word Religion, but that omission was atoned for by Father Roland Knox, who, because of the interest awakened by this and subsequent religious series, which this one evoked, wrote a book dealing with the phenomenon of Feet Street's sudden interest in religion. His title was uncomplimentary, though he was not unfriendly. It suggested that we were Calibans of Grub Street. There was no congestion that we might be practical mystics.

Father Knox showed us that religion was something which restrained us from doing what otherwise we might do, just as conquered people were restrained by their conquerors, foot on neck, in the bad old days when power was as much synonym for right as money is to-day.

Many beautiful passages were contained in the articles written by these representative novelists describing their religion. Outstanding among them, like St. Paul's Cathedral, was a marvelous symphony in prose by that delightful playwright, Henry Arthur

Jones, which is surely destined for immortality. Its sheer beauty stood out in clear relief as I read the article, and has haunted me ever since. I turned to my little staff and read it over for their delectation. Listen to the song behind the screen of words, the yearning and the heartbeat of a lovable Englishman:

"Whatever call to wander in strangely haunted spheres of ether, or fields asphodel, in new moods of being, amid new duties and new pleasure; whatever call to prolong and fulfill its existence my spirit may obey when it has earned its release from the flesh, it is to this earth that it turns and returns and passionately clings to-day; this earth that is the mother of all I'm know and feel, this earth where I have lived and sinned and suffered and loved and fought and stumbled and tramped and despaired and laughed and wept and eaten my fill and drunk deep draughts of pleasure and success and bitter cups of misery and defeat and shame; this earth whose dawns and sunsets and variegated pageantries are nicely suited to my eyes and her harmonies and discords exactly tuned to my years; this earth whose biting winds and angry hailstorms have buffeted me, but whose sunny skies and blue haleyon days have restored me -- this very earth, the only place where my foot finds firm standing and where my spirit feels at home."

Sir Arthur Conan Doyle and Henry Arthur Jones were friends; if otherwise, this article would have made them friendly. For in it Henry Arthur also declared that no future state would be intolerable for him if he found Sir Arthur waiting at the entrance to greet him. In rejoinder Sir Arthur quoted the "asphodel" passage in a public address and commented: "I have looked upon Henry Arthur Jones as one of the very first -- if not the very first -- prose-writers that we possess. He has that rare gift of rhythm which marks a great artist. For this alone his article would be memorable. There are few living men who can write prose like that."

Praise indeed of one master by another, both of whom have since "earned released from the flesh."

"My Religion" ran with smoothness from start to finish, with the staff more excited than I have ever seen journalists excited by newspaper articles. And this by a simple series on religion in a street swarming with Pagans.

As for the public, they leapt for it. During a part of the run the circulation-staff was unable to cope with the demand. Each morning for a fortnight Young England on its way to the office scrambled for, almost fought for, bookstall copies of the morning newspaper giving it something up-to-date in religion. Arnold Bennett tramped the streets of Liverpool vainly seeking a newsstand not sold out on the opening day, the day he led off. Then he returned to his hotel and wrote amusingly to the Editor gently lampooning our circulation department. Yet probably he, too, had not foreseen how vast could be the public demand for the sharing of religious experiences by celebrated novelists.

Arnold Bennett's opening article gave our church-going readers a tremendous jolt. And no wonder! Had he not been asked to modify his language he would have shocked them more. He only agreed to his article be modified when I pleaded that we might harm the baby -- the newspaper. I said that our church-going readers would think we were turned atheist and leave us. He spoke somewhat peevishly about one whose views counted with us and who might disagree with our request, and then decided to cut his articles lightly, though reiterating he was doing it against his better judgment.

As it appeared, his self-censored article was the worst attack on Christianity I have ever seen in a respectable and popular English newspaper.

"It is curious," said Arnold Bennett, "how bold some very ordinary statements seem when they are put into print in a popular newspaper. I do not believe, and never have at any time believed, in a divinity of Christ, the Virgin birth, immaculate conception; and heaven, hell, the immortality of the soul, the divine inspiration of the Bible."

Quite a comprehensive Cardinal-of-Rheims catalog of fearless belief. No wonder half of England rose up to answer him, many to disapprove his opening statements by his later admission of a leaning towards a future life. No wonder that he was vigorously attacked in the religious Press and in the pulpits all over Great Britain. Yet "the Unknown Man" (who spoke in the spirit of the characters of this book) was that among the critics. She understood exactly Arnold Bennett's attitude, the position he had reached, and the reason why he could not say more. To attack him, she said, was wrong when he was so obviously expressing his true opinion. How could a man who had not been born to this Spirit write otherwise?

The public interest awakened by the unusual feature was early reflected in the Editors mail-bag, which must have been about the largest ever prompted by a straightforward literary series. The letters were opened, but the staff was too small to read them thoroughly. They grew into a vast heap on one side of my room, into which I occasionally dug for interesting contributions.

London's society was aroused, as never before, by religious articles in popular Press. The provinces read widely and eagerly. Bishops and clergy swung into the debate. A swarm of novelists had invaded their realm. They had a right and a desire to be heard on the same all-important subject. Late Archbishop of Canterbury (Dr. Davidson), reluctant to be disturbed by newspaper religion, wagged his statesman's head and elected to make a public reference to the series that everybody was discussing.

From the first it had been my intention to give the feature a definitely pro-Christian bias, and the replies of the bishops, clergy and religiously-minded readers, as well as some of the articles, were more than adequate for that purpose.

The same series was afterwards sold to America, where it ran in a chain of newspapers, and it was reproduced in a book form both in England and in the United States. The theme was also adapted for America by the publication of a new series entitled "My Religion" by "Ten American Novelists."

Echoes of the original stir in London are still heard.

Rebecca West wrote in a London journal for writers saying that the author of "My Religion" had shown himself a journalistic genius. I thought so, too, and wished I could have given her the authors name. But the mysterious voice that came to me from the spirit-world had left no name.

What was the reason for the astonishing success of the series? In the shrewd opinion of the proprietor it was the emphasis on the word "My" in the title -- an opinion I was to hear endorsed again and again when investigating the Oxford Group and their practice of "Sharing" experiences.

We had induced celebrated writers to confess their religious convictions, and in so doing had merely re-discovered a simple truth which religion had learned years ago: there is always a public eager to hear a man's own story of his search for God, if haply he might find Him.

For was not a method by which the early Apostles spread Christianity through a Pagan world?

Chapter Two

The Three Troubadours

It was January 1931. Seven years had passed since the "My Religion" feature was released on a surprised public. For nearly five years I had held the managerial chair of our Sunday newspaper, to which I had been promoted possibly as a cynical reward for success in religion.

In January 1930 the newspaper was doing magnificently. Good features, bright news stood, bold, original publicity, and the developing momentum of past efforts had combined to double our sales, although the depression had descended upon Britain.

Only once during that seven years did I experience a repetition of the supernatural guidance which preceded "My Religion." But lest it be assumed that we expanded our sales only by supernatural suggestion, I should say here that afterwards an idea came to me without supernatural accompaniments which gave us a jump of over four hundred thousand in circulation, settling down into a permanent increase of more than one hundred thousand.

But the theme in this book is not the "scoops" that certain newspapers have secured, but the "scoop" that every newspaper missed.

I was still hankering after another series of the "My Religion" order to give the circulation of one of our newspapers a spring flare-up. One Sunday morning I was sitting in a Presbyterian church in Orpington, Kent, when the minister, the Rev. J. M. Fergusson, M. A., subsequently Moderator of the Presbyterian Church of England, dropped a few complementary words about a new religious movement emanating from Oxford University known as the Oxford Group, that he said was spreading rapidly through various countries, including South Africa.

A new religious movement spreading out from Oxford University! That was the only point in the minister's sermon I remember. Here was a fresh trail of thought. Several flourishing religious movements had started in this intellectual centre of England, as everyone knew. It was about time for another religious revival of sorts in Britain. The last had come from Wales. That the new ones should emanate from Oxford was befitting. Oxford would contribute the dignity so essential to a revival of religion. There was only one Institution in England more suitable as a starting-point when regarded as news, for Cambridge had never yet produced a real live revival. One had pleasant memories of visits to both Oxford and Cambridge, notably as a member of ex-President Roosevelt's party when "Teddy" was on his world tour, but mostly I thought of Cambridge as the sports University, and of Oxford as the home of new religions. A reversal of that order would be interesting news.

I've visualized "Oxford's New Religious Movement" with our columns thrown wide open for the views of every Tom, Dick and Harry in the land; yet a wisely-guided feature inculcating much sound and helpful religious teaching. Vaguely I was aware I should again be skimming the cream from both worlds.

But why wait until Monday for the start? That Sunday evening I telephoned the minister and asked for more particulars. He told me all he knew on the subject. Not much, but he believed that the leader, known to his intimates as "Frank," lived very close to God.

Next day a disappointment: having sent to our newspaper library, cynically known as "the Cemetery" for "clippings" about Frank and his movement, I discovered the Oxford Group had existed for several years; that it was vaguely known in Fleet Street, and had been casually referred to in our own daily newspaper. Then I remembered reading about the beginnings of the Group in Oxford in newspaper reports distinctly unfriendly which had repelled me at the time. But it had escaped my notice that a number of distinguished Oxford dons had joined in a letter to the Press protesting against the unfairness of these criticisms. Speaking from observation of the results, they said newspaper criticisms distorted the spirit of the work through the misunderstanding and unfounded rumor.

This was a blow! Not much hope of turning this old stuff into a successful religious series to awaken England. The news had already broken, strictures had been passed on the informality of procedure and the emphasis on sin. Now I understood why several years had a lapse and no journalist had been enterprising enough to advise his newspaper to espouse the Oxford Group. Still, I was unwilling to be put off. There could not be much wrong with teaching, or it would not be permitted in Oxford University. They professed to test all they said and did by the standards of absolute love to all, absolute purity, absolute unselfishness, absolute honesty. Surely there was not much wrong with a movement squaring up to those ideals. Old news though it was, when judged by Fleet

Streets up-to-dateness, I felt there was a good story somewhere in ancient times and that it is an unusual and growing movement -- spreading worldwide from Oxford. And good circulation as well.

The Journal's thought in a situation in this kind may be, "If you can't praise, punch." A lady novelist strongly advised me to attack. But how good was one attack on a religious movement which had the tacit approval of Oxford University? More than one reckless journalist has attacked this movement without understanding its genius, for the attack is always more interesting copy than the eulogy. There are so many opportunities for the latter and so few to attack in safety. For the English libel law is an inter-presence menace. Merely to ridicule a person in print is to invite an expensive law-suit involving big damages. Rarely do newspapers say all they think, for they may have to pay more than a penny for their thoughts. An occasional target like the Oxford Group, that does not shoot back is sometimes a most welcome discovery.

I had no wish to attack the Oxford Group, for I believed in Christianity, and a closer study of the "clippings" showed definitely that the leaders did too, even if they had a new and perhaps uncomfortable way of putting it over. Moreover, I believed it necessary and possible to modernize the Christian appeal, and perhaps "Frank's" unusual methods and teaching, already making a great headway in Oxford, might be just the way to do it. One is the 'been blinded' way by a little hostility and some ridicule; they were necessary to any new movement, religious or secular with a chance of winning through. Luther had lots of it. So had St. Frances. Wesley had his full share. Booth was ridiculed and pelted. This Group was in the right tradition of successful religious movements. And -- one could not dodge the fact -- it had a foothold in Oxford, the intellectual and cultural centre of England.

I determined to interview "Frank" without delay. Where did he live? No one seemed to know. After some difficulty, I located his quarters at Brown's Hotel, Dover Street, London.

The last time I was at Brown's Hotel I was the guest of a gentleman racehorse trainer with whom I collaborated in the writing of some exciting Turf reminiscences. Judging by the remark of "The Unknown Man" in the "My Religion" series that faith is natural to the born gambler, my return to Brown's Hotel to see a man of God instead of a racehorse trainer was the natural step forward in spiritual growth.

Frank's address at Brown's Hotel puzzled me, for it is a good hotel, much used by the aristocracy: the best county families were often to be found there when in town. But hardly the location, I felt, for a modern Elijah. Yet every man of God has to be housed somewhere if he elects to live in the English climate. He cannot deliver his message under a country hedge to the cows, or spend his energy preaching to the birds, like St. Francis. No one doubted that the Piccadilly area around Brown's Hotel needed more of a spiritual shake-up than a country village. Moreover, Frank was a Bishop of Souls, but had no bishop's palace, not even a vicarage, only a hotel point of contact with those people described as "the up outs," so often overlooked in the life-changing process, and so useful when changed, whether they be twentieth-century English noblemen or the Roman Emperor Constantine. And Frank was quartered in Brown's Hotel at specially reasonable terms. Sometime afterwards I discovered that he had often worked day and night among the unprivileged and "down and out," and was ever at home to all men and with all men, in palace or tenement.

At Brown's Hotel I was told that "Frank" was in South America, though three other leaders of the Group were in London. They accepted my invitation to tea in my office the next afternoon. I was anxious to look them over and take their measurements, and instructed my secretary to use her feminine powers of quick observation and to make notes about them in their presence, for they would not suspect her of doing it. She did.

I have lost her notes, but remember a good point she made -- their strangely natural way of mentioning God and Christ, without that apologetic halting so noticeable with most of us. My three callers were Garrett the I am, John Roots (both clergymen of the Anglican Communion and sons of bishops), and Charles Haines, a bronzed and athletic young Quaker; all in mufti.

These were three exceedingly likable young men, smartly dressed and radiating good feeling, kindliness and self-possession. Evidently "Frank" knew how to choose men.

We talked for two hours, or perhaps three, and they explained what their movement stood for. Their talk intrigued me. They had intelligence, zeal, culture and good looks. I liked their radiant appearance, their frankness and the way Garrett Stearly beamed at me through his horn-rimmed spectacles. I liked the well-groomed strength of Charles Haines and the boyish enthusiasm of John Roots, son of the Bishop of Hankow. Later I learned that John Roots was a capable journalist and a brilliant writer. Already their coming had brought an unusual feeling, a freshness and tranquility, into the rather soiled and sometimes sordid atmosphere of

Fleet Street.

Out of that strange first meeting came the impression that these men had voluntarily lost the world in order thereby to change the world. They are the exact opposite of the "go-getter" type one habitually encountered in business. Though they were no longer masters of their fate or captains of their souls, they had a quiet strength, a relentless purpose which were already bringing astounding results.

For them nothing was casual. God had a plan. They were trying to fit in with it. Knowledge of that plan, God's guidance and God's power were available for all who chose to work with that plan. This guidance is an eye and in every form of self-determination. God-guidance in God's strength could be the normal experience of everybody at all times, they asserted. When three B.A.'s arrive with the remark that they were specially guided to accept the invitation one must take the visit as complementary, even though doubting their contention.

Many extraordinary callers had come my way in journalism: a man sentenced to death for the most sensational murder in England and reprieved by Winston Churchill; another, afterwards hanged for a "good murder" -- as Fleet Street would express it; detectives who caught most of the notorious murderers of my time; famous statesmen; the "Man Who Won the War"; boxing champions and best-selling novelists; singers and famous players; the World's Fastest Motorist; film stars, sporting men, racing men and a galaxy of forgotten celebrities. Once the Prince of Wales walked up the stairs and interrogated the commissioner on the landing outside my room and was half-way down the street before he was recognized.

But the radiant Three were the first callers at my office to claim they had been guided my way by God.

When I asked one of the leaders of the Oxford Group who was the founder of the movement, he replied with simple conviction:

"The Holy Spirit."

So that was the amazing claim which had escaped Fleet Street's attention. *Not a man, but the Holy Spirit, had founded a new religious movement in Oxford University, and here were three of His representatives.*

Either the most blatant piece of post-war blasphemy, or a movement that might accomplish anything. And worth investigating, even though it was somewhat late in the day. Moreover, I had unearthed a fresh point. And that was NEWS.

There was nothing fanatical about the way the Three Troubadours stated their case, which they claimed to be strictly Orthodox. True, point for point, and to the New Testament, though for
me a new way of looking at the New Testament. They regarded it as
not so much a set of rulings that are arguments by the careful ob-
servance of which one acquired a safe seat in Heaven, but pictures
-- "movies" if you will -- or revelations of what was bound to take
place in any age, in any life entirely surrendered to the will of God.

If they were completely surrendered, as the Apostles were surrendered -- with Jesus Christ the Master in every area of their
life -- and inspired others to be likewise surrendered, there must
be kindred results. In Coleridge's illuminating words quoted by
John Roots, they were out to restore commonplace truths to their
first uncommon luster by translating them into action. They were
making a film of first-century Christianity by leaving it. Consequently they are impatient of preaching without practice. Also
they stressed witness before argument, my own method of putting
over "My Religion" with the help of ten novelists.

Nothing new, but a view which should give them favor with the
great army of non-Christians who defend their pagan living with
the time-worn excuse that Christians do not practice their own
preaching (as though confessing another's sin ever excused one's
own).

But their point about Witness -- which they happily called SHAR-
ING -- was new to me, in so far as it concerned University men.
True I once inveigled novelists into the witness-ring, but not necessarily a company of University graduates. They defined Sharing
as meaning two distinct things -- further definable as Confession
and Witness, one readily passing through the other. The former
meant the confession to God and also to any person if guided to
do so by the Holy Spirit for one's own release. It might mean talking freely to some Christian man or woman who could be trusted
to keep secrets and to give wise counsel as well. Confession to one
another was advocated by St. James and practiced by the Ephe-
sians during Paul's visit to Ephesus. It was practiced by John
Wesley's Holy Club and "love feasts." Frankness about one's faults
was also good witness to the world, for when Christians confess,
Pagans believe.

The ultimate aim of this Sharing was a right relationship with
God. According to my three visitors, we are in desperate need of
forgiveness; and in the last resort, whatever aids we may use to
help us to reach it, we must come to the one place where we stand

before God face to face, confess to Him our sins, and receive the forgiveness which He so freely gives. There is no other way to fullness of life, and in our hearts we know it. Now ideally such confession as this should be made direct to God without the need of any human assistance, receiving God's forgiveness then and there; obviously, in fact, this happens time and time again.

But in practical experience, and just because we are not ideal, instance after instance could be quoted to show that there are very many who need the help of Sharing with another, so that they may come directly face to face with God. For them Sharing is a practical necessity. Only so do they grasp that reality of their confession, of the God to whom they confess, and of the forgiveness which He bestows. The forgiveness itself does not depend upon the Sharing; its appropriation by the individual constantly does.

In practice it was found that confession one to another in the Scriptural sense was mutually helpful and the only way to true fellowship. It was one of those fundamental truths of life, like Christianity itself, never fully grasped until it was practiced. From its earliest days the Christian Church had been well aware of the value of such confession. Wesley and the modern Anglo-Catholic were at one in this, and in one sense the psycho-analyst, with his splendid technique was based upon exhaustive experiment, was simply bringing scientific proof to what the Church learned long ago under the guidance of the Holy Spirit, though she has often forgotten to practice the lesson.

The other aspect of this teaching was Sharing as Witness. Those who had been spiritually healed themselves had the necessity laid upon them to hand on the good news to others, for it was every Christian's obligation -- "By all means to save some." The Bishop of Leicester said a propagating Christian was a normal Christian; unfortunately to-day the propagating Christian was the abnormal.

Again I was skeptical. Perhaps because there were some persons I had no particular desire to see in Heaven.

That telling phrase of the Three Troubadours, "God has a plan for every man's life," came up continually that afternoon. Somewhere I had seen it stated that when each human being was born, the plan of what he could become was made for him in the next world, and one of his joys or sorrows when he went there would come from a comparison of his past with the original plan of his possibilities.

"Not only has God a plan for every life," said one of the trio, "but when through sin we spoil the plan, God is always ready with another." This, too, was a new way of looking at things for me. Unfortunately, most of us refused to follow the plan when we saw it's, or, if unaware of it, to pray for the plan to be revealed. Our sin of sins, embodying all other sins, was independence towards God; doubting God's interests in us, that He had a plan for us, that He would show us the plan, and that He would help us to carry out the plan which was the only satisfactory plan for our lives.

Here was strong teaching. There was much that attracted in the argument. But what about those people for whom there seemed no clear plan, or one that miscarried before the person had the chance to ascertain it? What of the unlucky child who had not even learned the plan of the street-crossing near his house and was killed in his happy youth? Was that part of God's plan for the child? The answer was: It must be left with God. Who could see more than we.

The New Testament answer, as put positively in the case of Peter and John, was, "What is that to thee? Follow thou me." Nobody could tell what was in God's plan for that child or if it was thwarted by the human will of child or driver. But death was only an incident, through a terrible accident, in a life which merely began here and continued "there."

The Three Troubadours positively asserted that those who attempted to live without God's plan, as revealed by the Holy Spirit, were as certain to encounter disaster as those living under God's daily direction were certain of success. Though this success must not be measured by the purely material results of their activities.

My objection to this argument was human nature's chronic inability to know when it was being guided. To that the Three offered the answer of two-way prayer: petitions and quiet listening for the reply, especially in the morning when preparing for the day's work.

They call this early morning listening to God "Quiet Time." The Oxford Group believes God spoke to them when they needed His guidance. I believe it to be possible that nowadays, as in the days of old, there are men to whom the Lord still speaks.

But I felt such persons were rare, and to that for a group of men and women to listen-in each morning hoping for a clear message from God on how to run their day was to expect a lot more than they would get. My views on this practice modified considerably as knowledge of the Group increased.

They emphasized that the condition of clear guidance was complete surrender of everything -- will, time, possessions, family, ambitions -- all to God. Christ had said that if we were unwilling to surrender anything that is most valued we could not be His disciples. Not that the Kingdom really took away everything we liked, or asked us to do anything most distasteful; often the things we were asked to do were those which we were most fitted to do. Nor was surrender always a humiliating leading thing. It meant a handing over of our little in return for God's All-Sufficiency. Each morning we lost our petty, disordered life to God and found the Real Co-ordinated Life all through the day. Accepting completely that the discipline of God brought not bondage, but the fullest freedom to do what we wished -- and that was always the Will of God.

I learned that it was a practice of the Group to keep a guidance-book and record in it those thoughts which came in periods of quiet listening to God. An Angelic bishop had quoted a Chinese proverb in this connection: "The strongest memory is weaker than the palest ink." The idea was novel, introducing the technique of the lecture-room into practical Christianity; interesting as news, but not convincing unless confirmed by definite results. Otherwise the practice bordered on the comic. Yet bishops were actually keeping guidance-books, and I, too, had received from supernatural sources (as I suppose) a remarkably successful religious series. "Through guidance," said the Three.

As our interview developed I elicited news of more interesting aspects of the movement -- just those unusual human things a journalist is always seeking, even when investigating a spiritual subject. Reaching back into the first century for their standards of Christian fellowship, they were ready to scrap any later practices they believe redundant or old-fashioned, and to substitute the earliest customs or something that met modern needs. They did that much of their work through house-parties, where the visitors shared their religious experiences and drew close to God.

HOUSE-PARTY RELIGION was a good headline, I thought!

Whether intentionally or not, I quickly saw they were working on the lines of true journalism; for one thing, they unerringly sensed the value of the very oldest and the very newest. Yet they are amazingly orthodox, holding sometimes by paradox even the interest of the heterodox. And so far no journalist had completely uncovered any real genius. I wondered why.

They were even so orthodox as to believe that everyone, parson as well as prodigal, must at some time come to himself, must experience the forgiveness of God through Jesus Christ. In short, the Cross was central and teaching. At the Cross man reached a turning-point when he decided to live as God directed and guided instead of according to his own human standards. Old-fashioned evangelicals called it conversion, but through misuse that word had for many minds lost its original potency, and so they preferred the simpler word "Change." As Hugh Redwood has it: they were out *to change lives on a colossal scale as the one solution of every world problem.*

Those who sought to change others were called "Life-Changers" instead of evangelists. While they paid tribute to much that was done by the old-time evangelists, they felt the new age required different words and perhaps less music to galvanize the religious interest. They believed that such phrases as "Are you saved?" were unintelligible to the average man. That the potency of such phrases vanished with a dead age. So did I. They also wished to break free from some of the mass efforts of old-fashioned revivalism. They had much evidence that men and women could be changed effectively without the emotionalism and the noise of a former day.

In fact, they believed in orthodoxy galvanized into new life in modern conditions. Just the same old Christianity, but one so intelligently phrased and sensibly though uncompromisingly presented that it became a fresh challenge to a Pagan world, still almost as far from God as in the days of the disciples.

As Christianity will again be a minority movement, they believed there that it was about time for the Church militant to show a bit of real militancy. My visiting trio made it clear that such a message as theirs must of necessity be both uncompromising and challenging, and so convincing that once more the agnostic would turn to God. They knew opposition would come, and were ready for it. You could never approve a challenge as you could approve the minutes of the last meeting. You had to accept the challenge to go all out for a maximum experience of Christ in the manner of the early Apostles, or you had to dodge it or put it out of the way. That was why a challenging Christ was crucified. The Oxford Group did not expect to be crucified, but they did expect to be strenuously opposed by those who were afraid or unwilling to respond to the challenge. It was inevitable. They challenged the world to turn back to God, to cut out sin, to make restitution for past sins, and to let God take full command of every area of life, just as the early disciples challenged the world.

Such a challenge must bring this consciences. The stung conscience must either be surrendered or endeavored to sting back. Man under conviction of sin might do anything. This challenge stung Christians as well as Pagans, parsons as well as prodigals. Christians were challenged to be filled with the Spirit and overflowing in love towards their fellow-men so as to change them. Most Christians were unwilling to accompany Christ in His search for the lost lambs, the normal duty and privilege of every child of God. Christians mostly preferred social service to the saving of souls. It was less intimate, more snobbish, socially more correct. While the Group practiced social service, they felt man's deepest need was not money, but God, for those who truly sought first the Kingdom of Heaven had all other necessary things added unto them. That was their own experience. Men and women were keenly hungry for the true God, who was more ready to manifest Himself to them and they to seek Him.

The work of life-changing was never more necessary than now. Anyone who was pure in the sight of God could become a life-changer. There was no joy in life so great as leading a prodigal home to his Heavenly Father, always half-way down the road to meet him. Men who really had the indwelling presence of God did not need urging to become life-changers; they were naturally so joyous they had to express their joy in changing others.

Life-changing was contagious. And it was more effective nowadays than ever before. The greatest piece of social service a man could do in his generation was to change a man into a life-changer. But *how*? -- By seeing that Christianity was again a minority movement. The Group had learned more of the How than past generations seemed to know or had the necessity for knowing. In their Schools of Life they taught how to avoid saying and doing clumsy things, as Christ also taught His disciples. And always there was a guiding presence of the Holy Spirit to assist and over-rule the teaching.

The best answer to the How of both sinner and potential Life-Changer was the Group custom of Sharing. Changed man might go wrong in trying to change others by arguments, but they were on safe ground in recounting their own experiences as the Apostles recounted theirs. Paul's method of founding a church was to start with this story of his own change. The Group did the same.

The extraordinary fact was that, in an age when, so far as I knew, converts to Christianity were practically nil in the churches, the Oxford Group were continually witnessing men and women being changed into highly-vitalized Christians. Some of the changes were real modern miracles: big sinners, key-men, intellectuals, aristocrats *and* commoners alike. Not emotional decisions, as witnessed in some of the old-fashion mass-revivals, but decisions taken in quiet heart-to-heart talks as a result of tactful personal evangelism by educated men and women courageously accepting, as they did two thousand years ago, the high challenge to give themselves completely to the cause of Christ, and telling their own experience of their indwelling Master.

Chapter Three

SEX AND MONDAY

My Three Troubadours now announced something which held for me still stronger news interests. They affirmed that most persons -- parsons and prodigals alike -- were facing two cardinal problems for which they possessed the solution -- Sex and Money. They sat in the Manager's room of a great London newspaper and coolly asserted that to be true. What journalist with his ears wide open for public interest could help wanting to know more?

A tonic band of people who could produce the answer to those two problems, or even thought they could, need worry about little else in the matter of news interests. They had the world waiting.

What were the solutions? They became more interesting and convincing later. My visitors recognized the sex-instinct to be God-given, and while they did not condone any perversion of thought or word or deed, they knew the real problem was not one of suppression, but sublimation.

"What exactly do you mean by sublimation?"

It was something which used sex energy for a higher purpose while producing complete satisfaction. Sublimation (according to Dr. Hadfield's definition) was the process by which instinctive emotions were diverted from their original ends, and re-directed to purposes satisfying to the individual and of value to the community.

There is no sex problem, they affirmed, nor indeed any problem, when it was surrendered to God. The desire for sin disappeared with the will to obey God. Purity was possible through a cleansing stream of spiritual life which followed a genuine change. As Christ was real and Christ's Spirit was real, there was no danger of fulfilling the lusts of the flesh when walking in the Spirit. This was psychologically explained as the expulsive power of a new affection.

Good theological and psychological stuff. But how could that satisfy sex hunger? I was to get the answer later.

Then we settled down to discuss the eternal problem of every household. How did the Group propose to solve the money problem? To relieve the anxiety of every housewife, dreading to open a letter which might be just another bill? The Three Troubadours smiled their confidence, for they were solving these problems every day.

"How?"

"By Faith and Prayer."

Was that old stuff the best the new religious movement spreading out from Oxford had to offer?

They said flatly it was.

That Faith and Prayer did not pay bills.

They differed. They knew what they were talking about, for thirty or forty in the Group were living on that basis.

"What! Trust in God and do nothing else?"

Not at all. Laziness is a sin. The Group taught that God would guide and provide, but God did not guide healthy, active people to be lazy. Changed man was named better than before he was changed: they wasted less energy and they received extra power from the Holy Spirit. Furthermore, the Group did not urge anyone to live on the Faith and Prayer basis, though everyone might have to do so at some time. And I must remember that the Sermon on the Mount was a practical proposition to-day as always. Still the old Faith, but Faith and uncompromising action. Here was news once more -- out of dear old Oxford! For a long time I had wanted to meet a bunch of Christians faithful enough and divinely courageous enough to believe and live the Sermon on Mount, expecting thereby everything needful to be added unto them.

Once, at the request of a millionaire, I evolved the dummy first issue of a new religious weekly: a paper that was to take England by storm because it would offer the solution of every housewife's main problem -- how to keep her larder stocked with life's necessaries.

The Sermon on the Mount was to me that editorial policy. Week by week we would tell our readers in a variety of brightly written and up-to-date articles the one simple truth, that if they would seek first the Kingdom of God and His righteousness all other things would be added unto them; their houses would stand when winds blew and floods came because they were founded on a rock.

There were many other ideas for this new type of religious journal, but on that foundation the publication would be constructed. My millionaire backer asked me to call and expound my views on the project. Together we paced the Green Park, with Birmingham Palace on one side and Piccadilly on the other, and thrashed out the prospects of a new religious paper -- millionaire and a practical journalist discussing how we could sell security to the British public on the strength of "Seek ye first the Kingdom of God . . . and all these things shall be added unto you."

"If we can put this paper over as the only comprehensive solution of the bread-and-butter problem, which it truly is, we shall have a sensational success," I argued, assured that anyone who had the courage to try the Sermon on the Mount would find it astonishingly practical. He rather liked the idea. He was impressed with the title. He flirted with the proposition. Presently he began to doubt.

"Isn't Christianity really Bolshevism?" he asked.

"Bolshevism grabs other people's possessions. Christ says give away your own."

Why I said that I don't know. He stopped in amused astonishment, turned full towards me and demanded, "Is that your answer?"

I said it was, and thought it true. We continued our discussion, but the religious journal never materialized. We examined those already established, and the prospects of an adventure in religious journalism did not look encouraging. My proposal was shelved. Perhaps he was right. Yet I was sure that was about the only type of newspaper which would thrive on depression. I have still a hankering to found that new religious journal, which shall bear the title SECURITY. Unless a wealthy backer comes along soon I may have to found it on Faith and Prayer.

And now here were three young religious adventurers bringing me the same thought, telling me that two of them had lived for a long time on Faith and Prayer without asking anyone for money. Confirmation of two convictions: that life on Faith and Prayer was really possible, and that news interest was plentiful in this Group. I pressed the Faith and Prayer men for stories of their experiences. How often had they gone hungry? No, they had never gone hungry, said Garrett Stearly, who added that mine was the typical question of the newspaper man. John Roots had been reduced to his last shilling in South Africa, but unexpectedly funds came unasked from his brother just when the situation was becoming desperate. One of the ladies in the Group, an Eleanor Forde, had got down to her last penny, but she prayed, and found a cheque in her mail the next morning.

Doubtless this was the ideal life for a believing Christian to live, but a little too jumpy for a married man with wife and children to care for. I preferred a balance in the bank. Better for the nerves, even though I had been ready to produce a newspaper to show the British public how to support themselves by the Sermon on the Mount. My visitors added that one could keep a family on Faith and Prayer just as well as oneself. The principal was the same. Garrett Stearly and his wife both lived in that way. And of course the immortal George Muller of Bristol had maintained a vast family some two thousand strong, three meals a day, and two suits each for fifty years, starting with a shilling, and never making a request for a penny.

"Don't you *ever* ask for money?" I queried.

Their guidance, said the trio, had been against asking for money. If anyone asked, he was informed of the basis on which they lived, and money offered was gratefully accepted. Those in the Group would sometimes share their needs with each other, as well as their religious experiences and their goods, for they were all one great spiritual family. It one suffered, they all suffered.

The more they talked the more convinced was I there was something brand new about these men, even though they claimed nothing more than primitive Christianity. Their movement might be first century, but it bristled with talking-points. They were not an organization, for there was no membership; not a sect, for they were interdenominational; not really a new movement, for they were but a continuation of early Christian fellowship; not a church, but aiming at an inner spiritual fellowship in all churches. They settled into my mind as not a noun at all. They were a verb, the verb "to be." An action! Really a life! They were out to end the twentieth century in a way the first began -- by living the life and by telling stories of other persons who were doing the same. Just as they did in the Acts of the Apostles when Christianity was first projected across the footlights into the darkness of a pagan civilization.

They were also against controversies. "We don't argue," said Garrett Stearly, "we leave conviction to the Holy Spirit."

A battalion of M.A.'s and B.A.'s, with no desire to argue the truths of their convictions anymore than Christ argued His case before Pilate, or Paul before Agrippa! I disagreed with their attitude at sight. But I could see that the Group practice of not arguing their views might be right, seeing that the Holy Spirit gave conviction, even at Christ's silence before Pilate was right. Yet there was a time for speech and a time for silence about sacred as well as about secular things, and I preferred argument so long as I had doubts. Silence might be anything -- sometimes golden, sometimes gilt, and sometimes guilt. To say they just accepted the New Testament and lived it, or tried to, seemed inadequate. My Three Troubadours answered that Christ and Paul thought otherwise. Further, there was no rigidity about anything they did, as the Holy Spirit might over-rule and change plans, as Paul was sometimes over-ruled and re-directed in other directions.

"But how are you going to convince the man who disbelieves the New Testament?"

I guessed what the answer would be, for it was my own answer to the skeptic. I had found it in the Gospel of St. John and in my own religious experience. My three visitors said that if one honestly tried to carry out the teaching of Scripture, one knew miraculously of the doctrine whether it was of God or man. The Holy Spirit was the Teacher. I believed that myself. In my spiritual egotism, I thought I was about the only one left who did, or had practical experience of "the witness of the Spirit."

But I still prepared to argue the reason of my belief as best I could: not to remain dumb on the debatable point.

They said it would be better for me to tell my own experience and let the Holy Spirit argue within the other person, as He did in the first century. If Christianity is real, that argument seemed unanswerable.

In their emphasis on knowing through doing intrigued me considerably. In fact, I once contemplated writing a religious novel around the title "You Shall Know," keeping as the solution of the mystery the plain teaching of Scripture that certitude can be miraculously discovered by obedience to known truth, which was quite scientific. The Group said that arguments would never save souls. One theological Professor said that the intellectual arguments for God and against God were about evenly balanced. There was not sufficient margin of theological proof to galvanize a man into action. He needed the proof in himself, and the scientific way to get that proof was to make the experiment. Those who obeyed Christ's teaching knew miraculously of the doctrine, through the witness of the Holy Spirit.

It was difficult to make the schoolboy with no use for love understand that in adolescence he would change his mind; it was just as difficult to convince an unbeliever that by obedience to Christ's teaching he would have the proof in himself that Christ was the Image and the Word of God.

When talking to the late Arnold Bennett about his agnostic contribution, I suggested that he could easily discover the truth of

Christianity for himself in this simple way if he chose. I think I said that a fortnight's intensive practice of the Sermon on the Mount would provide ample proof. "A.B." gave a start as though a fresh idea had come to him from a surprising quarter. Then he crooked his forefinger in that odd way he had and shook it decisively.

"Not for me," he said.

His religion was kindliness.

And now I was discussing the theme again with three modern young men, who are advocating the same ideas as I, but leading a movement to convince the world by those same simple pragmatical means. As they sat in my office that afternoon, I felt they carried a large measure of proof faces. With no argument to justify their belief but their own life, they appeared to have achieved a measure of Christian certitude and Christian radiance far greater than I, though I was treated as the expert on this subject by two important London newspapers.

Again, I wondered why. Was it because they had gone all out to win the great game, or because they had not encountered such adverse odds? Perhaps they had found some secret knack of keeping out of the rough, and always driving straight down the fairway. If so, what was it? They said, "Absolute surrender in all areas to God." Had I done this? Evidently not.

One had to be honest in sizing up these fellows sitting in this room. Regard them as one would -- the Saints, adventurers, fanatics, anachronisms -- unquestionably they possessed a good deal more than the ordinary cultured human animal. I had met crowds of the charming unregenerate type. And through many unpleasant experiences I had reached the stage of suspecting everybody until the contrary was proved.

What was there about these fellows which seemed to prove their claim? The answer must again be -- News. My Three Troubadours said it was the natural by-product of true fellowship, which included the most ruthless Sharing. Honest Sharing among surrendered Christians tended to produce the Apostolic glow which Christ left on the faces of His disciples.

To retain this glow, the principal of Stewardship must also faithfully be remembered: stewardship of time, lands, money, houses, things, family relationships, sex relationships -- in fact, of everything possessed. It might mean giving your time in a Sunday School or helping in your neighbor's garden if he were too ill or too poor to pay for help. It might mean changing the theme of your novel or modifying your attitude towards clothing or food or drink.

It might mean surrendering to God the entire royalties of a play or book, as Hugh Redwood did with his fine story *God in the Slums.* A great act of stewardship, for the royalties were considerable. The only thing about the book which Hugh Redwood did not give away was the excellent title, which, he told me, was the inspiration of a leader in the Salvation Army. *God in the Shadows*, the title of his still better success was his own happy idea.

My visitors explained that stewardship embodied the final answer to those two materialistic philosophies now holding sway -- one, that prosperity is the supreme value of life; and two, that the wealth is necessarily evil and poverty virtuous. The Gospel taught neither of these philosophies, but everything belonged to God, who asks His children to handle wisely His own property according to His wishes and guidance. The true Christian answer to Communism, and one more complete than mine when I said that "Bolshevism grabs other people's property, but Christ says give away your own."

The doctrine seemed too sound. Again there was nothing new in theory. But what would a wife, husband, children, parents say when they watched the responsible person giving away possessions with the excuse of doing it as a steward of God? The Group said that one would give under guidance and that God was more interested in the needs of everyone we were interested in than we were, and that was why the principle of stewardship was necessary. And a changed man or changed woman would probably have a changed wife or husband. In any case, we would invite the others views.

Pondering these principles, I seemed to be returning to where I was with that projected new religious Journal, only -- that journal was to be a consolation to the worried masses of impecunious England, while this uncompromising Group were becoming a challenge to myself.

I was certainly getting the hang of what the Oxford Group was after. First, there was absolute Surrender, bringing Guidance by the Holy Spirit; then there was Sharing, bringing true Fellowship and shining faces; then Life-Changing, bringing in God's Kingdom and Joy, in Heaven, in the Sinner, and in the Life-changer; then Faith and Prayer, bringing all things needful and helping toward God's plan to provide for everybody. Also those four standards of Love, Honesty, Purity and Usefulness, on which Christ had never compromised; and, of course, Restitution. Later I was to understand perhaps the strongest principle of all -- Fearless Dealing with Sin. Meanwhile, there were two other principles easier to swallow -- Team-work and Loyalty.

Jesus practiced team-work, said my callers. He and His disciples were a team. He sent His representatives out, not singly, but in twos and threes. After His Ascension the disciples moved about the Roman Empire in small traveling groups. They were doing the same. Great movements had lost their driving force because the principle of team-work was misunderstood. Founders wanted to gather all power into their own hands and retain it, oblivious to the truth that the Spirit bloweth where it listeth. No person can have a monopoly of the Holy Spirit. At some times men are more spiritual than at other times. Men grow in grace, but they declined sometimes in grace. The discipline of team-work irons out human eccentricities. Truth is presented more adequately through a team than through one individual. Half a dozen men recording their religious experiences cause more heart-searching and conviction than one man giving Christian advice.

Again reality was put before theory; life-interest before head-interest. In the language of Fleet Street, News took precedence over Views.

Then there was the principle of Loyalty. First there must be supreme loyalty to Jesus Christ, but that involved lesser loyalties as well. Those who were being used by Jesus Christ deserved loyal support from those who professed Jesus Christ -- a true welcome enough in theory, though not always so gladly received in practice. It was a strange phenomenon that so many professing Christians could be so disloyal to those trying to live in loyalty to Christ.

Above all, the Group was a Fellowship -- a first-century Christian Fellowship controlled by the Holy Spirit. And it was remarkable how the guidance received by different persons in the Group, when pieced together, made a perfect pattern, showing that the Master Mind of the Spirit was actively at work behind the scenes, not of the Group only, but everywhere that room was made for Him. That exquisite Fellowship of the Spirit, so often talked about, and so little understood, was actually being realized. All barriers in such a fellowship were broken down by loving understanding, leading to greater depths of human experience, more happiness and abiding peace. Man was otherwise obtainable in human association. That was why their faces glowed.

Because the Holy Spirit was the real head of this Fellowship, "Frank" did not arrogate to himself full control. When guided, he would preside at Group meetings. When guided, he would leave the leadership to another. Sometimes he would be seen at the back of the room listening to his colleagues whom he was training for leadership, occasionally breaking in with a quick, clarifying phrase when a difficult question came up. As at Oxford when someone asked the Group leader if she should confess all her faults to somebody, "Frank" interpolated, "Not necessarily. But everyone should be willing to do so if guided by the Holy Spirit." The decision rests with oneself -- always.

The Group's emphasis on Loyalty brought home to me one of the faults of my youth when, attending a Church meeting, I presumed to criticize a minister much older than myself in none too happy language. The Group said Loyalty was particularly necessary towards those more experienced in Christian living. And yet even with this point firmly recognized, they encouraged "checking" faults among themselves, in the spirit of loving fellowship, and not allowed to degenerate into the sin of fault-finding. A newcomer to the Christian experience might see a glaring fault in one on the way. For him outspokenly to condemn the fault before he had earned the right by loving, solicitous fellowship would be sheer presumption.

Undo possessiveness of husband towards wife, or wife towards husband, was condemned by the Group. Either should be free to do as either felt right, for the marriage relationship was not between two, but between three. Just as the advent of a third human being as a competitive factor produced the Eternal Human Triangle for the wrecking of marriages, so the advent of the Third, Jesus Christ, into the home, the non-competitive-guiding factor, requiring each to act towards the other according to God's standards, produced a new Eternal Triangle which saved marriages from ruin and established the ideal human partnership on earth.

Excellent in theory. But could all this Idealism work? It could and did, the Three asserted. Groups were coming into existence in many places, in many countries: England, Scotland, Holland, Germany, India, South Africa, China, Egypt, Switzerland, North and South America. And in South Africa it had taken, but not in the dimensions of a National movement. As far as possible, the Group was making their challenge through the Churches, and had the sympathetic interest of the Archbishops, and other Angelica and Nonconformist church dignitaries. They were urging Christians, congregations and clergy alike, to expel sin from their midst, as the Apostles did, stressing the need of surrender entirely to God, and to trust His guidance and support in every circumstance and vicissitude of life. Emphatically were they against being another religious "order" or "cult," or "sect" or "organization." They wished to be an inner church in all churches, irrespective of the domination, or the deepening of spiritual life within Christ's body and for the carrying of Christianity to its logical and practical limits. In fact, a power-house within and without the churches for encouraging everyone to have a complete experience of Jesus Christ.

There were Groups meeting in churches, Universities, and numerous private homes in many parts of the world. In Johannesburg one Group met in a fire-station. By meeting informally anywhere (not getting church hours) they reached people who were interested in religion but unready to attend formal church services. Their house-parties were an exhilaration, an astonishingly successful religious advance wherever they were held. No attempt was being made to organize the Groups springing up here, there and everywhere. None would be made. Each group was a separate unit linked to the others only by the Holy Spirit. Their only organization was the great historic churches. These were ample for the Group to worship in as they felt led. Here they found their theology and their preaching. There could never be a series of Group churches. As the Group thrived, so much the better for the churches in the neighborhood. If the Group died, that was unfortunate, but only a repetition of what sometimes happened in early Christianity. . . .

Before leaving, my Three Troubadours of God told me they had booked a tourist passage on the *Europa*, sailing the following day for New York. And they had just sufficient money left to cover extras for the voyage and get them safely back to their destination. As for the future, they had no fear. Money would come as it came in the past if they continued to pray and obey. At my Invitation they made a selection from my book-case, tactfully choosing one of my own stories and the life-story of George Mueller of Bristol. Departing, they left me a copy of *Life-Changers*, by Herald Begbie, which took some remarkable stories of lives transformed by "Frank's" efforts.

As I returned to my room, one of them dashed back to invite my wife and myself to their farewell-to-England dinner that night in the Chinese Restaurant in Piccadilly Circus. There we received our first lesson in the use of chop-sticks from members of the Oxford Group who had lived in China and had learned some of the ways of the Orient. A jolly meal it was. "God-guided" life-changers joked, told good stories of their adventures, introduced us to some novel dishes and gave us an entertaining evening.

With Fleet Street's atmosphere of awareness and suspicion clinging thick about me, I felt I had struck a note of fellowship an octave higher than normal. Too good to last! One would soon descend from that ethereal state of Apostolic fellowship into materialism and mutual mistrust. Then I should discover the snap in the new teaching -- just where the catch was hidden. Most men of the world looked for the catch on the door of their money-box. When the waiter brought our bill, there was a smart to catch. Garrett Stearly grabbed the bill and paid. So their faith and prayers were strong enough to provide for two guests as well as for themselves.

When returning later to Brown's, I first detected a possible catch. Garrett Stearly and I were discussing varieties of religious experience, and I, rather puzzled, mentioned one or two curiously ecstatic occurrences in my own life, once when studying the Bible, and several times afterwards, during periods of crises. I remember saying that these joyous experiences had ceased with me, and I could not understand the reason. That gave him an opening which he promptly took. Was it possible that I was allowing sin to wall me off from God? Then he quietly hinted that we needed to touch deeper reaches of fellowship before he could give me any helpful advice.

"Hello!" I thought. "Here, then, is the catch in the movement! Here is a man I have known for only a short time suggesting there is something wrong with my spiritual inside and wanting me to confess the facts. Quite premature, my lad." Sharing was all right in theory as outlined to me that afternoon. It was a very different thing as practice. "Never tell all you know," was the sage counsel once given me by a Scottish girl, which I now remembered. I decided on caution. One never knew. We continued our walk around the block, while I informed him rather guardedly that I knew of nothing particular in my life which might explain this hiatus in God-consciousness.

Garrett Stearly gave no expression of relief or belief. On the contrary, I sensed a mute incredulity in his emanations. "Which means," I thought, "that you will want me to confess all my short comings to you, a man two-thirds my age. Including those occasional slips which, because you would not understand the circumstances, you might harshly label sin." So I persisted in declaring there was nothing wrong, omitting to say I was not quite sure about it.

Moreover, there was another reason. I wished to chat with Frank when he came back from South America on a Christian-to-Christian basis. There must be none of the penitent-to-priest attitude about this interview. To disclose a few past sins to one of his friends might, so far as I then knew, be putting the unknown Frank in the position of advantage. Even if my life had not been a hundred per cent perfection, it had been lived for many years on a higher level than before, perhaps higher than that of the average Christian. I felt that was not me or egotism, but simple truth. As for the slips, they were explainable and even excusable. Though I was still not quite sure about them. Anyway, they were no concern of these young fellows, clean and charming though they were, or with my thoughts to link our paper and our movements for our mutual interest.

And was it perfect, anyway? I asked myself. Nevertheless, I wanted to put a long period between past imperfections and my meeting with the legendary Frank, so that if he did challenge me I could say quite honestly I was living his kind of life. Of course, I could say so at any time, whether true or not. In my early days as a journalist I had told more than one lie to secure a good story. Only -- lying was a peccadillo I had long sensed contrived to master.

During the interval which elapsed before I met Frank I was also successful in keeping those other graver faults which were defeating me under control. But you shall hear later how ineffective this trick of the conscience proved to be.

As Garrett and I walked on and talked on it, the sex problem suddenly reappeared, as it had done in the afternoon. I wanted a definition of the Group's view about absolute purity.

I had heard it argued that immorality was excusable in certain circumstances. What of two persons in love with each other and each unhappily mated to an unfaithful partner? What about the one who had an erring partner yet disbelieved divorce? What of the scientific contention that certain types of men and women could never mate, and so must develop wanderlust if they married the wrong type? Blood tests might even prove that two persons were absolutely incompatible. If a person married one of those incompatible types in some moment of blind love or uncontrolled passion, no amount of compromise could ever make that marriage a melting success. Both were doomed to incompatibility for life, since for such Christianity had still the empty message "Grin and bear it." To my mind, common sense and human nature joined in revolt against this inhuman creed.

Garrett Sternly said sex had to be surrendered to God. One of the test questions of true surrender was: Am I prepared to let

Christ master my sex life entirely?

Then that, I thought, would be a staggerer for Fleet Street.

He reintroduced the thought of sublimation. He sought to lift one to a higher plane of thought, to where (he seemed to think) the freedom of instinct and the restraints of conscience merged into liberty and complete satisfaction: to a level in the realm of grace which I did not believe in, though it was commonly taught in Christianity.

He told me an amazing story, insisting that it was true, of a husband and wife whose seemingly insuperable marital problem was straightened out by the Group message. The husband had suffered injury which took sex completely out of his life. The wife was young, gay and restless. She attended lively reckless parties to balance her barren life at home. Their home-life was about finished when they came under the influence of the Group. Instead of urging a divorce -- the natural thing to do, I thought -- the Group advised the complete submission of the problem to God's guidance. This advice was accepted, and clear guidance came to the wife to accept a situation, not resignedly as a sacrifice, but cheerfully as a means of grace consistent with God's plan. So for her, as well as for her husband, the problem was entirely removed from her life. Yet there was no sense of deprivation, for the sex instinct had been sublimated to a higher level of satisfaction on which truly happy souls had lived in all ages. Sex discontent had vanished through the expulsive power of a higher affection.

There were several answers I could have given to the story, for I was very skeptical. I expressed doubts as to her real happiness.

"She is perfectly happy," affirmed Garrett. "They both are."

One had no doubts about the husband. This sublimation idea had solved for him every husband's problem of keeping a restless wife at home contented. From his standpoint it was a satisfactory, if selfish, solution. I felt he should have urged her to seek divorce. That would have breathed the true spirit of unselfishness.

"She loved him," said Garrett. "God's guidance, her love and Christian teaching were all against divorce."

"But human nature is still human nature. And a wife craves for a child."

Those may not have been the exact words, but they convey the thoughts we expressed or were in our minds. And all the time the young troubadour refused to be moved from his high standard. One wondered what would happen to this sex-mad world if someone who really believed sublimation was a practical possibility could preach so simply and convincingly that others believe it too. The streets of our cities free from solicitation, from men leering at every passing opportunity. Women no longer eternally brushed aside the sex-laden overtures of men. Genuine friendship between the sexes at last. Sex wiles eliminated from every social gathering. Ended the eternal comedy of pursuing men and pursued women.

Of course churches preached sublimation when they mentioned sex at all. But I thought few virile persons ever willingly or consistently practiced it. This way of treating sex was all very well for the naturally stoical or weaklings, but not for red-blooded, vital men and women of the world whom the Group were out to win. Further, I felt rather sorry for the lady described by Garrett Stearly, for she must have settled down to a very bleak sort of married existence.

God's troubadour again disagreed. He was a married man. He understood the problem. He told further of a lawyer who had been in the habit of making large fees for divorce cases, but was now spending more effort privately showing his clients God's way to settle their quarrels, and with more success than he achieved in his divorce court practice.

Bad for legal business, but good for the Kingdom of Heaven! And as he was doing God's will instead of his own will, even if he lost some good fees, he was not injuring his true interests, since God's will for a man was always the best. Garrett argued doggedly. Fine, lofty teaching. Idealistic and intriguing, and definitely challenging.

I went back to think. How to adapt this extraordinary Group to a new religious series? If these people were right, then we were the newspaper to report their activities. So I thought at that time. I settled down to read *Life-Changers*, and to delve deeper into the origins, the arguments and the case histories of this remarkable movement.

Chapter Four

THE LIFE-CHANGER

Frank is a unique character. The story of how his own life was changed, as told by Harold Begbie in *Life-Changers*, is an absorbing and inspiring narrative. Frank is a character who grows on you -- in a book, and in life. After the first chapter you want to meet him. When you meet him you may have reason to wish you hadn't. But if you remove the reason, you will find Frank still there and that you have obtained release from spiritual defeat.

Life-Changers is now in its fourteenth edition. I learned from the publisher, who was well pleased with the sales that the movement is growing strongly. Though I never met Harold Begbie, the author, I knew him to be a man of fine character and from his writings, a clever journalist. He was engaged by our powerful rival to write a series of articles to answer our runaway "My Religion" feature. I thought the series dull. Instead of writing about the new religious movement at Oxford, he contributed a series describing the modern attitude towards God. I have since thought that our rival had in its office the best possible answer to "My Religion" and allowed it to slip through, non--recognition. And now, seven years later, the movement had come my way.

Harold Begbie scored several successes before he wrote *Life-Changers*, including (so everyone said) *Mirrors of Downing Street*, a collection of piquant sketches of the man from King George V during the Great War, but hiding his authorship under a pen-name "A Gentlemen with a Duster." One or two celebrities received a severe "dusting-down," possibly not altogether deserved, from the "Gentlemen with a Duster." I knew some of them.

Not so the founder of the Oxford Group. Begbie, at Frank's request, masked the name of his hero under the initials "F. B.", whom he portrayed with a master's skill. "In appearance," said Begbie, "F. B. is a young-looking man of middle life, tall, upright, stoutish, clean-shaven, spectacled, with that mien scrupulous shampooed and almost medical cleanliness or freshness which is so characteristic of the hygienic American."

He might have added, "Which is so characteristic of every one of the Oxford Group," as I discovered later when traveling with a well-dressed team, whose leader ran an appraising (or critical) eye over every one of us each time we swung into his orbit.

Frank is still as scrupulous as ever over his appearance. He has a tidy mind and dislikes untidiness at all times. "His carriage and his gestures," said Begbie, "are distinguished by an invariable alertness. He never droops, he never slouches. You find him in the small hours of the morning with the same quickness of eye and the same athletic erectness of body which seemed to bring a breeze into a breakfast-room. A few men so quiet and restrained exhale a spirit of such contagious well-being.

"A crisp accent marks his speech, and is richly noticeable only when he makes use of colloquialisms. The voice is low but vigorous, with a sincere ring of friendliness and good-humor -- the same friendliness and good-humor which are characteristic of his manners. He strikes one on meeting as a warm-hearted and very happy man, who can never know what it is to be either physically tired or mentally bored."

Then the writer strikes the happiest of all descriptions of Frank. "I am tempted to think," says he, "that if Mr. Pickwick had given birth to a son and that son had emigrated to America in boyhood he would have been not unlike this amiable and friendly surgeon of souls. Fuller acquaintance of 'F. B.' brings to one's mind the knowledge that in spite of his boyish cheerfulness he is of the house and lineage of all true mystics from Plotinus to Tolstoy."

Several odd experiences of my own (as I had mentioned to Garrett Stearly) had induced me to believe that I possessed something of the mystical quality; that "My Region" had come to me in the true mystical way. That made me all the more anxious to meet him.

Frank was baptized in infancy, and later confirmed, without any special religious experience to make the location particularly memorable. But illuminating crises were to come in his life from the time when he was training for the ministry, ardently desiring to make converts and puzzled at his ineptitude, on through humiliating change and mystical enlightenment to extraordinary triumphs among surely the most difficult material of Great Britain -- the undergraduates of Oxford and Cambridge.

The first serious crisis came in Frank's life when a fellow-student at Mount Airy Seminary, Philadelphia, accused him of ambition. This accusation smote him severely, indeed, he chose the most difficult quarter of Philadelphia for his initial labors. The invitation to his first church was not without humor. It said, *'The question of salary must for the time be left unstated."* Meaning there could be no stated salary, because all the money collected for the non-existent church was seventeen dollars, mostly in pennies. But someone gave a new corner shop, and this, under Frank's vigorous direction, grew speedily into the Church of the Good Shepherd. The locality was residential, but the hierarchy of the place was already well looked after when Frank arrived, so he decided to provide for the spiritual requirements of their servants, who had no shepherd. He set out to collect a congregation by ringing the door-bells of the big houses and getting into spiritual communication with the butlers and the housemaids, with such great success that more than one employer remarked to Frank at dinner that he had to remain friendly with him to keep the cook.

The Church of the Good to Shepherd flourished, and there grew out from it a hospice for young men which developed into a community of hospices spreading through other cities. After that Frank founded a Settlement House on the lines of Toynbee Hall, though differently Christian, which reached to several hundred persons. Frank still gravitates to this house whenever he returns to America.

Experience with the younger generation at the hospice taught Frank how to handle the grown-ups; especially never to lose his temper, as no one was likely to pick it up. From a child he learned later never to laugh at other people's faults ("You are just as funny yourself"). Frank's secret of getting boys up early on Sunday mornings was not to scold but to announce there would be pancakes on the table at nine sharp. After that all were down on time, some before time.

Sometimes boys drawn from the streets went back to the gutter again, or would disappear for days, perhaps to be found in the peanut gallery of some cheap theatre waiting for their stolen show to begin. These prodigals were welcomed home in New Testament style.

And now Frank had trouble. Both hospice and settlement were under the same control -- a committee of clergy and laity. After five years there came a clash, bringing about the second big crisis in Frank's life, and leading presently to the establishment of the Oxford Group movement. The business committee was strong on balancing the budget, as business committees always are. Sometimes the budget would not balance -- when the young folks were numerous. So the Committee requested Frank to reduce the rations. The spirit of Oliver Twist stirred within Frank, who resented the order, and nursed ill-will against the six persons who were dominating him in this respect.

"Here," he frankly admits, "I've failed. I said the Committee was behaving badly. Yet my work had become my idol. All I should have done was to resign and let it go at that. Right in my conviction, I was wrong in harboring ill-well. I left and came abroad, my health badly affected by overwork. *En route* I had a vision of 'Care' in Horace's Ode, following on a charger, always just behind. I could almost hear the horses' hoofs and feel their breath on the back of my neck.

"Traveling through Italy, and other parts of the Continent, I found my way back to England, and so up to Keswick, where a convention was in progress. And there something happened! Something for which I shall always be grateful."

That experience was the miracle which changed Frank's course of life and started a new religious movement that may achieve anything. True to tradition, the miracle did not happen at the big convention, or at some important church service addressed by a notable preacher. Again the old story of dipping in Jordan instead of the spectacular plunge into Abanah or Pharpar, rivers of Damascus. Although Frank attended church regularly, he was satisfied with a rather slim diet, and found comfort in a quotation in a recent sermon he had heard: "They also serve who only stand and wait." His life had become a big "I" Self at the centre of the picture! The refined sin which the average person condones while it walls him off from power.

A tiny village church. A tiny congregation. A special afternoon meeting. The speaker -- a woman! No thunder, no lightning, no cloud, no supernatural voice, but a simple, straight-forward, conversational talk to a gathering of about seventeen persons, including Frank. The woman speaker spoke about the Cross of Christ, of a sinner and the One who had made full satisfaction for the sins of the world.

This was "A doctrine which I knew as a boy," says Frank, "which my church believed, which I had always been taught and which that day became a great reality for me. I had entered at the little church with a divided will, nursing pride, selfishness, ill-will, which prevented me from functioning as a Christian minister should. The woman's simple talk personalized the Cross for me that day, and suddenly I had a poignant vision of the Crucified.

"There was infinite suffering on the face of the Master, and I realized for the first time the great abyss separating myself from Him. That was all. But it produced in me a vibrant feeling, as though a strong current of life had suddenly been poured into me, and afterwards being with a dazed sense of a great spiritual shaking-up. There was no longer this feeling of a divided will, no sense of calculation and argument, of oppression and helplessness; a wave of strong emotion, following the will to surrender, rose up within me from the depths of an estranged spiritual life, and seemed to lift my soul from its anchorage of selfishness, bearing it across that great sundering abyss to the foot of the Cross.

"With this deeper experience of how the love God in Christ had bridged the chasm dividing me from Him, and the new sense of buoyant life that had come, I returned to the house feeling a powerful urge to share my experience. Thereupon I wrote to the six committee-men in America against whom I had nursed the ill-will and told them of my experience, and how at the foot of the Cross I could only think of my own sin. At the top of each letter I wrote this verse:

When I survey the wondrous Cross
On which the Prince of Glory died,
My richest gain I count but loss
And pour contempt on all my pride.

Then I said:
"My DEAR FRIEND,
I have nursed ill will against you. I am sorry. Forgive me?
Yours sincerely,
FRANK."

"I received no written reply. But that apologetic gesture meant much to me in a new and complete friendliness when I met them later on. Some of them are now in Heaven -- and some more of us are going there soon."

Frank continues: "I was staying with some friends who had lately been worldlings that had been changed. They had a son who was not like-minded, a first year man at Cambridge, and now thoroughly bored with the Convention meetings. The family was puzzled to know how to interest him in Christianity. He came in to tea, and I began to share my wonderful experience and tell him how a rapturous joy had come in place of the ill-will I previously harbored with such inhibiting results. I said that all my old caterers had been dropped overboard. The young man was immediately interested. How had it all happened? When would I walk with him round Derwentwater and talk further about it? I said I would be glad to. It had been a whole year since anyone had invited me to that kind of a talk. Before we returned, he too, decided to make the surrender of his will to Christ's will. He went to church that night, became a good Christian, and later a successful barrister. And again, I had the joy of winning a man to Christ.

"A further test of this new experience came to me later on when I returned home. Attending church on Christmas morning, who should I see in front of me but the person whom I considered to have wronged me most of all. He had a bald spot on his head, and at one time, whenever I sat facing it in committee meetings, I used to think the letter "I" was written all over that spot. That morning I forgot even the bald spot itself, as the true Christmas spirit of peace on earth, goodwill to all, rained in my heart. I naturally wished this former opponent on the Committee a Merry Christmas, and meant it, though as I did so he was looking on the floor as if seeking a lost pin. But he, too, wished me a Merry Christmas, and appreciated the fact that at the Cross I had learned the great truth never to be resentful against anybody, including committees."

The foregoing story of the change in his life was told me by Frank himself sometime after I read the summarized version in Begbie's *Life-Changers*. At first I was not surprised to learn that Frank received no reply to any one of his letters, for it seemed to me that his religious zeal had outdistanced his common sense.

Perhaps the recipients thought so too. Or perhaps they still fostered unpleasant memories of the kind Frank had just torpedoed. But this did not daunt his unbroken sense of divine companionship or his conviction that he had done the only right thing, though it made him understand how impossibly hard it was for a proud heart to enter the Kingdom of Love.

For light and direction had come at last. As Frank puts it, he had turned the Big "I" of Self onto its beam end thus (-) which left him with only a big minus. He saw that Christ must be the Big "I" to turn that minus back into a mighty (+), and by continuing the line of Christ the symbol was now the Cross (+). Frank's suffering mind had immediately been healed by a decision to submit his will in future entirety to the Will of God. His crisis was not a crisis of the emotions, but a crisis of the will. Once the will had been surrendered, the emotional experience followed. The will is the root, the emotion the fruit. Frank saw clearly now that all success demands the whole will at the back of it. A man cannot be happy in a life of vice so long as he is conscious of moral scruples; conversely, he cannot be happy in a life of virtue so long as he compromises with vice.

Frank now realized that the demand of both worlds is identical -- the whole heart! And so realizing, he found a great happiness through the decision to exert his unified will and the service of One proclaimed the reality of the spiritual world and pronounced the values of materialism illusory. Now he perfectly understood that what hindered him long ago from making this decision was sin, which must be completely excluded from the life of the child of God.

Sin was anything done contrary to the Will of God, as shown in the New Testament or by direct guidance. There was no complete catalogue of sins for everybody, since what was sin to one might not always be sin to another. Sin might be drunkenness or pride, murder or dishonesty, selfishness or refusal to love God or one's neighbour, coveting another man's wife or loving the husband of another woman. It might be over-eating or vain boasting, laziness or over-calling your partner at bridge. It might be wasting money on the racecourse, at roulette or in a night-club, or refusing to trust God at all times. It might be high-hatting someone poorly dressed, lying about the time you left the office, as to what you owed the butcher or lost at cards. It might be unwillingness to play that Good Samaritan to a broken-down motorist, or being ashamed to offer your seat to a weary char-woman on the streetcar. It might be pride in the pulpit, a desire to make a hit with the congregation instead of to reveal Christ. It might mean graft or greed, pugnacity or fear, waste or meanness, aversion or perversion. Such sins and all others were included in the one major sin of independence towards God, Who should be first, last, and all the time as taught in the Ten Commandments and the New Testament.

In other words, Frank had undertaken a crusade to be absolutely for the absolute: to live the maximum life which all Christians held, but constantly essayed. To the average man a decision to let God so deal with sin that He would accompany them every day, everywhere is a terrifying thought. To Frank it was the only logical step. It was the starting-point from which Abraham, Paul, Francis, Booth, Muller, Moody and the other religious leaders all moved forward to great achievement. To Frank and his friends this unconditional surrender of everything between them and God meant the grandest adventure of all time: unquestionably the grandest possible adventure in an unadventurous age of dull poverty and depression, unbelief and debasing license. It meant for thrills of a Columbus voyage, pioneering trials in new countries, risks of going over the top, persistent poverty in the midst of luxury, living hour by hour on faith and prayer with exposure to ridicule inside and outside the churches, misunderstanding and ceaseless misrepresentation. It meant voluntarily facing up to every challenging obstacle that has lured the boldly aspiring and adventurous to triumph or disaster through all the ages.

Moreover, it meant a relentless crusade to induce other men and women not only to believe in the possibility of living the victorious life, but to live it. To found a new community of saints, always ready to be fools for Christ, always care-less and care-free in an age of blank and blind materialism. To call together an interdenominational band of lay friars, Spirit-guided and controlled, who would roam the world with no visible means of income, living on God's manna as God's warriors, while out-living, out-loving, out-laughing all in a glorious new crusade to redeem the world from the enticements of sin in a luxury-loving, security-seeking, sensual civilization.

This Pickwickian life-changer was well aware that he had undertaken a Herculean job requiring wise slogans and wiser methods. He pondered long on the problem of the ages: how to get rid of sin -- sin in black capital's; sin among Pagans, sin among Christians. He knew that sin was everywhere: in the office, in the factory; in the home, in the pulpit; in the college, in the theological hall. He must take a buddy for granted, because he was insidiously pervasive. Sin, which the preacher opposed perhaps without having mastered. Sin, which the Pagan took as a pleasant drug, while a Christian smiled, shrugged, and publicly condemned. There were few to warn wisely, and fewer still to show both Pagan and Christian how to overcome.

And pondering, Frank evolved what he thought was an answer to the eternal problem of sin, "The degree of our freedom from sin is the degree of our desire to be free. If we complain that we are slaves to sin, we are really saying that we love sin and desire it. Sin can only live in the heart that does not love goodness with all its strength. Only a feebleness of desire for God enables sin to be a tyrant. It will disappear as though it had never been; immediately one craves for righteousness wholeheartedly."

Sin happens between the look and the thought. First the look, then the thought, then the fascination, and then the fall. But it may be only the fall in thought, Frank argued. And so knowing that "blessed are the pure in heart, for they shall see God," Frank set out on what he believed to be his Spirit-given task of causing people to hate sin so intensely as to forsake it, and to love goodness so thoroughly as always to follow it. Consequently every reasonable opportunity must be used to expose sin as a loathsome cancer in a person's life, preventing him from self-fulfillment and from becoming a miracle-worker. So, Frank insists that should one sin, confess and forsake that sin. Confession has a treble effect: it raises an obstacle to repetition of the sin, since it may mean another unpleasant confession; it is a warning guide to others, and produces a sense of release and cleanliness of spirit. Thus the offense is purged by the Cross of Christ.

Further, he believes that wherever reasonably possible one should not only confess a sin to the person sinned against, but make restitution. Distasteful though this teaching is, it has a strong appeal to the highest spirits, and has often been used to change the lives of those confessed to as well as of those who confessed. For though it was Christ Who forgave, it was only the convert who could repair the wrong he had done, a duty as plainly obvious for the changed man as for the bellicose country that despoiled an inoffensive neighbor.

Here, and then, was the reason why Garrett Stearly was sensitive to the possibility of a sin that might be walling me off from God. If I had admitted such, he might have urged me to undertake a few missions of confession or restitution. Instinctively I'd disagreed with the doctrine, which seemed to contain much that was dangerous, particularly on my own self-esteem. Yet I saw no objection to anyone else making confession of the sins he had committed to or restitution for the wrong he had done -- except myself!

And now let Loudon Hamilton, one of Frank's friends and earliest captives, formerly a master at Eton, and at present leader of the Oxford Group in Scotland, tell you, as he told me, the inspiring story of how Frank arrived in Oxford, guided him to put his challenging convictions into operation in the intellectual centre of England. Especially do I recall the way in which Loudon expressed his feeling of boredom, with a tinge of vague curiosity, at being asked to meet "an American professor from Cambridge." (Frank had spent a short time in Cambridge at the request of two bishops before coming to Oxford at the request of a third.) The rest of this chapter is in Loudon Hamilton's words:

"Care to meet a man from Cambridge?"

This somewhat mystifying requests from a Rugger (football)-

playing Rhodes scholar floated across this quad one summer evening in 1921. We do have manners, so we said, "Yes." Our Rhoads athlete brought the foreword, a man of middle size with manners and clothes that gave no clue to his job; but his eyes were large and alert. Thus entered Frank to Oxford. There were no announcements, no advertisements. Yet there began then in Oxford an influence admittedly more far-reaching than most of the organized, patronized and authorized movements in religion.

One man had entered Oxford carrying a vital message, himself in tune and in touch with God.

We invited him to attend our Philosophic fortnightly meeting. At first, it was a serious evening -- in the wrong sense. The occasion was a philosophic debate -- we became very profound. Who was it who wittily said that in Oxford we don't always stop talking when we have finished what we have to say?

Eleven o'clock came -- so far Frank had said nothing. Coming from Cambridge, this was unexpected -- so he had to be asked. Picture the crowd: ninety per cent ex-officer undergraduates, from majors downwards; men with reputations from the Intelligence Service, from the Navy, veterans of twenty-one or twenty-two with rows of medals never seen or referred to; men who have since gone into important positions in Education, Civil Service, Diplomacy and Empire-building.

There was the man of influence in college. Most of them played games or rowed, some really well. On Sunday a few -- very few -- would go to chapel. Now we were deep in armchairs and the air was delicious with Dunhills. The moment Frank began, the atmosphere changed. He picked up some thread in the discussion and used that to weave his pattern. He began to tell of changed lives. His language was untheological. He described the changes in men so like ourselves that interest was riveted at once.

How else could it have been done? By sermons? By uplifting appeals? By philosophic subtitles? All these were familiar, but there was something new. Or, was it new? At least fresh and therefore interesting. Somehow our debate had been forgotten. We went out saying to one another, "What do you think of this fellow?" A saying of rare courage had been done among men accustomed to courage of another sort. It rather took our breath away, leaving more than a note of interrogation.

One of the men least likely to respond followed it up. He suggested we have Frank to breakfast next morning. Probably, I thought, he would ask us about our souls. That wasn't done -- certainly not at breakfast. So we ordered a large quantity of food then to keep him busy, a device that was only moderately successful. He began to tell us of a head mistress of the apparently dowager variety who wanted to know what to do with a girl who had stolen.

By way of making a disarming reply he turned to her and said, "When did you steal last?" This story delicately drew admissions from ourselves that we had been similarly delinquent. It suggested a shifted emphasis. Was this where to begin in the search for truth? Maybe it was. I had recent and painful recollections of having gone to the New College Commemoration Ball without paying for the ticket, and so I decided to send the money. The surprised committee replied by sending an invitation to the next ball.

A week or two later Frank returned to Oxford with three Cambridge men to spend the week-end. They came to tell us what their contact with Frank had meant to them. Yet they were not speaking about a man. These men were not the type that one generally associates with religious enthusiasm; one of them was a leading Cambridge Rugger Blue (football letter-man), the other two were ex-officers of the cultured, attractive type.

More than that, they seemed to have a radiance, subtle yet distinct, in their faces and manners and a good-fellowship among themselves that was as attractive as they were unforced.

That evening in our rooms these men spoke easily, yet convincingly, of a new power that had come into their lives to help them with their problems. They immediately captured the attention of the Oxford men. Granted that it was doing what was not done -- i.e., talking about personal religion -- yet it was done in a way that could offend no one, but only gain their confidence and sympathy.

Their words were the words of honest men out to share something good with anyone who had the sense to receive it. The Rugger Blue was walking round to the quad with an Oxford man on either arm. He seemed to get to know them better in one evening than we had in two years. There was something distinctly challenging in the quality of these men's lives and words.

Following their visit, groups of men would drift together in the quad and discuss this apparently new thing. Discussion rapidly changed to a deeper interest, even to astonishment, when it became known that some of the atheists and agnostics were different. There was abroad in the College an air of expectancy -- what was this all about?

The opportunity soon came to find out. Word came of a suggested house-party in a Cambridge College during the vacation.

It might be interesting to go and see it. A word here of personal explanation. That intervening month was one of those disturbed periods of my life. Plans had gone wrong and the future was uncertain. I realized that such efforts as I had made in philosophy to find a basis of life that after all proved very largely fruitless.

Going from school of thought to school of thought, I had found each to be a floating island. Already the noise of the cataract was sounding in my ears. The cataract for me was the abandonment of all attempt to solve the riddle of the universe and definitely to accept a cynical materialism as is the only solution. We had been caught up in the clouds of philosophic controversy and theological finesse; we had become academic, detached from life, and without any real solution for the questions of peace of mind, happiness, and the freedom from the bondage of temptation and sin.

I had been brought up to believe in the Christian message, and that conviction remained. Yet, I had never been able to find out how Jesus Christ Himself might become a personal reality in my older life. I naturally shrank from any such discussion with my friends. Conventional religion had failed; so one was thrown back upon a religion of one's own manufacture, the product of the code of behavior commonly accepted and in certain respects rigidly enforced in a Public School, the Regular Army and the Varsity.

Yet this self-made religion did not seem to work much better. There were still things wrong in my life and, more serious, getting worse. It was this last fact which the Group compelled me to face. I took refuge in flippancies and cynicism, yet they only intensified the difficulty. What was life all about, after all?

At this moment an invitation arrived from Frank to go to the Cambridge House-party. Providentially also an aunt sent some money. We had always understood that there was a University at Cambridge, and it might be rather interesting to see it. Also, what would Frank and his friends be doing at a house-party? It was all a little intriguing. We would have shrunk from anything emotional or sentimental, and we were bored with the conventional terminology of religion. The very word "religion" was anathema. Yet there was none of these things at the house-party.

It was a mixed crowd -- sinners, happy and unhappy, saints and would-be saints. They were all men, almost of an age, but with very different backgrounds and points of view. Religion would have been the last thing they would ordinarily have been willing to discuss or agree upon. We introduced ourselves, laughed very genuinely, and began to enjoy ourselves. There were some thirty men present. Very soon we were entirely at ease with each other.

Get the contrast. An older man of a different nationality was able in an effortless, unassertive sort of way to induce men hitherto strangers to one another to talk without affectation or self-consciousness of the things which most deeply occupied their minds. There was a rare freedom from pose or preaching. The language was colloquial.

It soon became clear that one of two things had to happen -- either one remained aloof and left, or else one stayed and was honest. Both these courses seemed equally disagreeable. By the last afternoon the necessity to decide was imperative. Four of us had been playing tennis and tea was just over. The discomfort of my false position had become intolerable. I had decided to be honest, with a full conviction that these men, clean, intelligent, healthy, would never have anything more to do with me.

Then an absurd longing to confess something dramatic or heroic; yet that would have been futile. There was only one thing for it -- to face the facts. To my astonishment and relief, the others were equally honest. False reserve had gone. Quite naturally we knelt down and prayed. That was the turning-point. Last there was a rift in the clouds. The meeting that evening was memorable.

The new quality of honesty became infectious. It continued to operate the following term at Oxford. Old friends began asking the reasons for new changes. A group of six met one night. A few nights later another six men were invited. Forty-four men actually turned up, and we adjourned to the Junior Common Room. Four of them had fortified themselves before coming and were slightly tipsy.

The vitriol of their attacks somehow failed to penetrate the charm ands reality of the atmosphere. We were definitely on this side of the angels. The message had established itself among us, and to oppose it was not primarily a sin against God, but a breach of good form. Prayer was offered publicly from a University pulpit thanking God for the illumination that had come to Oxford.

Chapter Five

THE FIRST HOUSE-PARTY

The scene is the Chinese Legation in a South American country. The speaker is the Chinese Minister, tall, angular, intellectual. After giving an official dinner, he is on his feet telling his extraordinary life-story and how he risked his head being carried on a pole down the streets of his native city (of which he was the Governor) rather than give up Christianity and at the behest of an all-powerful Soviet agent, just installed to communize his native providence. But he met Frank before he met the agent. Having imbibed Frank's message, he informed the communizer that he was quite ready to have his head taken down the streets of his native city on the pole, but unready to give up Jesus Christ, his personal Friend.

What so changed a Chinese Minister, one of the foremost men in his country, that he risked death rather than alter his basis of life, and incidentally gave the first house-party of a new movement that is developing largely through house-parties? Here is the Remarkable Story: Frank was working in the mountains of China when one day a friend said that since he was so concerned about changing people, why did he not try to change a friend of his. The future Chinese Minister was then described -- a fine diplomat and a great lawyer, in the foremost rank of the profession, and the legal adviser of the former President.

While studying abroad, this lawyer had become a Christian. On his return he was made a member of the Church Vestry and Treasurer of the Y.M.C.A. He surmised that it was because he would meet any debts when the financial year ended. He knew the church-people were criticizing his habits at the club. But as they failed to meet his deepest needs and were caustic about some of his practices, he kept to his club and Mah-Jong.

One day that Chinese diplomat invited Frank to his house to tea. The host brought cocktails to entertain the foreigner, and Frank said "No." A charming tray of cigarettes was likewise waived away with thanks. But Frank noticed the lawyer's hands were stained and his nerves were in a shocking condition as a result of too much nicotine and other things. His hands shook. The Chinese lawyer-diplomat talked a lot about himself and of his vast interests, while Frank thought here was another of the poor, rich men and tried to find some common bond of interest. His roving eye spotted a tennis-racket and they had a game. This led the lawyer to invite Frank to a feast. Frank had long since decided always to accept an invitation to a Chinese feast. (Long dinners of thirty or more courses beginning with eggs twenty years old, "tasting luscious, like cheese," followed by seaslugs, fish, fowl, and so on and on and on, until the chrysanthemum leaves dipped in marvelous sweets arrived.)

With the twenty-year-old eggs tucked safely away and the knowledge that he could skillfully dip his chopsticks into the great central dish, Frank began to feel happy. As his host took a different wine for each course, and as there were thirty-seven courses, he grew talkative as the evening advanced.

Frank had no need of his host's offer to send him home in a chair carried by six coolies; but he accepted. Next morning's Quiet Time told him to send his new friend an invitation to a return dinner, which was accepted too: just an English meal of soup, joint, cabbage, sweets, with no wines. A bishop and an archdeacon were present, and after the meal some of them began to share their religious experiences for the spiritual benefit of the visiting lawyer-diplomat. He, however, held aloof, sitting in one corner and looking like a huge question-mark.

Frank's story that evening was of an experience when crossing an American town and feeling impelled to accost a well-dressed man whom he sensed to be in deep need. Not being quite certain of the guidance, he decided on a compromise test. If the stranger stopped at the next lamp-post he would speak to him. The man stopped!

The Chinese lawyer-diplomat now grew interested as Frank told how he went up to the stranger and asked him if he was in need.

"Of course I am in need," he said anxiously.

"Then I think God must have sent me to you," said Frank.

"Of course it was God," he said, and told how his mother was at that moment dying in a near-by hospital. He had come out for a little fresh air.

Together they walked along with that sense of deep fellowship which comes when God drives one man into another man's life. Frank shared with the stranger the story of his own fathers and brothers home-going, and how he was convinced of the life beyond the grave.

The stranger said he had heard preachers talk about these

things, but not ordinary people, and was grateful for the consoling conversation. His seven brothers and sisters were waiting at the hospital yonder. Would Frank come and cheer them up? Frank went. The stranger begged him not to leave the hospital until they had prayed together in the chapel. Frank agreed.

At Easter Frank received a card, then a wire announcing the mothers home-going; and later a letter of deep gratitude.

The lawyer-diplomat was now intrigued. Frank says it is marvelous how all things fit in when working with God. At that moment a baby typhoon was raging outside, though not enough to raise the roofs, and there were sheets of rain. Frank invited his guests to stay the night. The visitor protested that he must go: his wife was waiting for him.

"You kept your wife waiting many times," hazarded Frank, and the guest smiled agreement.

Then he pleaded the coolies: they must get home. At that, Frank said that the coolies, also, would be welcome to stay, as three had been eaten by tigers over in the valley recently. But where could the visitors stay? This was the next objection. There was a spare bed in Frank's room, and the offer was accepted, none too eagerly. When they entered the bedroom, Frank reached for his Bible and invited his guest to read his favorite chapter. Most Christians, according to Frank, try to read the Bible to other people.

"That is the wrong way. Have them read to you."

The visitor went all through the Old Bible, as he called the Old Testament, trying to find his favorite chapter, and failed to find any familiar reading. He went through the New Testament with similar bad luck. The second time he went more cautiously, hoping circumstances would favour him. But luck was still against him. Then he did what a good many do -- he tried a lucky bit. The luck still went against him. He turned to a chapter in the Old Testament full of hard names and plentifully sprinkled with begats, but did what every good lawyer always does -- read it through from beginning to end. Frank suggested prayer. He replied:

"You pray."

Frank prayed, and they went to sleep. In the morning the boy brought tea, but the lawyer was unwilling or unable to awaken. The host made many attempts to wake him, but he was unresponsive. Presently, after a great deal of yawning and stretching, the Chinese guest opened his eyes and slyly asked Frank if he thought reading the Bible had put him so soundly asleep.

"Perhaps so," grinned the host. "Shall we read another chapter?"

"You read."

"I did," said Frank, "and his eyes almost popped out of his head, though I read only three verses."

The lawyer-diplomat asked for the verses to be read again, saying they just fitted him. Frank read them again. They were out of the sixth chapter of the First Epistle to the Corinthians. The reader may guess what the verses were. At this stage the lawyer revealed why he did not want to stay the night. It was because he had not brought his little pill. His doctor provided him with a pill to put him to sleep and another to wake him up.

"You are the only one to whom I've told this little secret," confessed the visitor, showing that the mask was beginning to come off.

After breakfast Frank told the boy to bring tea, the Chinese sign that the guest is now at liberty to depart. But the visitor was now eager to stay and talk. Frank had a meeting at 10:30 at a friend's house, and the lawyer decided to go with him. Frank's theme at this meeting was "Having too much of the good things of life."

"Those words apply to me," said the lawyer.

"That's why you heard them," said Frank.

"Then you planned the meeting for me?"

"Of course."

Frank believes in saying the right things to people who hear him. The lawyer was now intensely interested and asked Frank to lunch next day. Should it be English food or Chinese?

"Chinese," said Frank.

The other said he preferred foreign food, as Chinese was too rich, but that was not the real reason. Frank's Quiet Time that morning had solved for him the problem of what to say to this man in need, should they lunch together. The two things which had come to him were that the lawyer would be a great force in changing the life of another man, and that they would pray together before lunch was over. They had three minutes before lunch for a chat, and during that time Frank told him what his guidance had been. Whereupon the lawyer pulled out his notebook and told him that God had given him more guidance than Frank, for he had written down the name of the person whom he wanted to help. And he read out to Frank the name of a big industrialist. They prayed.

Then came lunch, at which were present the lawyer's Christian wife, Confucian mother, his children and governesses. During the lunch the lawyer shared with his wife and family some of the thoughts which had been in his mind, and said that when he married he led his wife to believe he was a real Christian. He had not succeeded in living the life, though the real hunger to do so was always there. But during the last few days he had made up his mind that Christ was going to have the first place in his life. Some of the things he did not want to do he was going to ask permission to do. One of these was to be a Chairman of the Religious Work Department to help the Chinese.

His mother was as deeply impressed as his wife, though she was a Confucian and took to her little cruse of olive oil and incense taper every morning as a votive-offering tube to the gods. She too became a Christian as a result of that memorable lunch.

The lawyer-diplomat had become a leading figure in China's Naturalist movement when Frank next met him.

And that time Frank and his team were helping a great Christian forward movement which added some four hundred members to the cathedral church of the city, and so astonished the Bishop that he became Frank's friend and admirer for life, his own son joining the Oxford Group as one of its leaders. The novel condition of entry for one cathedral service at this time was that each Christian brought a non-Christian with him. An official disregarded this stipulation, thinking himself privileged, and so was turned away. Instead of feeling indignant, he returned with three "tickets," his only comment being: "Why didn't you ask me to do this before?"

The Bishop's observation on this service was that he had now learned to see that every person in his diocese must be a force and not a field.

Next there came the first of a long series of house-parties through which the Oxford Group did much of its work, held in the country home of the lawyer-diplomat-Governor, who made a splendid host. Some of the eighty persons attending came from long distances necessitating six days of travel, and all brought together by the miracle of one changed Chinese lawyer-diplomat. From that gathering there sprang the first Chinese missionary society undertaking to man one of the unoccupied Chinese provinces with Chinese life-changers supported with Chinese money. And further, before the Governor departed for his high post as Chinese Minister abroad, he was instrumental in changing the prominent industrialist concerning whom he had as his first guidance.

Frank's early days in China are still a talking-point for Christian workers in all parts of the world. The late Bishop Lewis of China wrote saying the work Frank and his team did in the Far East had meant more to foreign and Chinese leadership than any single movement during his twenty-eight years in China.

Everywhere Frank goes he leaves behind him a trail of converts of all nationalities, which may open up for him a wider work, as in the case of the boy, Victor. Picture the Hanchenjunga Range of the great Himalayas, white tents of Abraham hanging in the heavens. Here in this wonderful country was being held a schoolboy's camp, including many who needed help. One of the helpers was a master from a well-known English public school. He invited Frank to assist him in the case of one Victor, the real problem of the camp. Victor refused to attend lectures, preferring to skylark about, releasing the tent-pegs and making himself happy at others' expense. The masters had met and decided that Victor must go home, but they thought he should first have a word with Frank.

"Have you talked with the boy?" Frank asked.

"No. We've talked about him."

Frank observes that some persons talk about another, but never with him. He suggested that was the first thing to be done, and promised he would see the lad at 10:30. The time came, but no Victor, and at tiffen (the mid-day meal) the master asked if Frank had had an interesting conversation with Victor.

"No Victor," said Frank.

"Oh, but he promised me."

"Victor may have said 'yes,' but he meant 'no,'" observed Frank.

Another appointment was made at 2:30, usually the hot period of the Indian afternoon when everybody wants to be asleep under the cooling punkah. Two-thirty came.

"Well, did you have a pleasant chat with Victor?"

The master received the same answer.

"He promised me," repeated the master, which suggested a rather wooden approach to a boy.

The master then invited Frank to address the meeting that evening, which he agreed to do, but could not guarantee to make his address just personal to Victor, as there were so many other needs requiring to be met in a variety of boys. That night he spoke in a beautiful little chapel, and in the middle of the talk in came the master, following an unsuccessful effort to lure Victor away from a boat on the canal on a liquid moonlight night.

"And who could blame Victor for staying away?" is Frank's aside as he tells the story.

The master was in dead earnest, for Frank observed him later praying for Victor and himself and for light on how best to deal with the errant lad.

On the following Sunday morning, at about eleven, the master came running in to Frank, announcing: "I've got Victor!" Frank must come at once. He went, expecting to find Victor seated in a chair ready to be interviewed. Instead he was shown a little knoll and Victor and another lad playing a farewell game before leaving on the two-thirty train. How the master expected Frank to lasso the elusive Victor and draw him back to the camp he did not know. But he stealthily approached, for Victor -- whose conscience was busy about those dodged interviews -- was very wary. The boys were playing with bamboo canes, which they twirled with cartwheel affect, requiring much practice and dexterity. As Victor twirled, Frank's cheering voice rang out:

"Hullo, Victor!"

Victor was completely surprised, and Frank followed up his advantage. "You do that jolly well, Victor. I wish I could do it."

"You try," said Victor, quite naturally.

Frank tried unsuccessfully, and Victor enjoyed his confusion. Frank turned to Victor's friend and said:

"Do you mind excusing us?"

The other lad walked away, looking regretfully back, like Lot's wife.

Frank and Victor went into a tent, and as they were sitting down Frank said: "I went to a camp once and didn't like it a bit."

Victor grew brighter. "Were *you* like that?"

"Yes, of course."

"I am, too."

"What's the reason?"

"I suppose," said Victor, "because there's something wrong inside. I feel rebellious."

"Was that why you pulled up the tent-pegs?"

"Yes. I felt I'd be in trouble, and so I didn't want to see anyone or be bothered with people."

Frank told the boy he understood and hated most things he hated. They yarned along. Then the boy said he was sorry.

"How much are you sorry? You know what remorse is?"

"Oh yes, I know. That's sorrow for sin when you go ahead and do it again."

"Then what do you think you need?"

"Repentance."

"What's that?"

"Oh, that's when a fellow's sorry enough to quit!"

The boy's destinations so impressed Frank that he has used

them ever since. He began to talk to the lad about having so interesting a companion that he always understood and so compelling
a friend that he never wished to run away from him.

"I know who that is," said the boy. "That's Christ. I would like to
be a Christian, but I don't know how."

Frank said he would try to show him. He explained that his difficulty had begun with the letter "I," which was the middle letter
of sin. "Sin blinds, binds, multiplies, darkens, deafens, deadens.
What we need is faith. When we are perfectly willing to forsake sin
and follow Christ, then joy and release comes. What we want to do
is to get in touch with Him and turn our lives over to Him. Where
should we go to do it?"

At once the lad replied:

"There's only one place -- on our knees."

The lad prayed -- one of those powerful, simple prayers which
are so quickly heard by Him Who made the eye and ear: "O Lord,
manage me, for I cannot manage myself."

They rose and talked about development in the Christian life,
Frank insisting that the real way to grow was to help other people.
As the lad said he felt as though a big burden had fallen off of him,
a lot of old luggage that was no good had rolled away. He wondered
why it had not happened before. The new feeling just suited him,
and he must go and tell his friends.

The master had gone to the railway station, and so Frank accompanied Victor there. On their way they saw a man being taken
off to prison. As Frank saw the rope binding him to the red-capped
guards, he exclaimed: "Oh, that's a sad sight! That man's a slave."

"I was a slave until this morning," volunteered the changed boy.
"Now I'm free."

"Is that how you feel?"

"Yes, I'm as light as air."

While Victor was buying the ticket, the master came up, saying
he had observed a wonderful change already in the lad. He looked
different. What had happened?

Frank said: "Ask Victor. We believe in keeping confidences."

But what was Victor doing at this moment? As Frank looked
down the platform, his curiosity got the better of him. Moving
down, he saw Victor talking in a friendly way to the shackled prisoner, who had become communicative.

"What did you say to him?" asked Frank, as Victor came up.

"I told him I was sorry about him and that I was like him once.
That I was a slave to sin and a prisoner. I told him that Paul was

a prisoner too, though he was really a free man. And that he could be a free man. And that I hoped to see him when he came out to tell him about it."

Victor had made a quick start.

As the man was hungry from his dusty walk, Victor bought him a curry and rice, which he gratefully accepted.

Several weeks later Frank was staying with friends in Victor's home-city and was invited to go for a Sunday afternoon drive. He said he preferred to stay in the city to see a young fellow who had experienced a real change. His host thought it a poor program for a hot afternoon. Frank went to the college and asked for Victor, and was elated to find he was down in the Mohammedan quarter conducting a religious service. That evening Frank told his host the full story, and found him so interested that it was difficult to get him to bed. He thought it incredible that so great a change could be wrought in a modern boy. It was like the miracles of the New Testament over again.

"Why not try it yourself?" suggested Frank. "People are hungry for someone to come along and do it."

Next morning Frank went early to breakfast with Victor, who brought in some of his changed college friends to whom he had passed on the message.

A few weeks later Frank was in a distant part of the country when he encountered a Bishop with whom he was to stay for a few weeks. The Bishop's first words were:

"I don't need any introduction to you. *I've seen Victor!*"

Because of Frank's success with Victor, that Bishop invited him to interview an undergraduate at Oxford; and that interview, in turn, developed into the Oxford Group Movement.

Chapter Six

THE OXFORD GROUP

Frank is a fine gentleman and a great missionary. An accomplished linguistic and a happy travel companion. He rarely stays in one country for a long period. Here, there and everywhere he is being used to start groups of changed people; then he hurries away to another town or country, according to the leading of the Spirit. When first I heard of him he was traveling through South America; he knows China like the Chinese; he is thoroughly at home in Germany, the Netherlands, India, America, Africa, and Australia. He has never penetrated Iceland, and knows what many Englishmen do not -- that Iceland is not part of the British Empire, but a Danish possession.

Sometimes Frank has been dubbed "a missionary to missionaries" because of his zeal and love for the Gospel message and his efforts to help every Christian to achieve maximum efficiency. When choosing leaders to supervise the Groups in his absence, Frank frequently shows himself inspired, as with the leader he left in charge of the Group at Oxford. Ken Twitchell is a handsome young Princetonian with engaging manners who suddenly changed, and later took his degree at Balliol, Oxford. He is one of those charming Americans who delight Englishmen.

One fine week-end in February I ran down to Oxford to see Ken Twitchell and the Oxford Group in action. Ken asked me to dinner, and I found myself in a comfortably-furnished home occupying a corner site just off the Banbury Road. For some years Ken and his wife, Marian and family have been living without salary on faith and prayer, which evidently did not mean they had to reside in a log cabin. For dinner there was no wine; a glass of water was placed before me.

"What is the Group teaching about smokes and drinks?" I asked.

"What do *you* think?"

That is the characteristic Group answer. The decision is left to you. Rigidity over details is unpopular. There are principals in the Fellowship, but no rigid rules. Throw a question at the Group and it comes back to you. Here are certain facts. Interpret them as you think best under God's guidance. "Do anything God lets you." That is the guiding theory of the Group, and that gives freedom.

Garrett Stearly was once a slave to cigarette-smoking. For him it had become a sin which must be surrendered, though not necessarily by others. Not an easy thing for Garrett. He won his battle -- with a struggle.

At another meeting I heard a newcomer ask for a ruling on liquor. Again the reply:

"What do you think?"

A dark, handsome Englishman said he had been striving to help some friends out of drunkenness. His guidance was to cut out liquor himself, or how could he hope to influence them? Unless he was prepared to sacrifice his own pleasure for their sake, he was not correctly interpreting the teachings of Christ and His Apostles for which the Group stood. Again the old teaching that Paul enunciated: if meats (or drinks for that matter) caused his brother to offend he would eat (or drink) no more of the offending food (or drink). Again, nothing about you in the thought, though a definite transition from theory to practice. And this is Oxford University, where nearly everybody smoked and drank. Here again, *now* and *had* become the verb: the theory -- the life. A truth commonplace in Christianity had regained its old uncommon lustre through transition into action.

Ken Twitchell brought out his car -- an aged Morris purchased when the open tourer was an English fashion. He drove me down to Corpus Christi College. It was half-past eight on Sunday evening. The night was beautiful and cold, with a full moon riding above the constellated roofs of the colleges brightly illuminating the great quadrangle of Christ Church -- college of the elect, where Frank had made his debut. As we passed under Tom Tower across to the flagged cloisters of Corpus Christi, delicate tracery of college pinnacles made a network of shadows along our pathway to the well-trodden stairs leading us to the Chaplain's rooms. I was too stirred by the beauty of old Oxford under a full moon to speculate on what awaited me as we entered. Was this a religious meeting, a lecture, or a concert? Very like the lecture-room of the Household Brigade, O.C.B., with the same fine-looking company of virile young men of the Guard type crowding the room, occupying every chair, or sitting, knees drawn up, on the scanty floor-space. Several sat about the door as we entered; others crowded the dais or tucked themselves into odd corners. A happy, homely meeting. No formality of clothes or conduct; lounge suits, plus fours, colored ties; good feeling, some healthy laughter, though nothing forced, ribald, or irreverent.

No juvenile Pecksniffs here, but faces that shone. This Oxford Group -- Number One Group of a chain of groups around the world -- was something very fresh and very modern. The atmosphere was religious but not sentimental. These young men were polished and sophisticated. Knowing the world, they had already elected to know only Christ, by deliberate preference. There was a Don or two present. A young man of 20-5 named Francis Elliston, son of an M.P., held open on his knees what I assumed to be his guidance-book, to which he occasionally referred as he developed his story.

A couple of chairs were immediately vacated for our benefit, while the room became more crowded as the trickle of undergraduates continued through the constantly-opening door. All the same cheery type. No roysterers attempting to disturb the meeting. I wished there were. Before the meeting ended we were to hear from one who first came in tipsy with a bunch of gay spirits, to find, not a new entertainment, but a new life!

The leader announced that if there were more arrivals we should have to copy the real-estate people and "move to larger and more commodious premises." Almost immediately we were ordered to take up our chairs and descend to a bigger room below. When the shuffling had subsided, the leader raised a laugh by giving the limit of accommodation of the new room. "If you get more than that," he dryly added, "we shall pass the safety factor again. And I would remind you -- the blast furnace is immediately below us."

There we sat in our first meeting of the Oxford group poised above a potential inferno, a Dantesque location for a new religious movement. Still the undergraduates swarmed in.

The meeting was thrown open for witness on the usual Group lines. I was doubtful if they would get many of the undergraduates on their feet. A lad on my left jumped up and began to address the meeting. He spoke sensibly, with feeling, while he quietly described his endeavors during the past week to lead a life lived by the early Christians. His story gave me a new thrill. One had heard reformed characters telling the old, old story in the market square, fervent evangelists speaking at revival meetings, old-fashioned orators in village Bethel's, young women volunteering good advice at Christian Endeavor meetings, and disregarded tub-thumpers in the parks. But this was different. The simple story told here at Corpus Christi seemed to make Christianity more real than before.

The life was being lived more earnestly than I had thought it was being lived anywhere. Though the voice was the voice of culture, the words were of true humility. Admissions were made which I had never heard made in any form of meeting. Young men were revealing their real selves, although saying nothing that offended good taste. Modesty, but no false reserve. Young aristocrats of Oxford were showing a masked world how to be honest by removing their own masks. They told of their daily fight with sin, indicated some of the sins -- pride, selfishness, dishonesty, laziness, unbelief, impurity -- admitted their slips and showed how, through the indwelling presence of a living Christ, they were achieving victory. Public testimony that life in close personal association with the Holy Spirit in Oxford University was possible. Here was something that was not done, being done: intimate personal religion talked openly and joyfully by young men who were happy because they were achieving victory over sin through walking daily with God. And for years I had nursed the conviction that if our religion was true, then Christians should lead care-free lives under the constant guidance of the Holy Spirit. News again!

There was no hesitancy. One undergraduate followed another quickly. Each spoke in the same easy style. Not the argumentative arrogance of youth in the debating society, but simple, compelling witness to personal experience. Each had something different to say. Each gave a new facet to Christian living because he spoke with candour and naturalness, and with many unrehearsed human torches, as journalists say. And as each spoke self-revealing things requiring courage to say publicly, the interest never flagged.

Some of the incidents narrated were, of course, trivial in themselves, but to the understanding hearer were important pointers to new principles animating in the lives of the witnesses. These young men had begun to learn what was rarely taught elsewhere -- HOW TO LIVE.

A well-grown lad in the far corner was an organist; he had learned to apply himself better to lessons through his surrender to Christ's teaching. Another, a dark-haired lad with rudy features, had discovered (if I remember rightly) that it was selfishness for the Group to hobnob together in Hall instead of mixing with the others and doing their spare-time best to bring prodigals back to their Master's Kingdom.

There were no blatant confessions. One tallish lad with a fine head did gratefully announce that only through contact with the Group had he been able to overcome impurity, an unusual admission in a religious meeting -- the first time I had heard it made. (Though once I had attended Brixton Parish Church when Dr. Lang, before he became Archbishop of Canterbury, dealt frankly with sex impurities when preaching in a gathering of men only.) One's sympathies were immediately evoked by this Oxford boy's frank confession. It was he who gave me fresh understanding of the word grace which I had previously heard defined unsatisfactorily as God's bounty to the undeserving sinner. This lad, telling of victory over sin, defined grace as God's strength which, to his amazement, had given him joyous release from his greatest weakness.

God's grace in action in Oxford University at that moment! What would be the effect of that story on newspaper readers -- if one dared print it? I could only tell the effect of that story on myself. I wondered if the same kind of grace would give me the same kind of victory over another kind of sin. Then -- doubts began. Wasn't grace another name for self-hypnotism? I had to delve deeper into the movement before I found out.

The words purity and impurity I heard occasionally at subsequent Group meetings. Sometimes the word lust. But though I have attended hundreds of Group meetings, I do not remember hearing anything in bad taste.

Presently I came to learn that spiritual anniversaries were a fashion at these meetings. Hardly one passes but someone rises and announces that just a year ago to-day he decided to surrender his life to God. Then follows a description of change from a life of worry, chaos and discord to one of peace, order and harmony. A relinquishing of every weighty burden and confident resting in the Everlasting Arms. A breathlessly interesting year of working out a new orientation of life, and striving to bring all thoughts and actions into accord with the challenging standards of Christ. And now a grateful testimony to the truth that Christ does change lives and does keep anyone on His narrow white road who wills it. These are happy stories of a new and exuberant way of living, sometimes interspersed with references to casual slips followed by remorse, repentance, and re-surrender of the area damaged by sin. But at the end of the year a cheerful and humble affirmation of spiritual growth, conscious progress in the kingdom of fitness which is the Kingdom of God. And a reiterated gratitude at being freed from the old life, which had never given real satisfaction.

One of those anniversaries occurred the night of my first visit to the Oxford Group. A fair-haired, rosy-faced youth, with horn-rimmed spectacles, speaking with a cheery and even rollicking reverence, if our Pharisees permit the description, told a jaunty story of his change from the prodigal life to one of sanity and serenity. Little more than twenty, he spoke convincingly, clearly, and well. Youthful polarity and youthful sincerity blended in the story he told. Weighing it afterwards, I wondered whether the hilarity predominated over the sincerity. Next day that doubt was answered when he gave up his afternoon to my entertainment, taking me for a run in his car, and then for a long stroll over the breezy hills to the south-east, amplifying his religious autobiography as he went with special reference to his victories over drink and impurity. As he reached the summit he stopped, swept out his arm, and proudly named each one of that stirring panorama of spires and domes which is Oxford.

But in his car he declined an invitation to tea for another reason which convinced me that he was the genuine Christian as well as the hilarious convert. He had an engagement with a young atheist undergraduate, who had invited him to discuss Christianity, through surprise at being frequently offered rides in the hilarious one's car when overtaken around the outskirts of the city.

"Giving Christianity away to another is the best way to keep it," said Ken Twitchell, looking after the energetic youngster as he departed once more to cast his life-story at the feet of unbelief.

But what religious experience could these young fellows have to share? This is the question which the average man wants answered. By the time a dozen undergraduates had spoken in the first Group meeting I attended, the question had been answered for me. Unquestionably these young fellows had an experience which convinced them, or they would have sat down confused. Later the Group leader of that evening (Francis Elliston) told me his own story of his change. He left school at the age of sixteen to go to Cambridge University, and quickly found that his public-school religion was unreal to him.

Francis always envied bus-conductors and other people without inhibitions. He had been jealous, for instance, of his elder brother's ability to play with children, dimly realizing that he ought to live a life that was unselfconscious and purposeful; and was bitterly antagonistic to a religion that seemed to offer an ideal without the power to live it. He was, therefore, ironical at the expense of those who professed to have it. He found an outlet for his energies in sports, amateur dramatics, and University journalism, but felt there was no coherence in his life. In the Group he was challenged by the simplicity of one man, and the peace of his expression. This man, then a medical student at a London hospital and now a doctor, asked him if he had ever made the experiment of writing down on paper what his life was like judged by the standards of Jesus Christ.

He sat down to write to his medical student friend outlining his attitude towards the accepted moral standards of society, calling upon psychological arguments to justify the avoidance of repression. He finished his letter and picked it up to number the pages. As he did so his eye was caught by one sentence he had written in which he said: "I have always been perfectly frank about my attitude in any company."

He was suddenly jolted into realizing that this was a plan of truth, and in accuracy wrote in the margin: "P.S. This is not true. I have never been frank about this in any company." He hastily re-read the letter, and by the time he had finished there were a dozen contradictory postscripts. He posted the letter, realizing that he was seeing the death-warrant of his own old life. The journey down to the office on top of the bus next morning brought home to him a startling truth of the text "Behold I make all things new."

Since that time, three years ago, he has been realizing something of the freedom of the Franciscan Friars, to whom every meeting on the road was a spiritual adventure, and he no longer envies bus-conductors.

A smallish, alert, and highly intelligent lad from Sunderland told how he came into contact with the Group in October, 1930, when he came up to Oxford, after a boyhood of conscious attendance at a Baptist church where he was baptized at the age of fifteen -- a step the significance of which he completely failed to realize. He had a shy and nervous temperament, a keen and absorbing interest in classical scholarship, a great love for good music, and an extravagantly high set of ideals of the kind typified in Ruskin's *Sesame and Lilies*. His ideals had been bruised under the rough and tumble of a modern University College, and he took refuge in an academic and the cynical exterior. His religious beliefs failed to stand the strain of intellectual examination, and with the opportunity of coming to Oxford he was glad to escape from a church situation rapidly becoming intolerable, because he was teaching children things which he had ceased to believe.

"At Oxford," he says, "I hoped to find an intellectually satisfying philosophy. On the first day of my first term I met a South African Rhodes Scholar, who asked me to go along to a religious meeting, and merely warned me not to be surprised at anything I heard. I was surprised at everything I heard. My intellectual vanity was tickled by the presence of a Don as leader, but what interested me most was the indecently radiant happiness of many of those present, and the conviction with which they spoke of the possibility of a life-transforming experience of Jesus Christ. Rather bitterly I wrote to an ancient friend of mine to the effect that I had met a crowd of people who said they had found Jesus Christ and signalized their discovery by laughing uproariously and calling one another by their Christian names. But I went again. At first I approved of a movement which was turning Pagans into decent members of society. Then I discovered that I wanted the power which these people had. Intellectual difficulties became irrelevant under a growing conviction of the sins of my own life -- dishonesty, intellectual snobbery, pride, a biting tongue, and an uncontrollable temper.

"Finally, I was faced by St. Paul's declaration, 'I determined not to know anything among you save Jesus Christ and Him crucified.' Then for the first time that significance of the Cross came home to me, and I made my surrender. Since then it has meant a growing sense of release and adventure. People have become more important than things. Sarcasm, criticism, and temper have disappeared. I have found that at the foot of the Cross pride, especially intellectual pride, vanishes. I am beginning to learn how to love people who are temperamentally different from myself. I have discovered an increasing victory over what has been my chief real problems -- conceit and fear. It has involved no loss of intellectual honesty. The discipline of reading 'Greats' has done nothing to shake the validity of the conviction I have had of the friendship of Jesus Christ, a conviction founded not on feeling, but on facts and on faith. In short, Christ is enabling me for the first time to live, as well as to know."

Listening to such witness, one passed through curiosity to astonishment, thence into unqualified admiration.

In his book, *Religion and Politics,* by Stanley Baldwin, the former Prime Minister of England, said: "I confess that I am not sure, if a Wesley or a St. Francis arose to-day, that to found a body of preaching friars would not be the best thing for the world. . . . . To-day the world seems more irreligious than it has ever been in the Christian era."

Yet here were three-score and more young men -- a body of preaching friars -- about to take their degrees, already dedicated

to the life of preaching friars, determined to follow Christ and pro-
claim Him wherever they went, as clergymen, ministers, or lay-
men, by the simple first-century method of narrating the story of
their own changed lives, and reliance on the direction of the Holy
Spirit. It will be for the next generation to estimate the results.

At Oxford a luncheon-hour Group meets every day in term in the
Old Library of the University Church of St. Mary. Another meets
every Tuesday afternoon. There is also a Women's Group. I attended the one held next day, when Ken Twitchell read a chapter
from one of the latest translations of the New Testament. All the
old truths came out of that translation with freshened force.

Here I had my first practical experience of the Quiet Time, a
first principle of the Group and one of the biggest obstacles to the
newcomer, but a principle on which the Group can make no compromise. The Guidance must come in all those who surrender to
Gods will. As Ken Twitchell announced the Quiet Time the undergraduates fumbled for pencils and guidance-books and began to
"listen in" to God. This was not simple meditation, which may be
concentration on some aspect of Christ or the Gospel, but something more: a lessening of definite messages applicable to present
needs. As they were committed to doing God's will, that could be
known for them at any moment of necessity.

Watching them quietly writing, one was divided by two opposing
thoughts. There was an element of humor inviting laughter. Surely
they were all crazy. Yet the lecture-room method of note-taking in
Quiet Time might be a happy idea. In theory what could be better?
This inspirational method had all other forms of communication --
wireless, aeroplanes, telegraphs -- clean beaten. If only it worked!

But who would believe that it worked? Most certainly not Fleet
Street. Once as a junior reporter I endured some scoffing for returning from an assignment with the story of how a sick girl had
been miraculously cured by her own prayers, although I had secured all the facts and interviewed the girl. She had been ill for
many years, had suddenly recovered, and of course had the face
of an angel. We printed this story -- with reservations. And now
what would Fleet Street say to this tale? I knew the answer: "Give
us the thoughts that come in Quiet Time, and if they are startling
enough to convince us we will believe."

There was nothing startling about the thoughts that came: just
such as would come from any young man dedicated to the Christian life, it then seemed to me. I asked Ken Twitchell about this
and how one could discriminate between what might be guided

thoughts and what were just floating human thoughts. The Group said the individual was guided by God both during Quiet Time and throughout the day in the following ways.

Through the Holy Spirit in attentive prayer by means of:

The Scriptures.
The Conscience.
Luminous Thoughts.
Cultivating the Mind of Christ.
Through reading the Bible and prayer.
Through circumstances.
Through reason.
Through Church, Group, or Fellowship.

The conditions of effective guidance where the whole-hearted giving of oneself to Jesus Christ. The tests are:

Does it go counter to the highest standards of belief that we already possess?
Does it contradict the revelations which Christ has already made in or through the Bible?
Is it absolutely honest, pure, unselfish, loving?
Does it conflict with our real duties and responsibilities to others?

It's still uncertain, wait and continue in prayer, and consult a trustworthy friend who believes in the guidance of the Holy Spirit.

Suddenly Ken Twitchell invited me to speak -- I, the representative of a group of newspapers which once cast a slur on the movement. The undergraduates listened with indulgence, without animosity. They smiled when I mentioned my religious discussions with my vicar at golf; how I won the arguments and he won the golf. I tried to make a point of Father Martindale's, that whatever one thought of long enough one was sure ultimately to do when the opportunity came. So if one thought of a sin, one would commit that sin. If one thought of goodness, one would do right. Then I forgot Father Martindale's point.

I said I objected to the phrase "Quiet Time," as it sounded banal, and preferred "Listening in"; and more trivialities I hoped would be helpful, but which, I sensed afterwards, were rather old-fashioned stuff with these new-fashioned youths. Evidently someone had been giving them such intensive training in vital Christianity as to leave me standing.

Afterwards I felt there was something elusive in the Quiet Time, and somehow a cleavage between my idea of Christianity and theirs. Twelve months afterwards I heard from my younger son at school that the worst part of college life was the hour for quite and study. I sympathize with the lad, three thousand miles away, feeling that he must be suffering from a family complaint.

Yet in the afternoon of that same day at Oxford I had my first results from the Quiet Time. We were discussing some difficult problem when Ken said, "Let's try the Quiet Time." We drew out slips of paper, relaxed, listened; confident that there was little in it, that inspiration could not be organized to solve a business problem anymore than to discover the name of a winning race-horse before the event. Then, just as we were about to put our papers away, there suddenly crossed my ordinary, tumbled, human thoughts one or another thought which seemed to possess a strong luminous glow, differing sharply from the rest. To describe a particular thought apart from what it expressed is well-nigh impossible. But I know that it had color, shape, feeding, and luminosity. It told me to do something that I purposely had never done, had no wish to do and, if I had previously thought of doing, I should have humanly rejected as useless and absurd. Yet, if the person I was told to see accepted my suggestion, which I humanly knew he would not, my particular problem at that time was solved. And perhaps another problem too: whether there was any sense in this amusing method of writing down your thoughts and kidding yourself they were messages from God!

The new luminous thought had come so unexpectedly and with such a peculiar glow of rightness that I went back to London and tried it. Within a few minutes of the thoughts being transferred to the person in great authority whom it concerned, he rang me up on the telephone thanking me profusely (as he had never previously done) for my splendid help, of which he was taking immediate advantage.

An unpalatable Quiet Time had cleared up one and perhaps two problems. So there *was* something in guidance, after all.

Chapter Seven

A MOTOR CLUB BLOWS UP

Let us assume the theme of this short story is a motor club in an English University, and that three young dare-devils are at its secret centre, bent on painting the town and countryside red, doing it so consistently that one of their number is sent down; that all three plunge heedlessly into all sorts of scrapes with all sorts of authorities; are modern disciples of Don Juan; organizers of illegal motor-races on the high roads, reckless riders in the Isle of Man Amateur Races; and are contemptuous of ordinary sinners because they have not the abandon to go hell-for-leather in a life of wild revelry.

And let us assume that someone alleged it possible, in these post-war years of unbelief, to penetrate that centre of profligate undergraduate life and change those three roistering prodigals into men who listen-in to God for His daily guidance and spend their lives changing others to their own pattern -- humbly modelled on the pattern of Christ, that these regenerated undergraduates had already become effective life-changers. Would anyone believe this possible in 1932, when the truths of Christianity are generally regarded as frozen assets?

Yet the truth is no less surprising than the assumption. These things have just happened in an English University, among the "up-and-outs," not in a slum mission among "down-and-outs." Because of their marvelous transformation, the heart was taken out of the wild life in the Carburetor Club (as we will name it for the purpose of this true story), the inner ring of a motoring club.

If there is still any adventure in modern religion, there is adventure in this tale as told me by the three chief conspirators -- who shall be called Bob, Rip and Sandy -- which seems to be one of the news stories that Fleet Street has missed.

The story begins with Bob, who is a tallish, upstanding, broad-shouldered young fellow of twenty-two with fair, curly hair, remarkably fair teeth, a pair of tortoiseshell spectacles, and a sphinx-like expression which leaves you wondering if he is on guard against you or hoping you will stay. He won a scholarship to Winchester and did amazing things when at that famous school. He annexed practically all the prizes for classical research, English literature, German translation, and a good many seconds as well. He was not a born athlete, but became one of the synthetic variety, by patient effort and determination. Good at rowing, at fives, at Winchester Football ("Our Game," as Wykehamists call it), he had sufficient merit to command a majority of what honors and positions there were. Of the four hundred and fifty boys at Winchester there are seventy-six privileged to wear the Scholar's gown. Five leaders of the school are appointed officers over the scholars, and over those five officers is the Perfect of Hall. And the one who becomes Perfect of Hall has to justify that pre-eminent position by weight of achievement, which Bob was able to do by dint of effort. Winchester expects that every scholar will do his duty at the Varsity by winning a first in "Mods" and "Greats."

Bob secured his scholarship into his college, and then his penchant for this study and sports, except motor racing, flopped. Surfeited with past achievements, he now felt the time had come to enjoy himself with Sandy and Rip, two gay companions. They founded the Carburetor Club and began to make things hum. Headquarters were conveniently situated near to several "pubs," all patronized in turn. That the Carburetor Love was not pictorially recognized, and was therefore an illegal institution, mattered little. In the first year Bob ran three motor-cycles for sport and a small car for pleasure.

The three went to the Isle of Man and two rode in the Amateur Road Races there. They had sport, some luck in their races, and still more merriment between, even to the extent in taking a public-house piano to pieces before breakfast. Back in College, Sandy continued to make things merry, once by throwing forty empty bottles into the main street, to the distress of the Dean.

Another exploit was for the three motor musketeers to hire a lorry and a temperance driver and tour all the public-houses of the city tasting all that was going, while the townsfolk, not unused to odd spectacles, looked on amused. Sandy became so offensive on the ride around that his friends threw him off. His language passed the Plimsoll line.

The Carburetor Club organized an illegal motor race at dawn on the high road, though the winner only achieved a leisurely 68 m.p.h. About this time Winchester's ex-Perfect of Hall quietly distinguished himself by climbing out of College, down the rain-pipe of an adjacent house, a difficult but not unprecedented feat, as other undergraduates know from practical experience. The difference between Bob's getting away and that of other undergraduates taking the same route was that he took with him the rain-pipe as well as his freedom! Though not for long! For a city policeman invited the ex-head of Winchester to the police-station, where he was allowed to go, after information as to identity had been checked by removing his coat for the police to read his name on the inside tab.

And now the Group began to get busy with the Carburetor Club; and the Carburetor Club with the Group. The three motor musketeers had heard that the Group talked openly about their sins, so Sandy was deputed to go down and tell them what it really is, since he was an expert in the subject, and to break the show. Perhaps the best way to picture Sandy is to say how he then looked to his pal Bob, who grinned as he said: "Sandy has a merry peal of laughter chiefly aroused by any form of iniquity. A moustache, slight and light, a hook nose, spectacles, somewhat receding forehead, sallow, a quick brain that can throw off smart slogans at command, and good organizing ability." Sandy returned from the Group meeting saying he had told them a few things they needed to know, as he was in the habit of telling Deans and other institutions before he finally left. Of course he still wore his old tweed cap, broken peak, plenty of oil on top, and his brown leather waistcoat. But the Group was good shock-absorbers.

And now Sandy ran into a Springbok (All-South African) Rugger-player, one of the Group, who began to take him in hand. He induced Sandy to go down to Chrowborough for a house-party which Frank had arranged there. "The people knew I was coming," said Sandy, "and I was ushered in by Frank with some ceremony, which rather fluttered my pride. That perhaps prevented me from being affected by the meeting. I know I was very disagreeable and obstreperous as usual. I had tea, and then looked all around for a few girls, and was rather disappointed at being out of luck. But I took a strong liking for Frank, and was struck by the kindness in his eye. I boasted to Frank that my amusements were women and drink, but I refrained from disclosing that I was secretly lonely and bitterly unhappy. He didn't seem very shocked, but said to cut them both out. We prayed together, and I went back -- changed! The first person to know the difference was my landlady. I had come in at three in the morning sober, and went out next morning still sober."

Sandy's first attempt at witness was a letter to Bob and Rip, telling them simply what had happened.

The earth ceased revolving for a while when the Carburetor Club received Sandy's letter saying he had tried running his own life and failed, and had tried letting Christ run it for him, and was succeeding; that as he'd tried two lives and they'd only tried one, he felt it right to tell them which was better.

"That made us think a bit," said Rip. "We put down our glasses and began to consider the amazing news. Our star had gone over to the despised enemy. Not having anything more or original to do, we jeered."

Sandy seemed to take that all right, which was rather unlike him, for he loved to answer back, and had a tongue like a razor. He merely said, "All right, you come and meet these chaps and see for yourselves." So Sandy arranged a tea-party at his house, and eight in the Club decided to go along. When the Group heard this they sent out a Flying Squad comprising three of the best shots, and -- most important -- backed by a battery of twenty-five men, solidly praying.

This Flying Squad stopped about one hundred yards from Sandy's house and held one of their deadly Quiet Times. Before entering, Ken Twitchell coached his two colleagues not to mince words, to avoid pious phraseology, and to talk in a language that Pagans understand. The eight lambs inside were unaware what was being prepared for them without. When the three entered, tea was served, and everybody was on his best behavior. At first the Group wanted to know of what the motoring game was like just now, how study was going, anything but the religious inclinations of the eight. But after tea all drew round in a circle, when the three broke into the main business of the evening, with Sandy, ex-ringleader of the revelers, the subdued link.

There was not much time to argue, for the Group jumped straight into their well-proven game of giving evidence. One began telling his yarn. A compelling story, that was. A parson's son, he had lost all his jobs in England, and had been sent out to Canada, where his progress was equally undistinguished. One night he had come home so tight that he indulged in a massacre (chopping off the heads) of all the hens in the chicken-run. That story was hilariously received by some of the wild men of the road. The speaker now found the climate of Canada a little too warm; he went south to New York, between trains gambling all his money on poker, with the exception of seven dollars. He picked up a job in New York selling china behind a counter. An English lady came into the store (a natural contact), and casually asked him if he had any use for religion, and he replied, "No." She invited him to Calvary Church, and he went. There at the famous Thursday night Group he met a young banker who had been in the depths of degradation and had been re-created by the power of Christ. But the speaker still thought he was beyond hope. So he was taken down to the Calvary Mission, where he heard some amazing stories of changed lives from men who had been right up to the edge or beyond. One man told of how he had been turned out of his house sick and ill and told to go somewhere and die. Looking for a suitable spot to die in, he was changed at Calvary Mission. This story at last convinced the parson's son that he could get the victory over his evil impulses, and that Christ was the real answer for him.

The former leader of Winchester, listening-in, observed the sinews standing out strongly on the speaker's brawny neck, while the story set him thinking hard. So did the way that another in the team shut his jaw with a snap of decision, showing that he too knew what life with God was, and intended to go on with it. Then the four standards of the Group were brought out -- and Bob's jaw dropped lower. Despite the testimony, he frankly did not believe it possible to be absolutely honest, loving, pure and unselfish. He said that he sometimes did an unselfish action in repairing motor-bikes broken down on the road, but that was perhaps because he liked motor-bikes.

"How about mending men?" asked Ken Twitchell.

"I get quite a kick out of mending a motor-cycle," said Bob.

"You'll get a greater kick out of mending men," prophesied Ken, hardly foreseeing that Bob would be used to mend a dozen directly and countless others indirectly before the next two years went by.

"Then we tried to argue," continues Bob, but after an hour and a half Bob came back to the evidence. "You cannot get away from the fact that Sandy's changed."

Following the Group Sunday evening meetings attended by the eight, Rip would noisily interrupt with some blasphemy.

"At those meetings," continues Bob, "I observed the radiance of Howard Rose when he said he was a free man. And that disturbed me a bit. So I used to draw my chair away from Rip because he was interrupting so blasphemously. I began to be ashamed of being near him. Then I noticed that one of the Group, after rowing two courses on the river, would be willing to sit up until midnight listening to a man's troubles. Here was a quality of unselfishness I hadn't seen before. At a Group tea-party I heard one say that impurity just slid off when Christ came in. I didn't believe it. I said I should always have to smoke and drink to hide my feelings when I became a diplomat. To which one of them replied, 'Suppose you haven't any feelings to hide?'

"The Groups are also unceremoniously punctured by my sentimental theory of free-love and eroticism by saying it might seem rosy to me, but it looks shabby to them. The next step came when a leader had guidance to read Masefield's *Everlasting Mercy.* I took a copy away, and my girlfriend and I read it over five times during the next fortnight. The line: 'And shut out Christ in husks and swine' caught me. Conviction of sin used even at the breakfast-table. It got me up earlier in the morning, because I found it uncomfortable to lie in bed and think about Groups. When I went into breakfast in the J.C.R. (Junior Common Room) I found myself grabbing food, instead of looking to see if my neighbor had any, and I felt how fundamentally selfish I was. It was a shock.

"Then there came a memorable Sunday night when I went out of the Group with the determination to try the standard of absolute purity they advocated. On Monday afternoon it occurred to me to go for a run around the parks with one of the Group leaders to get back into training. As I ran I determined to show no sign of distress, bad training, or bad condition. My theory was that one could get away with fast living with impurity. That run acted as a bracer, and I decided to get the impurity, the nicotine, and the drink out of my system. Then I decided to put God to the test that Monday night. On the bus I prayed and looked up into a grey sky clouded over and asked whatever Supreme Power there was up there to come to my aid.

"The power worked that night, and I prayed before I went to bed. Strange, but I felt conscious that Christ was standing there. Next morning I had the same sense of Christ being in my room. I always pictured Christ standing by the lake shore. Here in College He was standing by me encouraging, strengthening. I knew now I had emerged from a gilded cage. That morning the trees were greener, the sky was bluer, the birds were singing. The New Testament was alive for me at last. Afterwards I went for another run, and ran in the power of the Spirit, definitely faster and with less distress. During that run I said to my friend, whom I outran: 'I may be in with you before long' -- the first hint I had given him, although I had been taking the side of the Groups at our shove-halfpenny matches. While others cursed, I said that Groups were the goods."

Forty personal talks at tea-parties with others in the College was Bob's program for the next few amazing weeks. In consequence a young man training for missionary work learned how to achieve the kind of results the Groups achieved. Another, training for Orders found release from moral defeat and a jaundiced outlook on life. Then Bob went home, and grew much stronger on his new spiritual diet. "I witnessed there," he said, "and rather crudely, I fear. I also made some restitution to an insurance company from whom I had claimed too heavy damages for a motoring spill. For the first half of the interview I was uncertain whether I was to be prosecuted. I was asked why I owned up, and told the manager that I had invited Christ to run my life. He was a bit staggered and in the end quite friendly, asking me to get in touch with a nephew of his in the University. He said I must refund nine pounds instead of the twenty I thought would be demanded.

"That evening I had to do a little more restitution. I had been tutoring a son of a rich man for nine guineas a week on an out-of-date testimonial. I was guided to tell the man the truth about this, and stood to lose about thirty pounds from the act. Instead of losing, I found the man very pleasant and I was re-engaged for that vacation and given twenty-six pounds towards the Group's South African venture as well."

Within a week Bob was being eagerly sought by a number of men who wanted his help, and was seeing them up to two in the morning. Within a month he was on a team of twenty getting rich experience in action. One of his best friends came to see him almost immediately after his change and made a decision. Bob also went to South Africa, while his story went all round Britain and nearly all round the earth.

The third of the three musketeers of the wheel to surrender was Rip, who spoke so blithely at the first Group meeting I attended. Perhaps the best way to picture him, too, is how he looks to his pals. This is the description that Bob gives of him. "Rip looks like Harold Lloyd -- horn-rimmed spectacles, sandy hair, a fine voice, speaks rather loud through self-consciousness and so he attracts a lot of attention. Could hold very little beer. His c.c. (cubic capacity) was about a pint. The rest of us rather looked down on him because he had to be carried out before we really began to soak. Of medium height, he can ride a motor-bike well, and is a good jazz pianist."

And now for Rip's rollicking story of his change. "I went to my first Group," said Rip, "a bit cheerfully primed with ale, and with the few friends of my own school of religious thought, because I saw that Sandy was sober for long periods and that something had happened to him. I was an atheist, and had written a thesis recently upon 'The Impossibility of the Existence of a Personal Deity.' I heard that some people in the Group had found freedom from the same elementary moral problem that had beaten me for the previous six years, and which I had ceased to regard as defeat.

"I love arguing with the Group people, but the thing that struck me was their happiness, friendliness and non-paucity. I went several times on Sunday evenings, giving as an excuse to my friends that it was worth it for the thirst I acquired during two hours of total abstinence in a hot room. But I wanted happiness and the purpose in life that these people had; yet I didn't want to turn religious and give up the way of spending my evenings that I liked.

"I met Frank at Wallingford, and was frightfully tickled by his good humor. The whole of the Carburetor Club -- a tough little gang whose activities were not confined to motoring, though we made use of our cars in the evenings quite often -- went up to dine with Frank in London. During dinner Frank asked me to tell my best story, and I didn't have one I could tell at dinner with ladies there, though I was renowned in a small way for my repertoire. Someone there asked me why it was I didn't throw in with the Group, and I remember I answered, 'Because I'm too selfish.' Though that was not half the story.

Shortly after that I got Frank's invitation to Edinburgh. I decided that if the Group was going to play being a God, I was going to add interest to the game by playing a devil. Hence, the letter I wrote to Frank I signed, 'Yours, Sin, Ltd., per Rip.' I rode up to Edinburgh on a motor-bike, but only got as far as Derby when a blizzard forced me to take the train, and after an uncomfortable night trip, ending up at 7 a.m., very irritable. The first thing that happened was Frank telling me to buy 'Long woollies.' Ugh!

"Then came the first of the big evening meetings. It never crossed my mind that Frank would ask me to speak. It still didn't cross the minds of those in the team, who fairly clutched their chairs in horror when he did it. I know I sweated heavily, and I forgot what I said, but no one took any notice of it, anyway. Then I got fed up, bored with everybody else doing a job and myself not being able to. I wasn't at all convicted of sin, but I knew that these people were happier than I -- and that was the thing I was out for. That aim had to be dropped before I was in the show for a week or two, when I found it wasn't all gin and gaspers, so to speak.

Anyway, that was the thing for which I originally made my decision. I walked into the hotel and found one of the team:

"Are you doing anything for five minutes?"

"No."

"Then come and convert me.'

"This was the actual conversation -- I remember that quite clearly. We went upstairs and knelt down by a bed because I'd been pretty silly. I asked God to come and run my life and tell me what to do. The first thing that came was to tell this man that I had been telling a lie consistently; the second was to wire my mother, who knew all about religion but not the best way to put it across; the third to let my friends know where I stood; and the fourth to send back two books to the head man of my school and tell him why I was sending them back, and I didn't like that sort of thing very much."

With the capitulation of Rip,the three motoring musketeers were again reunited. They are still trying to paint up the town and countryside. But using white paint instead of red.

And that is the true story of how the Carburetor Club blew up in A.D.1930.

Chapter Eight

FRANK ACTS

May came, and with it came the legendary Frank, back from a fruitful tour in South America. Though Ken Twitchell had warned me the Groups sought no publicity at the time, for they had only the sufficient leaders to cope with the interest already aroused, he promised me an interview with Frank immediately on his arrival. One May morning Ken's voice on the telephone announced that Frank was in London and would be glad to see me.

I invited both to lunch. Frank's "guidance" was that I call at Brown's Hotel for afternoon tea. Unexpectingly I went, and met for the first time the well-dressed Doctor of Divinity, human founder of the Oxford Group, who received me with cordiality and even gaiety. Frank was stout, kindly, affable, and very active. He talked a good deal in that quick, crackling and not displeasing voice of his. He had experienced a great time in South America. He had been amazingly conscious of the presence and guidance of the Holy Spirit during the whole trip. He had seen a good deal of Bolshevism in South America. He was still more confident that the world needed the Holy Spirit's guidance, and not Bolshevism, to put it right. I had never heard a Parson -- and Frank is a Parson -- express himself so freely about the Holy Spirit before. Most Parsons seemed uncertain about Him. Frank paced the room, head and shoulders thrown back, hands behind him, using similar gestures and showing that awareness and intensity of purpose I had noticed about Lloyd George when I was introduced to him in our office. We discussed the religious articles that had appeared in our newspaper. I explained what was in my mind about an Oxford Group series, and Frank listened without interruption until I proposed to invite our readers to express themselves for or against the movement in a fresh newspaper discussion.

"Oh, dear no!"

Frank was flatly opposed to the proposition. The Group was not seeking publicity; they were prepared to give information if published correctly and this subject treated with reverence. Newspaper controversies on religion were never satisfactory. The New Testament was against them. They are roused to interest for a time, but did little real good. People whose interest had been quickened were left stranded, while the newspaper went back to its daily task of purveying news. That sort of publicity was useless for the deeply spiritual movement to which he was committed. And would do more harm than good.

Further -- and here he threw a ball at me -- the Holy Spirit's guidance was against encouraging me to write or organize the publication of anything about the Oxford Group until I myself was spiritually ready for the task.

This remarkable Life-Changer had courage. He had made the most extraordinary suggestion that I had received in twenty-five years of London journalism; although I remembered making a somewhat similar suggestion to a well-known celebrity some years before. Frank was turning the tables on me, saying that he felt the Holy Spirit was against my writing about the Group until I, too, was thoroughly right spiritually.

Did Frank know that journalists never ask outside permission as to what they shall write about? Evidently not. Nor did he know or seem to care that for many years I had been trying to live Christianity, read the Bible most days, prayed twice or thrice daily (like the Pharisee), was repentant of occasional sins, and tried to conform to New Testament teaching as I understood it while endeavoring to pilot myself and the paper through a daily maze of difficulties. I was an elder of a church, a treasurer of a church building fund, the organizer of phenomenally successful features (secular and religious), and not altogether a stranger to a little persecution, perhaps for righteousness' sake. And drawing the top salary on a newspaper which could give Frank's young movement just the help upward that it seemed to need.

For a time I wondered if Frank's uncomplimentary attitude was not merely clever charlatanism, an effort to hoodwink me by quoting the Holy Spirit, to ensure that we only published what he wanted, irrespective of our honest convictions about his teaching. At least my doubts about him were as honest as his doubts about me. After all, a man knows himself and the kind of life he is trying to live; let others say what they may who are unafraid to make the same effort, be their motives natural aversion, self-justification, jealousy, or common projection.

What could there be in my life which entitled Frank on our first meeting to say the Holy Spirit was against my touching the movement? Of course, it was a safe guess to make about anybody. The odds were on the side of the challenger -- always. He had got in the first below. But even if he were right in his assumption, was he still right in his objection? Ventilation of a new movement did no harm unless there was harm in it. Moreover, there were illuminating Scriptural texts concerning those who had nothing to hide being ready to bring everything to the light. Our novelists had confessed their religion and exposed themselves to the criticism of our readers. Arnold Bennett had endured a heavy barrage of loveless bigotry. If an unbeliever was ready to write openly at my invitation, why should Frank object when he knew I was on the side of the angels as well as he? If Frank really desired sin to be brought to the light for exposure as the vile cancer it was, how much more should his new movement be held up to the light for all to inspect its purity? And in any case we could do it whether he liked it or not it. The Editor was always the deciding factor.

Still Frank said "No." He was positive he was guided to say "No." And recalling that interview in the light of subsequent events, *I, too, am positive he was right.*

Frank was "guided" to say several unexpected things to me during the afternoon and evening. One thing he said at dinner interested me considerably. He had just taken a second helping of asparagus when I asked him to explain where common sense ended and guidance began.

"I don't pretend that every detail in my life is guided," said Frank. "For instance, I did not have guidance to take that asparagus. I was hungry, and I like asparagus. But if I am alert for guidance it comes whenever I need it. And so it does to anybody."

And other of Frank's sayings that afternoon as he walked about the big Red Room ticking off letters of the alphabet on his first four fingers was, "P-R-A-Y: Powerful-Radiograms-Always-Yours" -- one of the many forceful epigrams he is constantly uttering, just as a pedagogue teaching easily-remembered shortcuts to education.

And another epigram that came later was: "We must work with the chisel, the hammer and the rivet. Make an opening and then flatten in the rivet so there shall be no more weakness at that point." That was Frank's method with me that afternoon.

Christ was sensitive to the possibility of sin in the Woman at the Well and in the sins of many others.

But Frank did not ask me for a confession of my sins that day, though a live journalist might have been willing to relate a few as the easy price of a good story.

Nevertheless, my own sins came up as we talked, came up vol-

untarily, and the way of future victory was shown clearly, almost
before I realized what he was about. Probably my vanity did it. I
was so anxious to tell this unusual evangelist a few of my own
experiences with the supernatural, partly for enlightenment, perhaps more to let him know that I, too, had practical experience of
the subject to either impress him or to disprove his offensive suggestion that I was spiritually unready to translate his movement
into journalese.

"You can tell me what you like," said Frank, standing in the middle of the room, his large head and shoulders thrown back, hands
again clasped behind him, just like Mr. Pickwick. I told him first
of an ecstatic experience which happened several years before. I
had been studying the New Testament, a book I had dropped as an
encumbrance during my early years in Fleet Street. Though I had
returned to Christianity, I felt no great compunction in committing one or two breaches of the teaching, seeing my circumstances
were unusual and I was harming nobody. Closer study of the New
Testament revealed that some of my indulgences were uncompromisingly forbidden. Then one day, when there came along a temptation which usually defeated me, I took a right turn instead of my
usual left incline. It was that same right turn which resulted in
the remarkable experience which I now described to Frank. I was
in my room shortly afterwards, when I suddenly felt an amazing
exaltation, and unspeakable rapture, accompanied by a delightful
glowing sensation throughout my left side. The ecstasy of this experience is untellable. It outshone all human joys just as a search-
light outshines the light of a candle.

It was a delight; I was fully dressed and quite conscious of everything about me. But the transport of joy which accompanied this
beautiful experience was so wonderful, so celestial, so vibrantly effulgent, so transcending anything that happens as a consequence
of the average good deed of the Boy Scout order, that I sank quite
naturally to my knees in an ecstasy of inspired prayer. And then
as this extraordinary trance-state continued I seemed to be raised
out of myself into a sunlit region where I could observe humanity struggling blindly in shadow, and lovingly sympathize with all
because of the shadow preventing them from seeing the glorious
future which was their destiny and into which I have been so marvelously drawn.

At this time I realized that even joy can be intolerable and that
joy, like pain, when it becomes unendurable ceases to be borne.
No unfortified human being could endure more than half an hour

of the rosy ecstasy. Exactly what happened to me that day I never quite knew, but I shall always believe the Creator allowed me to pass a full have-hour on the fringe of Paradise. And if Heaven is still more glorious, I can understand Paul saying that eye hath not seen nor ear heard aught of what the Lord had prepared for those who love Him. Such an experience turned the joke about the golden harps of Heaven into bathos. Later on, when reading a book on English mysticism by Dean Inge, I saw that this state of trance was not peculiar to myself, but had been experienced by others, and described in some of the autobiographies of the mystics.

I may have thought there was something specially worthy about my attempts at Christianity, as distinct from what others were doing, to justify this foretaste of Paradise. Possibly I expected Frank to think so, too, as I told the story to him that afternoon at Brown's Hotel. He listened interestedly and waited; but made no comment.

Then I described another experience which had come to me just as surprisingly. But whilst the former gave me half an hour of such intoxicating joy that no earthly experience could compare with it, the other scared me out of my wits for the ensuing forty-eight hours. And it still gives me a shudder whenever I look back upon it. This second experience came as a glorified nightmare. It was midnight -- one o'clock summer-time (delight-saving time). I had been sleeping, but was awakened by a human face at my window. Between that face and myself was something black and evil. There was no one else in my room. The human face vanished, but in the darkness I had a strong sense of the uncanny and the sinister. My unseen visitor, that had separated me from the vanished face, if a living entity, and is not a black cloud of evil -- the incubus -- certainly had no rights in the world of man. He or it seemed to steal into the room, pervading the atmosphere above me; then descending to seep itself into my body, an inky odiousness pervading my left side just as that effulgent visitation had previously done. This second experience, like the former, lasted approximately for half an hour of wakefulness, during which time I was helpless to dislodge it -- a dark shade saturating me with its blackness, producing all the sensations of horror, guilt, and severance from God which surely must be felt by the lost soul. Once again I had no recourse but prayer, a series of repetitions of the Lord's Prayer with stress on deliverance from evil. At the end of half an hour I felt my body freed again, though how the incubus departed I cannot say. It had been; and then it was not. But the experience had been so poignantly real that it was sometime before I felt completely at ease when alone, fearing a similar visitation.

But what was it? Was I going mad? Or had I really had an experience of an evil spirit? I knew there were many incredible stories about them in the Bible which were explained away as meaning something else. Pondering over this odd experience, I received the idea that probably my visitor had been sent by someone dabbing in the black arts who had some unpleasant interest in me. Then later I came across a book by an English lady of title, *The Riding Light,* giving experiences of The Sinisters. Later still, I read a book by Lord Frederick Hamilton, *The Days Before Yesterday,* which also contained some kind of confirmation of my own experience.

When I had finished these two stories of spiritual light and shade, Frank suggested neither clairvoyant intervention nor the Black Art. But he quickly revealed to me what I should have realized from the first.

"Those two experiences," he said, "relate to the same sin which God wants cleared out of your life, so that He can accomplish his plans for you. He may have something for you to do which a mortal sin of yours is frustrating."

Light came. Even if the suggestion that God could have anything special for me to do was more flattering than reasonable, because one particular sin had produced the opposite poles of mystical experience I have described. Again, doctors might suggest active glands following protracted medication. Only -- the second experience happened to be accompanied by the features of a person whom I had never met, and whom I did encounter several years later. This showed pretty clearly that even if this were not a prophecy, my psyche had managed to project itself into its own future for several years and picture one character in a scene who was presently reproduced in life. Who that character was may be revealed in a subsequent volume as a kindly and fruitful worker in the Oxford Group movement.

Frank's voice called me back to earth. He was talking earnestly, urging me to drive stakes around myself as protection against further lapses. Mentioning a person whom I had wronged, he urged me to go and tell that person the facts. "Never mind if there is another side to the story," he counseled. "You do your part. The other person can confess or withhold. What is that to you?"

Frank's drive to get me to forsake every form of sin and to put a fence that cannot be scaled between it and me caught me unawares, although I should have been ready for him after reading of his tactics. I thought his request was unreasonable, as I was as much sinned against as sinning, perhaps more.

"Supposing it causes further trouble?" I protested.

And I explained the difficulty.

"I don't urge you to do anything that will hurt anyone." He paused for guidance. "If you are sure it will, don't do it."

I thought of him at this minute as a kind of a silver dynamo, sympathetic, but irresistible.

And then, of course, Frank suggested the inevitable Quiet Time. Taking two sheets of notepaper, he handed me one. We sat down and listened in prayerful silence. I tried to pick up another of those luminous thoughts. Nothing except it came: quite a lot of ordinary human thoughts, but no luminous ones. I had no wish to confess my sins to the person Frank had named, but I wished to see the thing through as an honest text. Yet my thoughts in that Quiet Time agreed with what Frank urged, though my wishes did not stand. I wrote down my thoughts; then read them aloud to Frank, who confidently and surprisingly pronounced them to be God-given thoughts.

"Oh, come," I said to myself. "That's much too strong an interjection." How on earth could a few wondering thoughts, unattended by mystical feeding or luminosity, scribbled on a sheet of notepaper, be catalogued as God's thoughts by anyone in his right senses? Still, I was determined to see the thing through, being a believer in the pragmatic method of learning by doing. I had always learned as I earned. Furthermore, my vanity was touched at being asked to do the most difficult thing yet, although Frank seemed unaware of it or entirely unconcerned. Later I told him that it was the most difficult task to set a man, and he jocularly replied, "Oh, that's nothing to what you might be asked to do on this basis of Christian living."

Was I going to do this thing because I was afraid to refuse a dare? To mask real cowardice? Or because I believed it might be the right step forward in the Christian life? Or because I saw a news story behind it? To this day I cannot distinguish between the four motives. All were there.

During our conversation Ken Twitchell had slipped from the room as a result of a glance from Frank. I thought his departure was pre-arranged. I learned afterwards that it was the custom in the Group to leave one of their members with any interested person when the opportunity offered. Ken Twitchell now reappeared, and Frank shared his guidance that all three might dine together, and that later Ken and I might go on to Harley Street for the Thurs-

day night Group meeting: typical of this modern evangelist who is
never so immersed in the present as to forget the future. Frank's
reason for staying away himself was that he had an unfortunate
person to see whose need might keep him far into the night.

I said "good-night" to Frank, having voluntarily taken on the
most unattractive assignment of my life.

Chapter Nine

RESTITUTION

Speak unto the Children of Israel, when a man or a woman shall commit any sin that men commit, to do a trespass against the Lord, and that soul shall be guilty;

Then they shall confess their sin which they have done: and he shall make restitution for his guilt in full, and add unto it the fifth part thereof, and give it unto him in respect of whom he hath been guilty. --*Numbers 5:6-7.*

The Harley Street Group meeting following my first talk with Frank was one of the most impressive gatherings I have attended: one of those rare occasions when one feels powerfully conscious of the presence and pressure of the Holy Spirit.

I had said nothing to Ken Twitchell of what Frank wished me to do. But there was a look of understanding in his eyes that evening which showed that he understood, for which I was grateful. That look, I discovered later, arose from an experience of his that is not completely dissimilar from my own.

Before arriving at my office next morning, I made a call on the person named by Frank and revealed the humiliating facts. It was not a pleasant interview, and the facts I disclosed caused no surprise. I was censured for the clumsy way I expressed myself and the early hour chosen for the task. I had no sense of spiritual exaltation at doing what I did. But it was done, and nothing could undo it. And I had driven in one of those protecting stakes that Frank is so keen upon to prevent his followers from repeating past errors. Furthermore, I saw that same person later register a spiritual change which probably would not have happened but for my frankness. I record this as a simple statement of truth.

Frank's practice of sending a person to make reconciliation or restitution is occasionally criticized by those who recoil from the high spiritual challenge of the Group. The criticism may arise as much from self-contradiction or cowardice as from an honest objection to a hard saying. For unquestionably, Christ said that before we bring our gifts to the altar we must first be reconciled to our brother, a difficult saying, but one perfectly reasonable if

Christianity is to realize its lofty ideals, though restitution should always be under guidance.

Sometimes harm may be occasioned by unwise and "unchecked" institutions. Nevertheless, the Group did not compromise on the necessity of reconciliation and restitution. Zaccheus told Jesus that if he had taken anything by false accusation he would restore fourfold as ordered by the Mosaic Law. But, for instance, how could a man with nothing restore fourfold what he had stolen? Why stir up trouble unless you were in a position to make amends? The answer to these questions was that each person must decide the thing to do on his own guidance, checked perhaps by the guidance of others.

Supposing a person to whom an apology or reparation is offered behaves badly? Usually he behaves very well, for the restitutional act has the psychological effect of raising the other person's ego, putting him in good temper with himself and with everyone else, including his humbled enemy. But should he act otherwise (say the Group), his behavior must be accepted cheerfully as the natural consequence of wrongdoing. *Nothing is born without pain; not even a soul born again.*

Everything must be subordinate to this new quality of life, even if it means the disapproval of others, since the Group rests in the Grace of our Lord Jesus Christ, the love of God, and the constant companionship of the Holy Spirit -- a benediction which means just what it says and is not a formalism.

Frank does not advise people to do what he is unwilling to do himself or what he has not found to be of great spiritual value in practice. Here is one of his own experiences of restitution as he told it to me in my room at Selwyn College, Cambridge, when I was attending one of his many house-parties. The Bishops of Norwich and Leicester and the Presiding Bishop of the Protestant Episcopal Church of America were there. Another Bishop would arrive the next day who was present at the Chinese house-party when Frank had his own sharp taste of restitution.

Frank said: "It was the very first religious house-party I had organized, and it was held at the house of a famous Chinese diplomat in one of the most beautiful spots in China, a summer resort where the old Chinese philosophers had their retreats. Its cragged peaks and sunny valleys were dotted with ruined pagodas destroyed at the time of the Taiping Rebellion in the middle of the nineteenth century. Our mountain beauty-spot overlooked the Yang-tze River, writhing through the valley below -- a yellow Chinese dragon.

"I used to go out and sit on the rocks and enjoy the glorious scenery. For the first two days I had a wonderful sense of communion, fellowship, and joy, and peace. My third day was uncomfortable. One word kept running through my brain: 'Restore, restore, restore.'

"I tried to brush it aside, but it came again and again. It referred to an old matter with the railroad company. I had accepted from them some former privileges, but a rider was introduced and the reduced rates privilege was canceled. I argued, was true casuistry, that I had the right to these privileges, owing to my prior claims, now only partly operative. At the time of the house-party I had hated and forsaken the wrong-doing, but I had neither confessed it nor restored. Therein lies the great secret of victory. A great many hate and forsake, but never go on to the larger victory.

"So my struggle continued. Should I restore? The vice-president of the railway, with whom I occasionally dined, might find out! What would he think? How would I know what money was involved? How could I own up when so many people had arrived at a house-party expecting me to lead them into larger areas of experience when I must admit my own dishonesty? Finally, I compromised by saying I would write anonymously now that I had found out the amount.

"I remembered that a check had come in recently to help me in any way I chose, and this had been forgotten in a multitude of duties and was adequate for the restitution. But as I went on to write the letter there was a sense of dissatisfaction and incompleteness. And so I knew I must do the costly thing, which meant signing the letter with my own name, revealing who I was and what I was doing. With it came a wonderful relief, but only momentary, for more disquieting guidance came, saying I must share with the house-party that afternoon.

I began to argue. How could I? What would they think? Could I 'lose face,' as the Chinese would picturesquely say? 'Losing face' was one of the things not done in China. But the insistent urge was there: 'Confess, confess, confess.' I did.

"With the pain of confession came a more complete message that meant victory to many in my audience, composed of people of national influence: members of Parliament, a General, several Bishops, well-known folk from the Foreign and Chinese communities. As the meeting ended I first doubted whether I had done the right thing. Have I had not yet learned that a confessing Christian is a propagating Christian? A costly confession may be the price of power. Certain things which concern the public must be publicly confessed. So many people have a false fear of confessing things in public which perhaps they should not confess. God often tests our willingness without asking us to do it.

"At that meeting when I owned up to the sin of dishonesty there was present a man who had come to that beautiful mountain resort to recover his health. The doctors told him he needed rest and quiet away from business. As he left he said that if he were to do the same thing as Frank he might have to pay out all the money in his bank. Then what would become of his wife and family? Fortunately, he talked to a friend who held him to his highest, and suggested that he look into all his affairs and put everything straight with everybody. A friend said his health might never be improved until he had put everything right. The Bible parallel is, 'Which is easier to say, Thy sins are forgiven, or to say, Arise and take up thy bed and walk?' This man made full restoration to all, which then left him with practically an empty bank account. Then the miracle happened. Coincident with his courageous step there arrived a note from his employers saying that the most important thing for him was to get well, and enclosing a check for a much bigger sum than he had paid anyway.

"Another person present had told a lie in Sweden. That lie followed her all the way to China, where she had gone to teach and help the Chinese be good and not tell lies. Wherever she travelled she found that lie turning up. Whenever she tried to help someone it burst in with 'You're a liar.' My telling that simple story of restitution made her realize she must do more than write anonymous letters owning up, not to a big lie, but to one that robbed her of the power of being a life-changer.

"There was a third person at that meeting possessing what is technically known as a dispositional temper. Her husband brought her to the house-party and suggested she enjoy the beneficial results while he went off to enjoy himself in his own way elsewhere. This contrary woman too heard this story, and it made such an impression on her that she went to her room and locked her door. Someone was concerned about her at dinner, but I said there was no real need for worry, as the New Testament enjoyed fasting. She did not attend the next meeting, sending to say she was not well.

"She wanted no breakfast the next morning, as she now had a slight headache. But at eleven a.m. she left her room radiant and triumphant, and went off to tell some of her friends with similar contrary problems of her new-found victory. Another miracle had come about leading to a procession of such miracles which were performed because I had now learned not only to hate and forsake, but also to confess and restore!"

When Frank had finished telling me that story, I asked him, "Would it not be better in the general interest for you to steal something every five years or so and then repeat the ceremony of taking, forsaking, confessing and restoring? You might start many more such processions of restitution."

Frank beamed.

"I learned enough from that first experience to be careful not to repeat the offense."

Frank has been setting his changed men and women tasks of restoration ever since he wrote his own difficult series of six apologetic letters to persons against whom he had borne grudges following his vital experiences in the Cumberland church. Because God floods in where there is no sinful obstruction to His coming, Frank sets his face against compromise which may also be sinful obstruction. He insists that converts should not only turn from sin, but take long steps to prevent reoccurrences. Voluntary confession and restitution bring home the seriousness of wrong-doing more effectively than any other curative method.

If a man's relations with the other sex are on a wrong basis, the Group say he should put them right immediately, and the obvious way to do so is to confess the change in his own life to the persons concerned. Even if he does not win them for Christianity, he puts himself on a comprehensible basis with his former women-friends. His changed demeanor is understood, and not considered a slight. Likewise, women who have been drawn to Christ are advised to tell why they can no longer live the old life of irresponsible pleasure. It is all to the good of the new convert, and possibly to the salvation of the companion in error.

Some graduates holding University degrees obtained by cribbing have been counseled by Frank to return to their College authorities and confess the devastating truth. Or have gone back voluntarily. One of these, a young giant, who, with his wife and two wonderful children, have been living on faith and prayer for some years, told me his own experiences over a luncheon which he insisted on giving. He said he was educated at a small, socially prominent college in New England, colloquially known as "snooty, snobbish, and high-hat." The Made Honors System for examinations was the rule here, and it was also "the done thing to respect the rule, to be honorable and never to crib, although there was none to supervise."

The system was controlled by a Students' Honors Committee, exercising the powers of a supreme court dealing with all cases of infraction of rules. If anyone was proved to have cheated at examinations, there was no option but to fire the student; the decision was automatic. Yet out of eight hundred students only one was sent down (expelled) every other year. From earliest boyhood the young giant had lived a life of expediency -- believing the end always justified the means. The reasons were laziness and fear of failure. With the Honors System of no other supervision during exams, he saw a splendid opportunity for indulging his laziness and getting clear away with it.

At prep school he habitually cheated, knowing he would not be caught. By substituting cheating for work he had more time for enjoyment outside the University. And illicit enjoyment at that. But it meant constantly inventing fresh excuses for absence from class for those extra outings. One day he fell on the stairs, and this gave him a new excuse for a free evening from study. He struck his forehead with a hammer hard enough to show a large bruise, which he passed off as the result of falling down stairs. He claimed to have been in a stupor when he should have been at lessons, and again was believed.

He was preparing for his degree when he ran into one of the Group house-parties, and became convicted of sin, as the old-fashioned evangelists used to say, and felt we must put things straight in his own life.

"Did anyone in the Group urge you to do this?" I asked.

"No," he answered, "I knew my duty very well without being told."

Tremblingly he asked to see the Dean, feeling so nervous that he wrote his own accusation before going in and tried to read it standing. His knees knocked so much that he had to sit down.

"It seems a sorry sort of admission," he said dismally, as he recounted this experience. I felt he was showing considerable courage in telling so much, and that I was showing the case-hardened indifference of the typical journalist over his painful recital. I said so.

"And what did the Dean say?" I then asked unrelentingly.

The features of the young giant broken to his habitual smile.

"The Dean said he was awfully sorry about it," he drawled. "Not so much for the honor of the University as for my own sake. He said he appreciated my honesty in volunteering the information, and omitted to reproach me for what I had done. At the end he said: 'Since you voluntarily told me this, and no one else knows about it, we will turn over a new page and forget it.'"

This young man is now a Presbyterian minister -- and a saint.

"Were you glad or sorry you saw the Dean?" I next asked.

"You bet I was mighty glad to get it off my chest. I now think it must have been God's special leading to do this. For not long afterwards several ministers of the intellectual type spoke critically of the Group at a Convention, when the Dean of my University stood up, and announced that he was a Unitarian with no strong leaning towards our teaching, but impelled to testify to its efficacy, since a number of young men in his University had come to him voluntarily with apologies for past misconduct."

Sometimes contact with the Group results in converts going to their parents to straighten out difficulties that have divided the home. Sometimes parents go to children and do the same reuniting thing. Besides seeing the Dean, the young giant had also been led to write a straightforward letter to his parents, telling them of how he had been behaving while they paid high fees for his studies, believing him to be a conscientious student. As he had always played a role at home, his mother was convinced he was the angel boy.

His letter home cost more than seeing the Dean. His courage ebbed so low that he waited until a few seconds to midnight, when the letter-box was cleared; and then he had to run his hardest to catch the post.

"And your parents said?"

Again things have gone smoothly for the student-prodigal.

"The same day they received my letter," he said, "I received a telegram thanking me for what I had written and sending me there love."

"So you are out to turn schoolboys into Saints?"

"That about says it," he replied.

Still I was unsatisfied.

"You say you were fearful and lazy by nature, when in fact there was plenty of courage and energy latent in you, which the Group, with their experience of psychology, knew how to stir up."

He would not have it. God's strength was made manifest in his weakness, he asserted. Being in Christ, he was able to do what he was unable to do otherwise.

"Has anyone ever regretted making such a confession as yours?"

I was prepared for another uncompromising "No."

"Only if they subsequently draw away from God. Those who keep near Him never regret obedience to His law of love to all. How low can anyone who professes to love God and his neighbor as himself, as Christians must do, how a wrong he has done to anyone can go unrighted? It would be a deliberate interference with God's scheme of righteous world-government as revealed in the Bible."

I probed further.

"Have you looked back into your life and carefully considered every wrong you have ever done anyone and endeavored to set it right? Or are there still some dents in your spiritual armour-plate?"

It was a searching question, one which very few persons, clerical or lay, Christian or Pagan, dared to ask themselves. But he was not to be caught.

"Wherever God has shown me that there was restitution to be made," he said, with quiet assurance, "there I have made it."

"That is to say, you have seen those in your neighborhood. What of those at a distance?"

He declined to admit exceptions. "I have either seen or written to all who are alive where guidance has come about them."

Hearing this, spoken not boastingly but hesitatingly, in answer to some very impertinent probing, I felt a sense of hopelessness. Such a state of purity and perfection seemed to be altogether too wonderful for me. Later I heard a Rev. Cleve Hicks (a former Harvard Chaplain) carry this point of restitution still further, when telling of a man, sixty-five, confronted with the Group teaching on this subject who said it would take him the rest of his life to straighten out all the crooked things he had done. And Cleve had cheerfully replied that, as guided, he could not embark on a more useful undertaking.

About this time I heard a fine young Englishman tell a story at a Group meeting which coincided with some of the things told me by the young giant. He had been to Oxford, but had deliberately kept away from the Group influence because he understood it would prevent him from enjoying himself to the full. Later, drunkenness and foolish squandering of an allowance from his father's depleted resources became his chief difficulty. Not long after that I was with him as he perused his father's letter just arrived. "'Your last letter made very unpleasant reading,'" he read aloud.

"Why?" I asked.

"Because I wrote and told Father the truth about my past life," replied the changed youth. "And now I'm jolly glad I did."

Sending prodigal sons back to their earthly as well as their Heavenly Father is a specialty of the Oxford Group.

One is constantly hearing stories of restitution from persons who have been attracted into the Group, including one from a very successful minister who preached a sermon which created a deeper spiritual atmosphere than I had sensed in a church for many years. He confessed to me that in his early life he had stolen money, and found it necessary for his peace of mind to call on the person he had robbed and confess his sin. That man to-day is one of the most fruitful Christians in the Group. A relative of mine was so struck by his sermon that she said to me, "The difference between that man and most preachers is -- he's real." When refusing a knighthood John Galsworthy said, "Literature is its own reward." The testimony of the Oxford Group is that absolute honesty by anybody is its own reward. George Muller of Bristol, who stole as a young man, and many another saint found that a confession or restitution is the gateway to power.

I shall never forget the greeting received by a company of the Group when we called on the Principal of a High School in an important town.

"You are the fellows who took formality out of religion and turned some of my students into honest boys." Or words to that effect. He said that about twenty-five school-books, purloined from the Library, had been returned as a consequence of our last visit to the city.

But what of the bad boy, the ugly duckling, with who nobody can deal? Garrett Stearly told me that in Africa the Group found such a boy; caned daily at school, moody and morose at home, his great claim to fame had been winning the junior swimming championship of his club.

He was bribed by his godfather to attend a Group house-party for the price of a cinema seat. At the party he was caught off his guard by the friendliness of the people he met, and soon found himself envying their state of abiding joy. He decided to try Christianity, though he saw it might be costly. First of all, there was that swimming championship -- he had been six months over age when he won it, but no one knew. He took his courage and his beloved trophy cup in his hands and made a clean breast of it to the committee.

The swimming coach was aghast. "You have more nerve than I have, my lad," he could only grunt as the lad walked out, shorn of glory, but triumphant. Later, with the minister's permission, he witnessed in his family church after the service, and promised to restore seven pounds that he had once stolen from the collection plate. A man in the congregation was so convicted that he sent back five pounds to a department store in the capital -- value of goods quietly stolen some years before. The store sent the money on to the Oxford Group team, telling them to keep up the good work.

Another convert restored jewelry stolen from the house of a friend at which he was a guest.

"Was he really a friend?" I queried.

"There are friends and friends," was the laughing reply. "He's a real friend now."

In Asheville, North Carolina, I ran into some more lads who had been captured by the Group's high challenge. One of them told the following remarkable story:

"I believe, without a doubt, that I was the worst pupil ever in the Asheville Senior High School. That is not only my opinion, but the teacher's and the Principle's, too. I wasn't mean, but I took a great delight in telling lies and seeing them through, which took bigger lies to make the little ones seem true.

"After a year of lying, I began to have enough confidence in myself to steal. I got money from my parents to buy books, then kept the money and stole the books. Every day I would go to school with a troubled mind and not quite satisfied.

"Then one day we had Chapel, and the Principal announced that the Oxford Group was going to speak to us.

Well, I thought, here goes another lecture, and I guess it will ruin our freedom with the girls for a few weeks.

So my buddy and I took a back seat and began to amuse ourselves. We carried on until Frank Bygott, the Englishman, got up and spoke. We thought his talk 'rather funny,' so we listened to him. When he finished, we also finished listening. Well, when the talks were over we all went to our classrooms and forgot about the Group for a while.

"After supper, the same day that I had heard the speeches, my buddy and myself decided to go over to our Sunday-School league, to get a couple of girls after the meeting, and go for a ride. When we got there, who should we bump into but Cleve Hicks! The next night up in Cleve's room we surrendered our lives to Christ.

"Well, I 'took off' and made up with my friends. I humbled myself to the Principal, and in doing so told him what I had found in life. He was in a hurry to be about his business, but when he found out that I had asked Christ to run my life he took time to give me a lecture on keeping it up. When he had finished, I thanked him and walked out, saying to myself, 'Well, isn't that funny, making a friend of somebody I never liked until to-day?'

"He wasn't the only friend I made. I confessed to everyone I could recall telling a lie to, therefore making friends out of enemies. And I also took back to the coach of the school some football equipment I had stolen, and straightened out affairs with girls. I have also been used to win fellows to Jesus Christ."

The influence exercised over the typical lad by Cleve Hicks is one of the many astounding facets of Group activity. Cleve told me the story of a Boston boy whom he had known before he was sent to a Reformatory. The boy's parents, anxious about their son, wanted Cleve to see him when he was released. Cleve agreed, making the proviso that the boy voluntarily come as he knew the danger of compulsory religion.

The boy came, and a heart-to-heart talk followed. Not long afterwards the boy suddenly turned up again, face beaming, altogether proud of himself; bursting to tell something important.

"I earned thirteen-fifty this week." (Spoken proudly)

Cleve has his own methods.

"So?" (Spoken casually)

"All gone!" (Defiantly)

"Yeah!" (Humorously)

Cleave's casualness merely stimulated the boy to burst out with the facts. When not stealing motor-cars, the boy and his pals went in for petty thieving. One particular store in their neighborhood often suffered from their depredations. As one of the young hooligans engaged the salesman's attention, the others lifted what they could.

"I went back to the store and gave that man five bucks," proudly announced the lad.

Another of this young Bostonian's rackets was to break into an elderly woman's house and damage her property. He told Cleve:

"I went back to that old woman and asked her if she lived there two years ago when the house was burgled. She looked at me scared like, and said 'Yes.' Then I told her I was one of the fellows who did that, and she looked more scared. Then I gave her five bucks, and she almost died."

The remaining three dollars and fifty cents of the boy's earnings that week had gone to another store from which he had once stolen a portable radio set, *carrying it brazenly out while the music was still playing.*

Of course, the best story that Cleve tells he forgot to tell me. When he reads it here he will wonder how I got it, and where. The Oxford Group was visiting a school in South Africa, at which Cleve gave a clear presentation of the message to the whole assembly. Some teachers afterwards were very skeptical, and one master cynically asked if the Group could do anything to help them recover school muskets which had been stolen.

"Look here!" exclaimed Cleve. "We are not the detectives." But he added that one never could tell what would happen when the Spirit of God was working to make someone honest.

The boys listened intently to his address, and one of them at least felt God was giving him another chance. Nothing happened for several days. Then a boy came and tapped on Cleve's door.

"Come in," said Cleve cheerily. "What are you here for?"

The boy was nonplussed. "I expected you to do the talking, sir," he said. "I came to hear what you got to say."

"Bless your heart, you heard me in chapel. Now let's hear you."

For half an hour the boy poured out the heart Cleve had cheerily blessed. Still he seemed unsatisfied. Then Cleve had an intuition.

"Do you know anything about the rifles around here?"

"Yes, sir," the boy blurted out. "That's really what I came for."

And the theft of the muskets was admitted, as well as of many other items belonging to the school and the students. From being the worst boy he developed into a spiritual force and influenced strongly for good the lives of seventeen other boys and that school.

Sometimes people become less-honest men. One of my best friends in the Group offered a former employee approximately a thousand dollars as payment for a thousand hours stolen when he should have been working, an offer which was refused, though the honesty of purpose was recognized.

These stories of reconciliation and restitution all point to new principles at work in the lives of persons encountered by the Group, and are quoted to illustrate "the take off" of the quality of life which this movement is striving to achieve. For a long time I felt the Group was erecting far too formidable barriers in the way of potential Christians; and were turning a simple leisurely flat race into a mighty Grand National Steeplechase, with appalling fences, wide brooks, and sudden turns to negotiate, which only the courageous few dare attempt, and a tiny minority of them achieve. Those on the verge of a change-over, I argued, might be driven away by this unsympathetic and uncompromising teaching.

The Group replied that persons attracted to Christ could not be driven away by an obvious Christian duty, since Christ supplied the strength as well as the incentive. Nevertheless, I had read no story of the disciples running around making restitution. I thought Christ had said they were clean through the word He had spoken unto them.

But the disciples may have had nothing to restore, or the act of restitution was omitted from this story; while the law of God unquestionably enjoined restitution, and Christ did say to Zaccheus, "This day salvation is come to thy house," when he announced he would fulfill God's law and restore fourfold.

"Listen to the guidance of the Holy Spirit," said the Group, "and you will hear Him saying, 'Be ye reconciled one towards another.'" I began to listen again. At first not too attentively.

Chapter Ten

THE OXFORD HOUSE-PARTY

About this time I left the group of newspapers I had served for eight years and devoted myself to a smaller rival prior to making a long-overdue visit to America. Once more I attempted to get Frank's co-operation in a newspaper series about the Oxford Group.

Frank knew I had taken his advice and seen the third person he had urged me to see. I wondered if he now thought my own spiritual life sufficiently cleaned up to entrust me with all the facts of the Oxford Group. Evidently he did, for when I called him on the trunk wire (long distance) he seemed quite eager for me to come down to the Oxford house-party which had just then started and begin work, although the newspaper I then directed was not so powerful as the one I had just left.

I went down twice to the 1931 house-party at Oxford, once to describe the event, the second time to introduce some of my friends.

My second visit to that twelve-day house-party gave me further insight into the intensive methods of this consecrated human engineer. I told Frank I wished my friends to meet some of the men I already knew in the Group. Frank gave me to understand that he would see to things, although I knew he was carrying the weight of the whole house-party. Instead of introducing us to those I knew already, he collected several other prominent figures in the Group to entertain us: one of the surprising things that happens when you work with guided people.

Furthermore, he had reserved a seat for me for lunch at High Table, Lady Margaret Hall, between himself and a young man he suspected of having the same problem to conquer as the one I had revealed to him. And so, instead of spending a leisurely luncheon-hour making interesting conversation in the accepted way of host to guest, Frank whispered in my ear a point about my neighbor on my left, and bade me get busy telling the old, old story in the autobiographical way common to the Group and the early Apostles. So zealous is Frank in setting his friends working for others by the simple means of narrating one's own experiences with problems common to both. Mentally I handed Frank the blue ribbon as an organizer of amateur evangelists.

Having recovered my breath, I turned to my neighbor, the son of a man I knew, whose book publisher had also been my book publisher, and endeavored to be helpful. I was not sanguine of the results. I felt no sense of the Holy Spirit telling me to talk, no freedom from natural inhibitions. Moreover, my neighbor was not at all interested in expurgating his possible besetting sin, but far more interested in proving that it was not a sin at all -- my original view. I'd tried to quote a text or two from the New Testament which had changed my opinion, but at that awkward moment could not remember one correctly.

Then the door swung open, and a member of my own staff, deputed to work the three colleges with the newspaper containing my first article on the Group, noisily intered and began hawking the papers around the lunch-table, to my added confusion. And this while at Frank's bidding I was trying to cure the soul on my left of sinning the sin he said was sinless. Another of many incongruous situations in which one occasionally finds oneself as an enterprising journalist.

The incongruity developed. I began talking to Loudon Hamilton, a former Master at Eton, an elegant *beau ideal* of the Guards officer type, who gave me the story of Frank's advent in Oxford which appears in an earlier chapter. Lunch ended, and the party dissolved, while we still talked. The friends I had brought disappeared; I hoped they were happy under Frank's genial guidance. Loudon Hamilton was absorbingly interesting; more so to me because I have never met a lay-evangelist who so thoroughly and convincingly in every respect does *not* look the part.

I scrutinized his aristocratic features, listened to his aristocratic voice, watched his aristocratic figure, and said to myself, "Everything about you makes me discredit you in this unsuitable role." And yet Loudon Hamilton is one of the most completely-surrendered, fully-consecrated member in the Group. He is a tremendous character. (Read his talk on sin in a later chapter.) He has undergone the most severe self-discipline, has given up "absolutely no end of things"; he is "completely in the saddle," and allows nothing to stand in the way of his helping other men. He has learned to believe absolutely in God, and trusts himself all the time to guidance by the Holy Spirit.

It was a long time before I understood Frank's attitude towards newspaper publicity. The Press is invariably judged by numbers, and has persistently missed the spiritual genius of his work and his great achievements with individual lives. At first the news-papers ridiculed, criticized or made a futile attempt at exposure. Never with anything to expose. The same attacks from every type of assailant are directed against every deeply spiritual movement, stimulated by the undoubted fact that known charlatans are lead-ing quack religious movements both in England and America. The extraordinary thing about the attitude of some newspapers is their complete inability to distinguish between the genuine and the counterfeit.

In rare cases Press criticisms, like individual criticisms, may be occasioned by the high challenge of the teaching; but usually that is not so. The Press knows there are more scoffers at, than believ-ers in, a new religious movement, and are generally on the side of the majority, until passage of time, public recognition, and the pa-tronage of the elect have convinced them of the movement's suc-cess. For the Street of Ink is also the Street of Snobs. Rarely does a newspaper courageously investigate and accept the risks involved in a daring espousal of a new religious stirring. Records show that the work of Moody in the British Isles had powerful and lasting results among countless thousands. Yet Moody had his baptism of Press opposition at the start. His success was all the more amaz-ing because he arrived in England to find that three persons who had invited him over had all died during the six months elapsing between his acceptance and arrival. So Moody started his great Crusade in the open air with no money and no backing.

It was not until after King Edward VII had sent for the aged Wil-liam Booth and congratulated him on his work for the submerged tenth that one dignified English newspaper would print the word General without quotation marks.

I heard some of the pioneering experiences of the first General Booth from his own lips when a guest in his house at Hadley Wood. The blind and aged warrior emphasized his points by thumping my knee with his bony hand.

King Edward asked the old General how he got on with his bish-ops.

"Sir, they irritate us!" wittily retorted that General, thinking of the Church Army. A remark which tickled King Edward. But be-fore that interview had taken place in Buckingham Palace Wil-liam Booth had undergone great ridicule and persecution without much support from Fleet Street.

Frank's desire to work through journalists who understood his ideals thoroughly and could be trusted not to misrepresent them was quite understandable in the light of past experience. Sanity suggested that the best way to help the journalists and the movement was to change the journalists, if they needed changing. As we are mostly a hard-boiled fraternity, nobody is likely to dispute the general need. The percentage of changed journalists is probably lower than the percentage of changed publicans.

Though this circulation of the London newspapers in which I ran the articles on the Oxford Group was small compared with the vast sale we had built up for the newspaper I had just left, we did quite well from our advocacy of the new movement. My staff was tiny, and there was no appropriation for advertising. Yet the circulation jumped immediately, convincing me that had I run the series in a big way with the great resources to which I had been accustomed it would have been another outstanding journalistic success, even though my booming methods might have developed more public interest than the Group leadership could have coped with at that time.

We opened a new series with a banner line on page one announcing:

REMARKABLE RELIGIOUS HOUSE-PARTY AT OXFORD

Then under the sub-titles:

"OXFORD'S NEW RELIGIOUS MOVEMENT"
"B.A.s WHO LIVE on FAITH and PRAYER"
"FIREBRAND COMMUNIST'S CONVERSION"

I stated that: During the past fortnight there has been taking place in three of the colleges of Oxford University a gigantic international house-party that may eventuate in a world-startling religious revival.

Oxford may be the home of lost political causes; it is indisputably the home of several religious awakenings that have stirred the five continents. Already the new religious movement centered in this remarkable house-party is awakening the most somnolent of all sleepers -- the intellectuals. B.A.'s, M.A.'s, LLB.'s, M.B.'s, honors men and women in great number, and many Oxford Dons are to be seen at the meeting-rooms in the three colleges or strolling together arm-in-arm on the rose-bordered lawns discussing nothing more intellectual or scientific than "Christ the Wisdom and Power of God," and the need of a daily self-surrender to Him as the solution of life's riddle.

Yet the house-party is not forbiddingly highbrow. The mid-brow visitor notices immediately the absence of any sign of intellectual snobbery; indeed, of every human affectation or mannerism likely to drive the curious and pagan inquirer hurriedly back into his protecting shell. For whatever he first thinks of the teaching, he has no alternative but to like the product of the Oxford Groups forming the house-party.

A healthier, livelier, gayer, more courteous and unselfish band of cultured men and women does not exist. Here at St. Hugh's, St. Hilda's, Lady Margaret Hall are groups of young and middle-aged men and women who are taking Christianity to its logical limits and practicing the faith, courage and recklessness of the early Apostles.

These five hundred or so, drawn from all churches and no churches, do not stand for a point of view as the price of a safe seat in Paradise, but for a quality of life. They accept the New Testament as marching orders for daily activities, interpreted and guided by the constant directing presence of the Holy Spirit. And all unitedly claim that Christianity, when put into unrestricted practice, becomes not the impossible ideal of popular belief, but the only working basis for a joyous life.

A new automobile may stop, a race-horse may die, the wireless may fade out, and a watch run down. But the Acts of the Apostles continue; they appear to continue impressively in many acts of the groups now gathered at Oxford University, who find in the New Testament the secret of perpetual motion galvanizing any man, any woman, any type, any class, in any age, into unexpected vitality and startling power.

Oxford's new religious movement is neither Methodist nor Tractarian; it includes both wings of the Christian religion. Through a unity in common action, many of diverse religious beliefs and more, have reached an attitude of Christian experience which may hold the one possible solution for modern world problems.

The man through whom the movement came into being is a buoyant, alert, broad-shouldered, vital man of middle age -- one who gives the impression of holding a reservoir of secret power, which he would explain as "being filled with the Spirit." He is a single man. I asked him why he had not married. Frank beamed through and around his spectacles.

"Just because I have never been guided to marry."

Oxford's new religious movement started because Frank found he was not making converts as the early Christians made converts. What was the matter with Christianity or with Frank? He found out, and evolved a technique to put his discoveries into practice, with such astonishing results that he seems to be capturing the cream of the world's universities for vital Christianity.

The Group has the blessing of Anglican and Nonconformist Churches. The Bishop of Leicester and Chancellor R. J. Campbell and Dr. Herbert Gray (Presbyterian) are but three of many well-known clerics and ministers visiting the house-party.

Most of the "cloth" present are in disguise. They conform to the informal nature of the Oxford Group by wearing mufti, although there are no rules as to dress or conduct. Visitors may smoke, drink, do what they like. Yet nobody takes intoxicants, and a visiting lady novelist had the utmost difficulty in borrowing a match from what seemed literally a matchless group.

There are probably a thousand groups scattered around the world to-day, each meeting informally as a little house-party where we soon can be talked to naturally without formality. New groups are constantly springing up under the Holy Spirit's guidance. There is one in Harley Street, and another in Fleet Street, and one for prisoners in a British gaol.

Some of the changed lives are so outstandingly interesting that books containing stories of a few have already become good sellers. Men and women who have seen little in church membership suddenly challenged to surrender everything -- time, money, ambitions -- to God and order their lives by Holy Spirit guidance are constantly capitulating, including those in the higher walks of life.

But there are picturesque captures mingling with the scholars, including James Watt, until recently the firebrand Communist organizer for Fifeshire, a miner, who once lived on the dole and used it to propagate the principles of Bolshevism; who admits that when least satisfied with his own moral code he stifled his conscience stirring up disaffection at open-air meetings, invariably resulting in clashes with the police. This ex-Communist namesake of the inventor of the steam-engine, proud of his sandy hair and his new life, has four months past been living on faith and prayer without the dole, while propagating first-century Christianity.

Being a Scot, he decided to move with caution in his new faith. He carefully tried out all the teachings of the Oxford Group to see if they worked. Discovering that some lived by faith, he and two others, feeling guided to do the same, spent the little money they had in furnishing two rooms in Glasgow. They read the New Testament, prayed, had Quiet Times each day listening to God, moved among the working-class preaching vital Christianity, asked for no money, and waited to see if supplies arrived. Food came, clothes came, money sometimes came. James Watt reached Oxford with a few schillings, and spoke in Mansfield College chapel last Sunday to a congregation of astonished highbrows.

Although it is not the practice of all in the groups to live by faith -- nor does teaching enjoin it -- there are many at the house-party who are actually doing so. At least thirty-five of them have been living without an assured income for several years; some for ten years. All have piquant stories to tell of their faith being tested to the last penny and the last minute; though none has ever gone hungry save through voluntary fasting. Nor do they ask for money or take collections. And this is an age of insurances and tumbling dividends.

A woman novelist, pretty, but skeptical, challenged one of those who lived on faith with the accusation:

"You mean, you live on others?"

He quietly replied: "We all live on other people. What counts is our own contribution to the world. You may work eight hours a day. Some of us work eighteen with no salary."

Frank has lived on faith for ten years or more. A working day in his life would appall the average businessman. It usually begins about 5:30 every morning. From then until 6:30 he spends, to quote his own words, "one hour of quiet alone with the living God" to obtain direction for the day. During house-parties at 7:30 a.m. he attends the first meeting of the Inner Group, some of whom live on faith, and all act on the principle of the Holy Spirit's guidance. Plans are received and discussed, speakers for the day are appointed, and work is allotted. And so on for a full-length day of speaking, guiding, counseling, until nearly midnight -- meetings to discuss the principles of Christian living, others for Bible study; more for witness, for converts to announce changed lives and to share experiences.

Though it is not claimed that every thought received and expressed is inspired by the Holy Spirit, there are innumerable proofs (when the work is reviewed over a period) of supernatural guidance, the divine leading that might be expected when a body of men and women meet often together courageously obedient to any indication of the will of God. All are receptive to the Inner Voice, which they say is one voice unfolding through them, though not through them alone -- not a five-year plan, but a majestic eternal plan for the redemption of humanity.

The first article so pleased Frank that he posted it to nearly ten thousand people. His enthusiasm amused me, seeing that not many weeks before he thought I was not spiritually capable of writing about the movement. The article was reprinted in part or in full in several American and English journals. It was quoted in several pulpits. I constantly heard echoes of it as I moved about the Western World.

Chapter Eleven

THE HUMAN ENGINEER

Though Frank knew everybody and everybody knew Frank at the house-party he was never in the forefront of things, and pleasantly evaded my attempts to draw him out for journalistic purposes. So I began to collect stories about him from his friends -- in case he permanently escaped my attempts to put him "on the spot." Presently I was in possession of such a sheaf of remarkable stories about him that in self-defense he had to verify them and modify them with me. But they still remain remarkable.

At first I liked Frank very much, then not so much, until I began to understand him thoroughly. Afterwards I discovered my experience was similar to that of many of his firmest friends.

Ken Twitchell's brother told me that when he first saw Frank at a Group meeting bustling about, talking gaily to everybody, he disliked him; yet he is now one of Frank's best friends and greatest admirers.

And the irritation shown against Frank by some was explained to me by Sam Shoemaker of Calvary Church, New York, who said, "It is like this. You go to a doctor and he gives you medicine. You don't like the medicine, but it is none the less good for you."

Moreover, Frank does not attempt to dominate meetings or house-parties or people. He uses meetings as a means for training his young men to become leaders and to carry on the work when he is gone.

"I don't know how you manage to make your parties go so well without leading them!" exclaimed the Bishop of Norwich to Frank, when looking admiringly at the Cambridge house-party in Selwyn College in April 1932. Frank smiled acknowledgments, but still kept in the background.

While traveling in a railway train in Canada, just before one of his early visits to China, there came home vividly to Frank the recognition that Christianity has a moral backbone. That moral Bolshevism precedes political Bolshevism. And that to make Christianity vitally productive he could not afford to miss making the moral test with persons who consulted him. To speak with a person about his thought-life is considered indelicate by the old-fashioned and the mock-modest; yet, apparently, the results completely vindicate the practice.

Frank's object is merely to strengthen the man in his weak spot. He finds it the most effective way of putting religion over to people who have no faith, only problems.

Frank has had many experiences of the wisdom of taking nobody for granted. He may be a clergyman, an elder or a vestryman in a church, a Sunday-school superintendent, and yet need ruthless moral surgery. Frank declines to accept the division of the world into two classes -- saved and unsaved. Christ was emphatic as to which of these two classes -- the professionally religious, and the publicans and sinners -- most needed changing, for with scathing irony He said, "I came not to call the righteous, but sinners to repentance." Frank believes the Pharisee is still as much in need of spiritual attention as the publican. One of the best stories of Frank, told in this connection, is by H. A. Walter, in *Soul-Surgery:*

In New York City a University student leader came to talk with Frank about entering the Christian ministry. He had just been attending a conference on the ministry at which brilliant addresses had interested but not convinced him. . . . Frank answered his questions to the best of his ability, still the man seemed to him unsatisfied. They had finished dinner with very little accomplished, and Frank then invited him to his room for further conversation. In time the student opened a little more and said, "I'll tell you why I couldn't enter the ministry. I want my own way too much."

"Isn't there anything else?" Frank asked, and the student said, "No."

And Frank was told what he should say as suspicion became conviction; and, leaning forward, he said quite naturally

"Isn't your trouble . . . ?"

The barrier of pride crumbled away . . .and a new beginning was made on a sure foundation which transformed the young man. . .. As they were walking together to the Subway, the student said (and it is worth remembering):

"Frank, I'd have cursed to-night If you had not got at my real need."

One of many examples of wisdom Frank shows in taking nobody for granted.

Frank was attending a conference for students when he heard the story of a piece of life-changing work in which was the inspiration for his future. A young fellow of limited means told how he had worked hard to help a well-to-do freshmen known as Dick (in with a fast set), who was so busy getting into mischief that he was unable to prepare his lessons.

The speaker rose early and worked through his own lessons, and then at 7 a.m. knocked on the door of his prodigal protégé. Naturally Dick was much too tired to wake up; he sleepily murdered his intention to cut lessons for that morning. Nevertheless, the student entered, got him dressed, and so helped him through his preparation that his recitation was the best he had done for a considerable time. After about six months of this assistance Dick observed that he would give the world to be as good a student as his friend. To which he replied:

"Well, so you can."

"But you don't know *my* problems. I'm a different type from you."

His friend insisted there were no types who could not live the life through the power of his Friend Jesus Christ -- as Dick, too, found from that time onwards.

Frank heard this story told, and said to himself that if a poor student could take so much trouble to help another man, he could surely do the same. Hitherto nobody had told him how. But he decided that his life's objective must be to win men no matter who they were. Immediately he drove a stake in, vowing to win a man before he got home. He thought this would be easy, although it had been a long job for the student.

On the way home, Frank was to visit New York, where he assumed he would have plenty of opportunity. In New York things began to crowd in on him -- those things which are the great enemy keeping us from men -- so that he forgot about his vow until he was on the point of leaving the city. As he was buying his ticket, he suddenly remembered he had not won his man. He grew hot and cold and bothered. How could he go home? He must find one needing changing on the spot. Frank caught sight of a colored porter, in a red cap, looking as fat and shiny as butter. "Here's my man," said Frank, and started in, feeling very scared about his first adventure in life-changing.

"George, are you a Christian?"

"No, bawss," said the darky, startled.

"Then you ought to be a Christian."

"I know, bawss. Other people have told me that. But I don't know how, bawss. What's more, I'm scared."

Two people scared of the same subject, comments Frank. Everybody seems scared to talk sanely about religion, which is why we fail.

"Why *are* you scared?" asked Frank, hiding his own fright.

"My brother's coming down the river from Sing-Sing. He's got religion up there, and I don't know how to handle him." Frank's own attitude towards George.

"Now, George, you've got to be a Christian," commanded Frank, not knowing what more to say, or how better to express himself at that time.

"Yes, bawss, I will."

"Thus ended" says he, "my first crude attempt to bring the unsearchable riches of Christ to another man. Whether he became a Christian or not in time to meet his brother coming out of prison, or afterwards, I cannot tell. But that day the ice was broken on a new life-work. Another crisis had passed which released me for one of the most glorious adventures open to man. It showed to me what ordinary men like myself may be privileged to do in life-changing on a big scale.

What is the secret of Frank's amazing power over himself, over his colleagues, over everyone who knows him well? Just the power of a positive personality, is the first assumption. Then one discovers that is not so. He is a long way from the domineering character who carries everyone with him by sheer force. Pleasant, suave, obliging, eternally merry, active, strong-willed, if you like. But not an overwhelming force breaking down all obstacles by the ruthless drive of the leader born. Whence, then, the secret of his astonishing power over others? He revealed it to me on the afternoon of Easter Day, during one of his gay chats over tea at Oxford.

I was very busy (Frank began) working eighteen to twenty-eight hours every day. So busy that I had two telephones in my bedroom. Still I was dissatisfied with the results. There was a constant coming and going, but the changes in the lives of my visitors were inadequate, and not revolutionary enough to become permanent. So I decided on a radical procedure -- to give that hour of the day from five to six in the morning when the phones were unlikely to ring, to listen for the Still Small Voice to inspire and direct.

The only thing that came to me during the first morning hour of listening to the Living God was three words, really the same word repeated three times: The nickname of a happy-go-lucky fellow in the University --

"Tutz , Tutz, Tutz."

This young man's grandmother used to call on my mother and ask if Frank couldn't do something to improve her grandson. I had prayed that Tutz would be changed, though until that time I had not the inclination to cross his track. But that same morning the first person I met on the green was Tutz, coming leisurely along, smoking a cigarette and just late for lectures as usual. My first thought was against speaking to him -- that I was not sure about my message, as the word Tutz might just have come to me out of my subconscious self or from the evil one. But there came again the same insistent message of the morning, "Tutz, Tutz, Tutz."

Knowing I must not evade, I said to Tutz, "Would you like to have a chat with a football friend of mine who knows how to put the great truths of life and make them effective for ordinary people just like ourselves?"

"Yes," he said, "I'd like to," showing that fine sense of abandon of the interesting sinner -- always ready for a new adventure.

Now Tutz had come from a normal Christian family, had been confirmed, but the strain of prep school life, and later the University, had veered him from the straight and narrow. He had talent, and did well in Dramatics, in which he always played the girl's part, and made a great hit with the audience, for he knew just how to swish his train to create the maximum comic effect. When the Dramatic Club went on tour, the show would always conclude with a dance, into which Tutz would put a lot of kick and go. And when he returned later to their private car, he would never forget to say his prayers before going to sleep.

I accompanied him to the football player, and so readily did my friend understand him, his problems, his open faults and secret sins, and the divided life that goes with them, his sense of defeat and unhappiness, that Tutz made a decision to surrender his life to Christ, the great Friend of sinners. He gave himself to God to have and to hold from that time forward for better, for worse, for richer, for poorer, till death. Later he came to me radiant with his new experience, whereupon I challenged him: "How about telling your friends the story?"

"Tell my friends! They'd all laugh."

"But you like the laughter of your friends at the play. The more laughter you get the more you are pleased."

The thing I like about interesting sinners like Tutz is -- they have imagination. Give them a chance to look, and they leap. He went back to his club, and found all his friends sitting about the hall waiting for the luncheon-bell to ring. The game or young Tutz breezed in and announced, "Well, I suppose you will all laugh when I tell you what I did this morning."

Everyone was most interested. Tutz usually had something to

say that was spicy and amusing. He may have been pulling the leg of some Don or picking up some good new story. He simply said: "Well, I decided to change my life this morning."

Here *was* news! They waited eagerly. He must tell them all about it. They sat on the edge of their chairs listening breathlessly to the happenings of the morning, and the gong for lunch clanged unnoticed.

One of the auditors -- named Bill -- who had a racing car with room for someone next to him and something in the rumble seat behind, said, "I'd like to see that football fellow." Tutz said, "Right. I'll telephone and make an appointment." He came on to the constantly ringing telephone, "Can you see Bill, this afternoon?"

"Certainly."

"When?"

"Any time."

Frank continued:

That's the marvelous thing about the busy college men. They can always make time immediately for something they really want to do. Bill came to see my friend, and he, too, found the new power that day and became a changed man, with Christ as his King and Guide. Later the same day I was standing with the Chaplain, whom everybody called Bob. His popularity rested on the short sermons he preached and his interest in sport, but he rarely met men's deepest needs.

Tutz came up with Bill and said to me, "You know Bill's with me on this." I said, "Bully for you, Bill." Bob the Chaplain added that it was about time he made a change. Then Bill rounded on Bob something like this: "We've known each other a long time, Bob. I used to admire you for your Varsity letter. Then you came up here as our Chaplain and coach and played around with us, but you'd have let me go straight to hell for all you cared about my real need."

This indictment of the Chaplain by Bill made me shudder (says Frank), as it might very well have been said to me -- that I was looking after men's bodies instead of their deepest needs -- had I not been listening to God for an hour early that morning, although only three words came, from which two souls were reborn in one day. But that day I found the secret of true education. The Holy Spirit is the Light, the Guide, the Teacher, the Power. What I am able to do I do through the power that comes in the early hour of morning quiet, waiting and watching for the voice of the Living God to break through the shadows of the night.

There was a sequel to the story of Tutz. Seven years afterwards I was asked to preach for a Rector, who advised, "Make it short, so they will come back for the second service to-night." As I was about to close I felt the Holy Spirit saying to me, "Tell them the story of Tutz. Tell the story of Tutz." Seven years' experience of the Still Small Voice taught me the necessity of prompt obedience. So I told this story. The church was large. There was much stained glass, and the congregation was difficult to see. As I got into the story I noticed a movement on the left half-way down the church. At the end of the service who should come up to see me but Tutz, Mrs. Tutz, Baby Tutz, and Father-in-law Tutz, all of whom had been in the church without my knowing they were present.

Tutz had held faithfully on for seven active, fruitful years. His wife was on his side too. And his father-in-law. And Baby Tutz would probably be coming along later.

"That went big this morning," announced Tutz, as he came up to me, adding, "I wouldn't have been teaching a Sunday-school class in this church but for your accosting me that morning on the College green."

And somehow, because I had enlarged my theme with the Tutz story in the morning, the congregation enlarged itself automatically for Evensong (adds Frank).

Frank learned long ago that he must never scold. To scold is not to understand. To scold is the negation of the story of the Prodigal Son. It is the whole question of nagging, he says, that makes the average home uncomfortable. The home atmosphere must be lifted above that undesirable, all-pervading human sin. One way to do that is to remember with Kipling never to look too good or talk too wise. Frank has developed the art of looking into the face of a man and reading like a book the life he is a leading. He has developed the sense of never being shocked.

"I am quite unshockable," he told me.

"Has a man ever confessed murder to you?"

He laughed.

"I knew you were going to ask that. I have been in condemned cells, but I think I had better not say whether I have heard murder confessions. We mustn't be sensational."

I mentioned that a clergyman told me he had listened to confessions of murder by four persons, and I had published these under his name in a signed article in a British publication. Had Frank received such a confession? But he still avoided the question.

If a murderer confessed he might say, "Tell me all about it. How did you do it?"

Frank's reluctance to disclose another's secrets is understandable. All ministers of the Gospel hear extraordinary confessions from sinners and treat what they hear as confidential, a practice adhered to in the Group unless the person who confesses himself takes it public.

Fear of a censorious attitude by the listener often prevents honest sharing which might end the chaos in many homes where the ideal life could quite easily be led.

Frank believes it possible for sons and daughters to return home and frankly disclose the story of their daily life, instead of contributing to the general conspiracy of secrecy as to the real doings of the day so common in many homes; secrecy inspired by an artificial restraint first introduced by the parents. He knew a mother whose chief hobby was temperance, but all of her children became drunkards. If she had known better how to get into the lives of her children by confessing her own weaknesses, instead of warning them so often against theirs, she might not have driven them all to drink.

According to Frank, the same judicious practice of sharing would prevent many sons and daughters from being driven away from their home by misunderstanding parents. There was as much need for prodigal parents to return to their forgiving sons and daughters who had been driven away by nagging and the unwillingness to share as for prodigal children to return to their earthly parents. Furthermore, there was too much assumed horror by parents at their children's repetition of their own early sins. Sex problems would cease to exist in homes where parents were honest about their own problems in an effort to help without affectation or censoriousness.

Frank learned the necessity of avoiding scolding when helping George through one of his early problems. George was sixteen with blue eyes and blond hair, a slight figure, a blue suit with long trousers. He was a double orphan. On the day of his mother's funeral his two sisters were sent to an orphanage and, there being no where for George to go, Frank invited him to his own home.

"I tried to make him feel comfortable with me," said Frank. "I sat next to him, told him my best stories and tried to make him interested. That was Tuesday. On the Friday night after dinner George said he would like to go downtown. I said, 'Yes,' but I knew I had not yet got his confidence. You can sit at the same table with a person and learn a lot of things, and yet not know him.

"It was a long summer evening. About nine-thirty I looked out the window, and saw young sixteen-year-old George zig-zagging up the street with the pavement not quite wide enough for him. I watched him as he tried to get into the house. He missed the bell, and so no one came, which made him furious. Then he began to shake the door violently.

"Most people shake the door when they ought to shake themselves. I felt very unhappy about George as I went to the door and let him in. . . ."

When Frank has reached this point in his story, he usually asks, What would you do with George? Some suggest a shower, aspirin, black coffee, soda-water, a school evening. Frank left George severely alone for a while, after making sure that he had gone safely to bed, without George knowing he was looking after him. Nor did Frank go down to breakfast next morning with George, knowing that if he saw the bloodshot eye he might say something he would regret later. During his Quiet Time guidance definitely came that he should go down to the wholesale millinery store where George worked and meet him there. He asked the Jewish manager if he could see George.

"Certainly, sir."

George came up a hall-like corridor, and immediately when he saw Frank his head fell and he blushed, although Frank had said nothing. Most people, Frank observed, who want to help others seem to think they must publish abroad their sins. He asked George what about lunch together.

George said, "Excellent."

They went along to a restaurant with the manager's permission to take a full hour. They started the meal with oysters, George as silent as a clam. They came to the fish, and while picking the bones George said, hesitatingly:

"I was drunk last night."

Frank heard the admission in silence. Presently George mustered up courage to go a bit further:

"You know it didn't cost me very much."

Frank again said nothing, but his comment to me on this excuse was, "There are people who think it mitigates the offense if the sin is not too expensive."

Presently George said, "You teach a Sunday-school class?"

"Yes," said Frank, and left it at that.

Frank observed that most people would think the occasion was now ripe for a pious talk, which would probably have satisfied their conscience, but not cured George, for his full confidence had not yet been won.

Finally George said, "I made up my mind last night as I came up Twentieth Street that If you scolded me I would go out and do it again."

Most people, according to Frank, are sober enough for some clear thinking even when drunk. As it was, George dropped his drink, turned up at Sunday-school next Sunday, and became a worker with remarkable talents who could do for boys more than Frank was ever able to do, as he was nearer their age and had a ready point of contact. In time, George came to be the Secretary of a national chain of Bible-classes organized by a well-known amateur pugilist who belonged to one of the old families.

"I saw Frank from another angle when discussing him with Cleve Hicks, a former Chaplain at Harvard.

"Frank is nobody's fool," said Cleve. "And he can deal trenchantly with anyone if needful."

"Has he dealt trenchantly with you?" I queried.

Cleve has a merry smile and a jolly, well-upholstered figure.

"We were having a Quiet Time, and I was feeling very undisciplined," Cleve admitted. "I had a lot of fear of the future and had been slack about morning devotions. Frank asked me if I had anything to share among a big Group, and I said, 'No.' Frank looked straight at me and said, 'Cleve, you are sleek and unconvincing.'"

"And what did you tell him *he* looked like?"

Cleve regarded me sleekly and replied convincingly, "I said nothing; but I had no fear of him. I knew he was right."

"On another occasion," continued Cleve, "we were having a Quiet Time when Frank announced, 'Cleve needs dynamic change. Hold him lovingly to maximum experience of Christ. Opposition results in great fruitage in years ahead.'"

Cleve was intrigued by this prophecy, and made a note of it. The prophecy is already being fulfilled.

Frank is a stickler for courtesy and good manners. A young man attending a house-party in Holland omitted to thank his host as Frank and team were leaving. On the way to the station, Frank discovered the omission, and insisted on the car being driven back and the host properly thanked. Immediate restitution!

If any of his young men are leaving England for another country, he warns them to learn the customs and fit in with the social code of the land they visit. For these international house-parties he always endeavors to see that the people from one country are

agreeable to those from other countries, and that everyone Is comfortable.

While he is sensitive to unfair criticism of his work, and has the
settled conviction that the Holy Spirit is with him, he dislikes arguing about the rightness of his methods of teaching. He prefers to
change his critics, thereby giving them a personal demonstration
of the practicality of his work. As, for instance, when a gathering of
American psychiatrists ask him to come and explain his methods,
he used all the time of the interview endeavoring to turn them into
Christian psychologists like himself.

If he could have been harnessed to any organization he would
have made a Napoleon of organizers. His Oxford friends told me
that when he arrived at a house-party he would ask a few questions and immediately gathered together all points in his well-or-
dered brain, quickly infusing more life and hilarity into the pro-
ceedings. And withal so simply and so naturally that you were
always in danger of overlooking his bigness.

Only after you had left him, and one of his apt sayings -- "We are
an organism, not an organization" -- or kindly just-right actions
recurred to you, would you observe, "Ah, Frank said that!" Or,
"Fancy Frank doing that just at the right moment!"

Frank insists there is no difference in sin wherever it is committed. He crystallizes the point by saying, "Crows are black the wide
world over" -- a favorite slogan of the Group. Immorality in Paris or
theft in China is just as sinful as immorality or theft in England.
But when a team was addressing an audience of Negroes in South
Africa, the slogan was changed to, "Grass is green a wide world
over."

I asked one of Frank's friends if he had ever seen him angry.
"Only once," he replied. "Frank was addressing a public meeting,
and waxed very angry with those selfish, lazy persons who want
their relatives changed to Christians but were unwilling to do the
tackling themselves."

"That's your job," is Frank's uncompromising rejoinder to most
of these petitions. A rejoinder which makes him temporary enemies because of its truth. A young man who confessed that his
trouble was sex was given the slogan, "Watch your eyes." Frank
believes that Christ meant what He said that "every one that loo-
keth on a woman to lust after her hath committed adultery with
her already in his heart." First the look, then the thought, then
the fascination, then the fall. It was better to look away, to think
of other things, and better still to be actively engaged in changing

others, which produced the highest joy in life.

The number of religious books Frank has given away would fill a public library. His traveling-cases are packed with Group publications suitable for different spiritual diseases. He uses so many that he buys wholesale.

He is a religious colporteur freely distributing samples of the commodity most needed by everybody. Those who accept the books usually allow him to pay for them. Occasionally one more thoughtful will leave him the price.

"Were you guided to leave that?" he crackles.

As you were merely refusing to accept goods for nothing from one who lives on faith and prayer you reply:

"Yes."

Though you are not quite sure about it.

A point that his friends stress about Frank is the utter selflessness of the man, the absolute identification of his own personality with the intangible development of the Body of Christ on earth. He is perfectly willing to be out of the picture, to be humiliated, scandalized, or, if necessary, to assume and exert all authority. No Group meeting ever goes with quite a swing and vitality as one run by him. Frank is fearful of putting too great dependence on personalities, and is out to modify rather than insult himself or his friends, since the humility is the true Christian characteristic. He believes in perfect freedom of action even without the money to buy it. He has been known to take his last penny out of the bank to help some person whose urgent needs seemed to entitle him to it. When Frank has no money he prays for it.

When first I met Frank he had been praying for money to help a man with whom he was sharing his linen.

The money came.

He prayed with the person who brought it. Frank thanked God, first for telling him the money would come, and then for sending the money.

He is scrupulously careful not to waste money on anything. Frank asks guidance for expenditure on postage. Yet without a qualm he will spend a thousand pounds if he feels he should do so and if he has the money. He emptied his pockets to help a team visit South Africa to found a Group there.

Sometimes persons who have little or no money, but are touched by his zeal, express a wish to help him.

For instance, a devoted maidservant in a house in Scotland, where Frank was staying, told him the only way she could help him was to wash his linen, which she would be glad to do.

And so every week when Frank is in England his laundry goes to Scotland and is washed free by "a braw Scott lassie."

It is impossible to understand Frank at all unless he is thought of as always in God's presence, listening for direction and accepting power, which he says is the normal way for a sane human being to live. Frank is an example of the psychologically mature men, thoroughly integrated round the highest relationship possible to man. An interesting part of this is the amazingly practical way his guidance works out.

If a man's life is thoroughly integrated in God, he finds a dominant purpose in which everything fits. It does not mean rigidity, but being so flexible as to be responsive to unexpected opportunities giving further opportunities to serve God, whose ways are not men's ways, as Paul found when he was going his roundabout way to Rome.

Frank is perfectly undisciplined. He does not wander voluntarily in his spiritual life: he goes direct to the Source all the time, and expects the Source to come direct to him. Whatever he does he feels must be right, since he is doing what is the guided thing for him to do.

Through his constant practice of losing his life daily he has come to find himself. He awakes in the morning with the idea that today is not his day, but God's day. Losing his life, he finds it all the time. The result of his discipline is abounding energy -- which he is confident comes from the Holy Spirit. This discipline at the heart of the movement means complete freedom. The paradox of Christianity.

Frank is a child listening to God and obeying Him implicitly, and getting all those around him to do the same. And no one will ever understand this movement who does not accept this as a working hypothesis, whether he needs it or not at the start. After a time he begins to see it is true.

As I thought of Frank living this listening-in life, I felt that it was excellent in theory, but impossible in general practice. And then the former Master of Selwyn (Dr. Murray) lent me the notes of one of his lectures on Prayer, in which I found this paragraph, which gave me a better understanding of Frank:

"For our life here is not meant to be a monotonous and lonely tramp on a treadmill. If it is meant to be a brisk, an intelligent and adventurous march onward towards a goal which, however distant and however dimly discerned, is certain because God has appointed it. But it can only become this in proportion as we hear and respond to the call of God, to cooperate with Him in the bringing in of His Kingdom. And when you come to look under the surface of our Lord's teaching on Prayer, you see that it is all directed to secure just this harmonious and effective co-operation.

"It was, of course, as we learned especially from St. John's Gospel, just this kind of life that Jesus Himself lived in the flesh. His meat was to do the will of Him that sent Him, to finish His work. His old being was supported by conscious communion with His Father. His life was brightened by the consciousness of His Father's approval. He was always watching for a signal from His Father's hand, so all that He did was not His own doing, but His Father's. The Spirit of His Father taught Him what to say."

Frank, following his Master, is always waiting for his Master's signals.

Everybody associated with Frank, like Frank himself, gets a new quality out of this basis of life, as well as some pain -- the pain of the Cross. Frank gets the disappointments which come when someone for whom he has an enlarged vision fails to obtain to Olympus. But he is supremely human, and is not harden himself through other's failure. He is never too busy to think humanly. He lives more of an objective life than anyone I know. That is one answer to any who suggest that he encourages introspection.

He is always thinking of other people. He loves festival's; his birthday list is long and growing; he is a great man at any celebration. He is a dominating character, but does not believe in domination, for that kills initiative. Meet him and you may not like him, because he does not appreciate you too much at your present worth, the reason being that he wants to get you to a higher altitude: more spiritual exercise and more spiritual air. For, says he, the spirit, like the body, needs food, air and exercise.

Frank has a way with him for every occasion. A young Presbyterian minister told me that when traveling with Frank he repeatedly noticed his amazing solicitude for the welfare of others. He had seen Frank stop suddenly in the midst of a discussion to inquire if a fire had been placed in somebody's room, or adequate preparations made for another's arrival or departure. When the last Oxford house-party was breaking up, I observed Frank stealing round the dinner-table to some of his friends with fine singing voices arranging a farewell chorus for the housekeeper at Lady Margaret Hall. Under Frank's vigorous direction they sang heartily:

For *she's* a jolly good fellow,
And so say all of us.

Typical of Frank's spontaneous good-will and rightness of action.

Once Frank wittily amplified to me his teaching about Sharing by saying, "Love's blind, but the neighbors ain't." We may think our sins are securely hidden, but directly we begin to disclose a few, we usually find our neighbor is already aware of them. If anyone doubts this, try it and see.

Frank has a counterpart of his saying about the neighbors in the aphorism, "Read men more than books." If you really want to help men, you must get oftener into their lives than into the bookshelves. He once asked the late Dr. F. B. Meyer (of Christ Church, London), a famous saint and a powerful preacher, how a man could have power in the pulpit.

"By answering on Sundays the questions your congregation ask you on week-days," was the answer.

That meant he must be getting into the lives of his flock all week to know their real needs when Sunday came.

Sam Shoemaker (Rector of Calvary) told me that when someone accused Frank of having no interest in the Second Coming he flashed back:

"Why talk of the Second when so many know nothing of the First?"

Not that he is less interested in the Second Coming than other ministers; he urges men and women to cut out sin and keep it out; then they know what it means to hope for and always ready for the Second Advent.

"I have never seen a man so completely surrendered to God as Frank," said Sam Shoemaker. "He is the most disciplined personality I know. Everything he has is absolutely given up to God. I have seen him at night seated in his chair thoroughly done in with his day's untiring labors toward God, pale and utterly exhausted. Then the door opens and in walks another opportunity for service. Tired though he is, Frank is on his feet instantly, his face glowing, his merry smile back again, hand outstretched, his whole being a-quiver for further effort for his Master, ready to go on right through the night if he can only help another from shadow into light. He allows himself to be just carried along without effort on a wave of the Holy Spirit.

"He never seems to tire. His life is entirely without conflict or worry, except when deeply concerned over someone else's problem. Occasionally he gets pained with sin, and can deal drastically with insincerity and compromise. He has amazing patience in the face of the incredible, persistent and blind stupidity of persons who consult him while unwilling to take his advice and surrender the sin which prevents them from fulfilling their destiny.

"Frank is no quitter. He is never through with a man. They may talk and part. The man may go away interested but unconvinced, and may forget, but Frank doesn't. The day may come when that man returns, perhaps prepared to go a step further. Frank remembers him and patiently endeavors to help him another step forward."

I asked Sam Shoemaker if Frank never grew tired of the strain of continuous personal evangelism. Did he never want to break out and paint the town red?

Sam laughed at the impossibility. "You bet he doesn't. Why should he when he is so thoroughly happy? I have never met a man quite so merry as Frank. He once signed a cable to me -- in a time of the greatest stress --'Yours merrily -- Frank.'"

Some of the New York toughs have a too-familiar custom of walking by your side in the street, thrusting a revolver at you, and demanding that you "shell out" all your money, in the good old Dick Turpin way. I asked several leaders of the Group what they would do in such a disturbing event. One or two thought it would be better to pay out than to be shot, for in New York those fellows stood no nonsense. The prospect of forty or sixty years in Sing-Sing was not encouraging. Only the fool fought when taken unawares, said my friend the Spider, who knew all about prisons and gangsters because he was changed.

I asked Frank what he would do if accosted by a man with a gun. We were in a London cab making for Bond Street. It was rather a tickler, I felt, even for Frank, who pondered a while. Then he said:

"I should invite him to say the Lord's Prayer with me. If he were a Catholic I should ask him to say the Paternoster."

"And suppose he fired?"

Frank gave an enigmatical smile.

"I don't think he would."

Frank likes to think in the plural when organizing a life-changing campaign. He would much sooner take a hundred life-changers into a city than one or two. Musical-comedy touring companies, he argues, take fifty or sixty into a town. Why should not the Groups do the same?

He foresees the day when an army of five hundred or more consecrated life-changers may descend on a town or city and set to work winning it to Christ. "Maximum effort -- no loan-wolfing" is his motto.

Though Frank has no money, he also has no worries, and so when he does go to bed, which may be at any time, he is asleep as soon as he has turned out the light.

In the morning he is astir with the birds. He came into my room at Cambridge before seven in pajamas to wish me good-morning. His face was hidden behind a foam of shaving-soap; yet merriment broke through. That morning Frank told me he not only believed in getting up when the cock crowed, but he believed in crowing as well. He was crowing with joy that wet April morning. The Lord was so good to him, he said.

I watched him as he prayed during the seven-thirty Communion service which followed, his eternally happy face lit with smiles.

Frank is one of those rare human beings who really love God.

Chapter Twelve

A JOURNALIST'S STRANGEST JOURNEY

There were divided opinions in my office as to the new movement. "I hate it!" affirmed the best writer on our staff. People only
hate what matters most to them. Hatred of religion is often the
beginning of faith. Christ came with nothing but love in His heart,
and succeeded in stirring up more towering hate than any other
man in history.

The time seemed propitious for my long-deferred pilgrimage
to the New World, and for fuller investigation of the work of the
Group outside my own country. I sent a cable to Ray Purdy, told
him of my projected trip, and asked what were the chances of cov-
ering the expenses of an American tour by writing. Back came the
answer: "Come on a basis of faith and prayer. Check your decision
with Frank." I wired Frank in Germany. He advised: "Go in faith
and prayer, and rely on the Holy Spirit's guidance." It all seemed
very unreal, possessing a mixed flavor of sand and sawdust, tasting more dry than prohibition. Nevertheless, although more interesting than journalism in the working out.

Europe was in semi-chaos when I left. My liner might have been
Noah's Ark floating on the Deluge to ground with me on a new
Mount Ararat, the Empire State Building. A panorama of pyramids glided by the porthole admitting me to a titanic city of con-
fusing right-angles and glittering towers. All incredibly thrilling.

New thrills produced queer effects. This is what the thrill of entering New York did to me:

Out of the storm
And to the quaking East,
Down the Atlantic bend
To a terraced city,
Lofty, geometric,
Fantastic as the dream
Of a drink-maddened tedious.
City of New York:
Dream-city,
Devil city,

City of Satan and God;
Gliding by my porthole,
Skyscraper after skyscraper,
Cluster following cluster;
Tall giants at the Battery.
Elder brothers in their prime,
Then the part-grown children,
Plump infants passing now;
Here come Father and Mother --
Empire and Chrysler,
Monarch of Fifth Avenue
And slim Mistress of Lexington:
Jupiter and Juno
Gazing proudly Down-town,
Excusably admiring
Their grown children,
Sons of an improved race
Of Anaks,
By whose courtesy
I enter
Gratefully
The Promised Land.

For some reason inexplicable, Frank was delighted at this; he learned it by heart and quoted it often.

One of the Three Troubadours who had come to see me in my office, Charles Haines, met me at the dock and introduced me to New York. We spent a delightful week-end -- on the Woolworth Power (Prince George had just been up, said the attendant), the Empire State (too giddy at first to look over, though on the next ascent I dropped off to sleep on the eighty-sixth floor in the warm February sun), Coney Island (America's great Yarmouth), Bear Mountain (no bears), and the beautiful West Point (America's Sandhurst). And a jolly day and night at Summit, New Jersey, where John and Alec Beck and their sister "Marge" gave me a true Western welcome as I first entered an American home. So did Grace and Howland Pell, and Peter; and Mr. and Mrs. Biscoe, the ideal married couple.

Later I was hospitably entertained at Bill Wilkes' home in Summit. While Bill's pretty wife provided welcome hospitality, Bill sorrowfully offered me much-needed advice on the sin of selling short. Crowded days followed. Charles Haines took me to his fine gold University, once controlled by the War President of the United

States, and proudly showed me Princeton from every one of Woodrow Wilson's fourteen points. John Beck drove me up Broadway -- the hundred-mile street -- to Albany, the State capital. I soon observed that America uses knives rarely at table, presumably keeping them for more effective use in the street; I've discovered that Babe Ruth was a greater national character than Al Capone, that millionaires walk about with armed body-guards to save themselves from kidnapping and torture, that Fifth Avenue is undoubtedly the finest street in the world, and that New York made nearly every city I knew seem painfully provincial. I have seen no more thrilling site than New York City and Harbour from Brooklyn Bridge. In Washington I met an Irishman who affably pointed out the scenes of British defeats!

Before my first week ended I was invited to take part in a tour with an Oxford Group team -- one of those faith-and-prayer trips, this time to the Southern States. There would be some hospitality, I was told. My expenses would approximate a pound a day. And there would be twenty dollars divided between the five speakers at a meeting in the Orange Presbytery in North Carolina. Four dollars apiece for a three weeks' crusade.

The tour attracted; the work scared; the pay amused. They mentioned romantic names like Indiana, Ohio, Kentucky, Tennessee, Virginia, North Carolina. Haunts of Raleigh, Lincoln, Lee, Deerfoot, and Daniel Boone! But a religious tour. Traveling with four men who said they had planned the journey under the guidance of the Holy Spirit. Four men who lived on faith and prayer. I expected Quiet Times in the morning, life-changing in the afternoon and evening, confessing a colored past and praying with people about their future and mine, perhaps morning, noon and night. Too much realism for real romance.

We started, four evangelist and a pseudo-evangelist; three of them -- Sciff Wishard (leader), the ubiquitous Cleve Hicks and Levering Evens -- were fully-fledged parsons; the fourth, John Beck of Summit, an ex-engineer. No apparent difference in the mentality of the four. All kindly, cultured, lovable. None wore clerical clothes and dog-collar as most clergy and ministers do in England.

One of the most entertaining travel companions, and one of the most liked and inspiring, was Cleve Hicks. His round, merry face, all smiles and generosity, is a proof that one can live on faith and prayer and still be free from all worry, even with no money in the bank. Cleve looks so youthful that one assumes he has only just graduated, instead of years ago.

Amazingly successful as a personal evangelist, he was most apt-ly described to me as "A mischief-maker for God" -- by the Rector of Calvary. Cleve's good nature is undiscourageable, his industry indefatigable, his humour unquenchable, and his ingenuity for God incredible. And always the merry schoolboy still rejoicing in tuck (sweets) and in English tea at all hours of the day and night.

At the end of a long day's drive I had gone to bed in a country home in the mountains of Pennsylvania, and was just settling into sleep when Cleve's merry face stole round the door and in a loud, almost guilty whisper, he called:

"A. J., would you like some tea?"

The American way to an Englishman's heart! He had been rum-maging in the kitchen and found a saucepan and crockery and teapot. He boiled hot water in the saucepan and brewed midnight tea in my bedroom. Whatever good thing comes his way he enjoys with the rollicking zest of his religion; enjoys it most as a means of sharing. Cleve would never have sat lonely in a corner hugging a tuck-basket to himself.

I was descending in the elevator at Calvary Home one afternoon when I again heard that loud, half-guilty whisper: "A. J., I've found some tea!" The Vestry was in session. They had just had tea. But there were spare cups and plenty of surplus cake in the adjoining room. Cleve had discovered this, and he wanted company to share his good fortune. I shared while he went upstairs to find another friend, Sciff Wishard, who came creeping down to participate in the spoils. I suggested that we three should have confessed our theft at the Group meeting that evening, and was informed that Cleve had secured permission before he distributed his invitations.

Although Cleve is a successful evangelist, I can never completely dissociate him from Friar Tuck. The first day I met him he came bounding down to breakfast, saw a tempting morsel near his plate, and asked his hostess ("Marge" Beck) if he could start on it. She smilingly announced that he must wait until grace had been said. "But can't I say a special grace now?" queried the former Harvard Chaplain, unabashed.

We were nearly two hundred miles away by lunch-time, and hungry with the journey. There were seven of us to lunch, and a smallish pie came in. Cleve okay regarded it with apprehension. "Is that all you've got?" he demanded, while everybody roared. Sciff's attractive wife produced another pie, and Cleve was content.

At one Thursday night Group meeting in Calvary I heard Cleve Hicks tell the story of how Sam had first intrigued him with his wonderful narratives of men and women who had been won for God. To capture men alive for Christ! That had become his motto. And he is capturing them almost every week. He told of his experiences in South Africa, and how he had attended a Quiet Time held in the Cabinet Room of the Government and of the unceasing fun and adventure and zest of letting God run your life as He wished to run it. Trusting to God for everything was not a worry, but a stimulating thing to do, he proclaimed, adding that if God let you down you were finished.

"But God never lets you down." Cleve's round, beaming face and well-nourished body confirmed his words as he smiled around.

Inseparable from Cleve Hicks is Sciff Wishard, who lead our team round the Southern States.

"To watch that fellow firm up and move forward in discipline since he came into the Group," says Sam Shoemaker, "is an inspiration! He has developed a knife-cutting edge like steel. What a change, he says, from when he used to stroll negligently about the campus at Princeton as though he were doing the place a favor to be there."

Sciff is tall and handsome and greatly generous. I heard him tell the story of his contact with an Anglo-Catholic clergyman in America which had some remarkable results. At one house-party he overheard this clergyman saying to another clergyman: "These fellows are getting after the clergy."

Sciff leaned forward and asked if some of them didn't need getting after.

"What you mean?"

"I'm a clergyman and I need getting after."

The clergyman suggested a talk. They spent most of two days discussing the principles of the Group. Then one morning the clergyman was trying to steal away quietly when Sciff Wishard encountered him and urged him to stay longer. The clergyman stayed against his inclination. He became a good deal rattled as several others spoke to him. Cleve Hicks asked him to come and read the Bible with him.

"No, I won't," he snapped.

"Well, you mind if I pray with you?"

"Yes, I do!" (Another snap.)

But the upshot was he returned home changed, where, through persecution and misunderstanding and loneliness, has been started a work which has changed many lives in town. For several months the Anglo-Catholic, the Methodist, and the Presbyterian ministers there have been holding weekly meetings to share their experiences and needs and sins. And the outcome of this new fellowship was a Group dinner for two hundred and fifty persons of the three churches, with the same number unable to secure seats. The clergyman said he was none less than Anglo-Catholic, but his encounter with Group had made a Presbyterian tolerable!

Both John Beck and Levering Evans had good stories to tell of their experiences, were convincing speakers, and lived the life. Never have I met a quartet of such happy travel-companions.

I soon found that the best way to discover North America was to travel south! Our first halt was at the Birmingham School for Girls, a lovely blue-and-white institution nestling in an area of the Alleghenies, where a Group had been established. The staff entertained us, and we talked quite freely, shared our experiences, and continued on our way next morning in brilliant autumn sunshine. I still feel like a sort of tame wolf in sheep's clothing.

There was then such a gulf between my colleagues' stand-point and my own. They claimed to have surrendered their wills to God, and always to seek His guidance. I believed in Christ, and thought perhaps I had been led to America. But I wasn't so sure about it -- as they seemed to be about our trip, for instance.

The first favorable thing about them was their unanimous state of mind; they never squabbled. Once I surprised one taking another aside to discuss something dividing them, and the tiff was over immediately. They had to act thus because the Group say, "Sin is that which keeps a man from God or from his fellow-men."

At Wooster, Ohio, we explored the Presbyterian College, and then, in a terrific heat, to the flat, curveless road to Indianapolis. Here we were welcomed by the First Presbyterian Church of the city, and entertained most hospitably by Sciff Wishard's parents and brother William, who figure prominently in the medical life of America.

I had heard some amazing stories of the early settlers from Skiff Wishard's then venerable Father. Though over eighty, he had just performed an operation with the sure touch of a surgeon half his age. A movie was taken of this notable performance.

One of his grandfathers, said Mr. Wishard senior, had been chased in a canoe by Red Indians and shot. His body fell in the Ohio River at Pittsburgh (then called "Fort Pitt"), and the Indians swam out to get his scalp. A beautiful collie dog lunged in to protect his master's body, and was also killed before the Indians secured the scalp. Those were the days when men were men.

But the story he told of another grandfather and his sister was still more thrilling. As a boy and girl, both under ten years old, with their mother and a baby, they had left Scotland to join their father in New York. They were aboard a sailing ship which took the usual three months to cross the Atlantic. The hardships of that journey were so great that mother and infant died on the voyage. At last land was sited and brother and sister were put ashore, but they could see no signs of their father. The girl began to weep, and the inevitable elderly stranger inquired the reason. They explained.

"Did you say you were to meet your father in New York?" asked the elderly inquirer.

They were sure of it.

"But this is Philadelphia," announced the stranger.

Their skipper, mistakenly or purposely, had deposited them at the first port he touched and made off.

There were no telegraphs in those pioneering days, and all efforts to trace the father were unsuccessful. So were the efforts of the father to trace the children. The elderly stranger adopted the pair and they grew up. The Revolutionary War broke out and the young man enlisted, went through unscathed, and was being demobilized at Pittsburgh when one of the officers called him into his office and asked if his name was McGohan.

The young soldier regarded the officer intently. Then, "Father!" he impulsively exclaimed.

His great-grandson was my host at Indianapolis.

It was while we were staying in Indianapolis that things began to happen which made me personally a little uncomfortable. The Presbyterian minister invited us to take his pulpit in the evening and talk frankly to his congregation on a frank subject. Not about our journey, nor the principles of the Oxford Group (on which I could have given a possible talk), but our personal experience of Jesus Christ. Though I had sat judiciously by and heard this being done by Oxford undergraduates, I had no great desire to do likewise. All right perhaps for our traveling and practiced foursome. Probably they liked it. But something unusual for the pen in the pentagon. Twenty-five years before I had spoken in a church pulpit. During the years that followed I had been everywhere but in a pulpit.

Nevertheless, during that time I had undergone a remarkable religious experience which the Group would describe as an experience of Jesus Christ. And as others were standing up telling about their experiences, I could see no honest reason for dodging a possible Christian duty. So I told the story of how before I went to Fleet Street I had been interested in Christianity, but, in the mistaken belief that I could do better as a journalist without it, I had let what I held slip overboard. Later I found myself beaten at three salient points -- my private life, my pocket, my ambition. At one period those points converged into a crisis. In adversity, I sought consolation and also something to still an intolerable and frequently recurring ache of the spirit. That spiritual ache had been more are less constant throughout life, asserting itself at the most unexpected moments -- when confronted with panoramic beauty, watching an emotional scene in a play, reading great literature, or when breaking the higher laws of the Universe. Afterwards I came to know it was the natural longing of the finite for the infinite, since man's true environment is God.

At this time I was a "confirmed unbeliever," arguing that my brain had come to me before the Bible, and as my brain could not honestly accept the Bible, I felt I was behaving quite sensibly in disparaging religion. Then one day I thought I would read the Bible again. Just as literature. But with a mind quite open to be convinced if I read anything convincing. Critically I read through the Gospel of St. John, not knowing then that some theologians have their doubts about this non-Synoptic writer. What a superb journalism was that simple and solemn opening! "In the beginning was the Word, and the Word was with God, and Word was God. . . All things were made by Him; and without Him was not anything made that was made. . . . He was in the world and the world was made by Him and the world knew Him not." Who in modern Fleet Street could open a story of such magnitude better than the simple Hebrew fishermen? Yet when I had finished reading the whole Gospel, I concluded that St. John was an unconvincing witness, a poor recorder -- the gaps in his narrative would make a cub reporter blush -- and an undeveloped poet. His testimony confirmed my unbelief. But I read St. John again -- as a fisherman-poet. How far I progressed in my second reading I do not remember, but I do know that at one stage, in some surprising manner, *his words suddenly sprang to life!*

A bright incandescent light seemed to have been turned on in my brain. It lit up every doubt-darkened corner, completely driving away all the grim shadows of unbelief that had haunted me for years. A bright white light -- soothing, cleansing, convincing. Possibly, I thought, a ray of the same light that shown about Saul on the road to Damascus. Besides dispelling, illogically perhaps, the cynicism and skepticism of years, it had a positively physical effect. There was a certain explosiveness about its manifestation which produced the same soothing result as when menthol is rubbed into an aching forehead. Once before I had felt a similar light bursting in my brain, giving unexpected relief from a long-continued worry, accompanied by the feeling that all was well, that some unseen power was watching understandingly, and although I had been breaking God's laws, the benevolent Unseen perfectly understood, sympathized, but completely disapproved.

Having those two experiences in mind, I was naturally interested to read the following in a New York evening newspaper when I returned from the tour with the Oxford Group team.

"Readers who follow John Masefield will find a little essay bound up in the covers called *Poetry*. It was originally an address, and can be read in a quarter of an hour. In it Mr. Masefield defines poetry as an inner illumination, a certain ecstasy of understanding, a flash which comes when the poet communes with the source of all life outside of himself, the Supreme Being of the Universe. After describing Shakespeare, Dante and Homer, Mr. Masefield writes:

"'Brave, proud, gentle and blind alike had access to an illumination which came within their beings, as sunlight comes within the sea.

"'I believe that this illumination exists externally and that all may know it in some measure, by effort or through grace. . . . Those who deny it can never have felt it. It is so intense that, compared with it, no other sensation seems to exist or to be real. It is so bright that all else seems to be shadow.

It is so penetrating that in it the littlest things, a grain of sand, the flower of a weed, or the plume upon a moth's wing, are evidences of the depth and beauty and unity of life.'"

The writer in the *New York World Telegram* who quoted this made the skeptical comment: "Such definitions interest me chiefly for the manner in which they are spoken. They do not convince me. If Mr. Masefield adheres to this type of mysticism, well and good, but he does not alarm anyone by declaring that 'those who deny it can never have felt it.' That is the usual excuse of a devoted priesthood when its arcana are challenged. Mr. Masefield's definition is the essence of a beautiful dream and nothing more."

But I know better. What England's Poet Laureate said of the illumination that flashes within our beings as sunlight comes within the sea, so bright that all else seems shadow, so intense that compared with it no other sensation seems to exist, or to be real, had flashed in me on two memorable occasions.

The life of that world, said John Masefield, was all ecstasy of understanding; all that instant perception and lasting rapture which we knew as poetry. Not as poetry did I touch the life of that world, but as consolation and conviction in a religious quest when reading the Gospel according to St. John. That flash from the world of Divine order and beauty -- the Kingdom of Heaven -- told me convincingly, what I cannot prove to anybody else who does not pick up the same flash, that the Beloved Disciple had really walked and talked with the Son of God.

That was the true story of my experience I told when addressing the congregation of that Group Meeting in Indianapolis. The others told their stories, all different, all convincing, and sat down, each of us following the simple practice of the early disciples, who publicly witnessed to their own experiences and left the work of conviction to the Holy Spirit. After the service we were surrounded by members of the congregation, who expressed deep interest in what we had said to them, re-emphasizing the Group contention that an audience is always awaiting those who will tell the simple truth about themselves for the spreading of Christ's Kingdom.

Yet I somehow felt more pleased that persons had been ready to listen to me than to hear about Christ's Kingdom. When the devil enters the pulpit his name is Vanity.

Social visits in Indianapolis further showed how deep was the interest of the individual in personal, rather than formal, religion, when men and women preachers and elders, instead of standing on a self-erected pedestal of virtue, are prepared to tell the truth about themselves as Paul did, so that others, hungry for peace and serenity in a jaded world of pagans, seeing themselves in another's mirror, may also be inspired to develop along the lines of their true destiny.

True, a delightful Society leader petulantly expressed regret when one of our party took off his mask and admitted having once cribbed at a college exam, although he had since made restitution. Yet she was swift to add that we possessed a quality of tranquility, unlike many of her guests, that we need not fidget, and that we were enviably united.

On the way we were continually hearing echoes of the changed lives resulting from activities of the Groups in the South. When driving me across Indianapolis, a captain of the National Guard, with no special use for religion, was most enthusiastic about the work done by the Group when they swept through Louisville in the spring.

The Southern States had been opened in the previous year through the initial activities of Levering Evans, grandson of Joshua Levering -- one of the four in my team. Levering went down to Louisville, made contacts there with strategic people; and then Ray Purdy and a small band of fervent men and women in the Group followed to prepare the way for a still bigger effort. This is how the editor of a local newspaper caustically described the situation in Louisville about that time:

In the spring of 1931, Louisville was nursing wounds that cut deep, fatally in some cases, and from which few were exempt. Men and women of all degrees and stations, white had colored, had about reached the uttermost depths of disillusion and were tumbling down the last rungs of the ladder of their descent. Their morale was worse than shattered, their reserves of courage as dissipated as their reserves of cash. They believed, in the successive, cumulative blows which assailed their well-being and bruised their self-esteem, that, granted all men were fools and some of them knaves, none were so foolish and few as rascally as those who, with no profit to themselves, had led them into the morass and left them there. Seeking a way out, craving leadership, avid of plans of betterment, concrete and not empty, all they encountered were the snarling conflict of ambitions, of angers, of rancor unappeased. A personal feud had ruined great institutions, closed banks and precipitated a general bankruptcy. And still its fury raged careless of all save only the satisfaction of a private vengeance.

The guidance came to the Oxford group that a strong team would be sent into Louisville, where the conditions were symptomatic of the national emergency. Invitations to join the team were sent to a good many people, one to myself in England. According to Sam Shoemaker:

Ninety of them came. They ranged from wealthy society people to tradesmen and students. There was a Scotswoman who had run for Parliament at home and who had traveled to America for this series of meetings; and an Oxford student. There was a distinguished minister, for many years a missionary in China. There was a young married couple from Rhode Island whose lives and home had been completely changed by the message three years before. There was a young Episcopal clergyman who had a perfect genius for winning the confidence of boys and helping them to understand how Christ could aid them with their problems. There was a New York woman with a European title whose whole existence had been remade through finding that an old friend of her husband had been brought to Christ through the Group.

Pentecost saw no motley crowd in its human composition, and they met with one accord in one place. Each had somewhere arrived at a decision for Jesus Christ in surrender, carried through the early stages of learning to live by guidance from God, helped to win others for Christ, and learned the price and the necessity of full sharing fellowship with like-minded Christians. This means that there were ninety people ready to function as a phalanx under God's Holy Spirit. There was a human leader (Ray Purdy), but he could not possibly have carried the details of all the hours in the day of all the workers who were there. Yet there was not a single bit of individual sharpshooting; we worked almost like one person, because unity was there at the beginning. Noiselessly the members of this group slipped into town by train and car. A church sexton from New York took several in his car and witnessed with great power in the meetings. Some were quartered with families; some stayed in hotels. There were daily groups for special interests: one for business men, one for women, one for girls, one for boys, one for younger married women, and one for ministers; each was led by someone belonging to his particular group. There was daily Bible study. In the evenings we gathered for a united meeting. This began with 300 and ended with 2,500. The theme was not preaching nor exhorting, but simple individual witness to what Christ had done. As a result family tangles were unsnarled, personal problems were solved, hundreds of people found a new power in Christ; the level of confidence in that city, depressed by the business slump, was enormously lifted.

A wonderful atmosphere remained behind when this Group of ninety, mostly lay evangelists, left the stricken city. It persisted during our own visit as a flying team, for Louisville, Kentucky, was our next stop.

News of our arrival spread quickly. Brown's Hotel placed a meetingroom at our free disposal. The Women's Prayer Committee of the Presbyterian Church (a strong organization), meeting again that morning after vacation, turned themselves into an impromptu Group meeting. There were many interesting witnessings from men and women whose lives had been changed in the spring. A social leader of the city was one of the most telling speakers. Once set on having a good time, she was now leading a Group.

We were offered true Southern hospitality at Louisville, beginning with a wonderful first evening picnic at Nitty Yuma, on the foothills above the Ohio River, and continuing until the last morning. That first picnic is unforgettable. Dusk was approaching as we arrived. We plunged into a large open-air swimming-pool and reduce our temperatures from torrid to temperate.

As we came merrily out, we observed the picnic preparing: a welcome campfire, under maple trees and mock-oranges, at which was grilling a vast joint cut from the side of an ox; sandwiches were prepared; corn was cooked on the cob; pies arrived in plenty and variety. And meanwhile the red sun curved down a mulberry sky behind the Ohio, while above, so new as to be but faintly visible, a baby moon, thin and crinkled at the edges, a pale papoose trailing his Red Indian father to his happy hunting-grounds across the river, where real Red Indians used to disport not a hundred years ago.

Southern stories, Southern games around the campfire, with benzine flares in the trees, and perhaps rattlers in the undergrowth, and always the ghosts of Red Indians stealing around, harmlessly lifting our scalps.

On again. We moved so fast, and covered so many towns and meetings in such hectic temperatures, that we felt ourselves a sort of Halley's Comet -- almost responsible for the baby heat-wave accompanying us. Everywhere we were received with double warmth, and our message was heard with kindly interest. At one important co-educational institution, Berea College, where students earn their education by manual labor, we were invited to address the staff, and the silence was so pronounced that Cleve Hicks, who led the meeting, and others in the team, felt the message had misfired, especially when he said: "We are just playing a little game of truth among ourselves."

Only when the meeting broke up, and we were conversing with the head and members of his staff, did we appreciate the depth of interest awakened by our simple attempt to revive a first-century Christian fellowship and a modern civilization.

Before reaching Berea, we halted at Danville, and received a hearty greeting from the President of the college there. Then a thrilling drive through Southern Kentucky, with its memories of Daniel Boone, past a replica of the old fortress against Indians at Harrodsburg, thence through the famed Cumberland Gap into Tennessee, shaving a corner from Virginia as we dropped into North Carolina to stop at Asheville, the "City of the Skies," which is really the old English watering-place of Bath (and Beau Nash) planned on a more majestic scale.

At Asheville again we were on the trail blazed by the Oxford Group. A picked team had visited this town in the previous autumn, and another in the spring, and found much the same conditions existing as in Louisville. The arrival of the first team was dramatic, as it synchronized with the suicide of the mayor and the closing down of banks. The results were not so astonishing as in Kentucky, but were again extra ordinarily interesting, especially among people in key positions.

We assembled at Battery Park Hotel, the highest point in the basin, ringed with fine mountains, dominated by the Peak of Pisgah. And here we effected a junction with another team from Washington, which included the Revs. Norman Schwab, Howard Blake, Al Campbell (Al Capone, we called him), and Mr. Eugene Scheele.

Doctor Elias, of the Methodist Church, welcomed us to Asheville. The City Group, meeting the same evening in the hotel, provided an occasion for sharing spiritual experiences. The witnessing was impressive; the joy of religion and zeal for evangelism were abundantly manifest.

Sciff Wishard and I spoke on the radio to North Carolina the next morning, which was Sunday, and in the evening there was a large Group meeting in Trinity Episcopal Church, followed by informal conversations which continued until late. A feature of this gathering was the presence of lads who had previously come under the influence of the Group, and especially of Cleve Hicks, and were continuing steadfast.

Asheville to Jonesboro, in North Carolina, to an experience different, but none the less delightful. Jonesboro is a village on the bi-way, in the centre of cotton-fields. It has a white Presbyterian church, old, stately, Colonial, which had not housed the Presbytery for half a century, and was then being used for the annual two day Assembly, presided over by the Moderator. Outside, under the trees, was a long, improvised table of wire-netting on which I dozed in the torrid heat.

The meetings inside began early, and continued until late in the evening. At lunch time the open air table under the trees was loaded with cold delicacies, not forgetting the fried chicken of the South. The pent up hospitality of half a century seemed to come, concentrating itself on that loaded table. Under two near by trees a pair of water tubs provided a constant stream of ice water for the thirsty assembly. The cotton was white in the fields around; the community was eager for the message, two astonishing days were passed among the kindest Christian folk, in a shade temperature topping a century.

And now the party divided, one Group returning to New York, the other, including the writer, continuing, with the Rev. Howard Blake in charge, to Washington, where we met the Group in the capital, heard how they had passed their vacation, and their plans for the winter. Here a Group hostel is being capably run by a wonderful lady, the mother of the Rev. Howard Blake. Here, too, a successful house party was held in May, 1932, with Frank in charge of a visiting team from England.

The next Sunday, a two hours' run over to Baltimore, where the reconstructed team gave witness in a Baptist church, after which the pastor impressively asked what would be the verdict on the power of Christianity of any fair-minded jury who had heard us.

Half way through the tour I complained that life of such spiritual intensity as we led was too strenuous for an ordinary journalist.

"Don't worry, you are just being stretched," I was told.

Perhaps he was right. We returned to New York -- I to meditate on the unusual experience, and still only three parts convinced, though I had seen, in a number of States in the Union, groups of changed men and women who were living new and happy lives. And most of these had been educated in the Universities, men and women with brains trained to test the things they saw and heard.

Chapter Thirteen

BILL PICKLE

During my American travels with Group, I was constantly hearing the comic name Bill Pickle in relation to some marvelous work that Frank had done at Pennsylvania State College, following his vital experience in a Cumberland church.

I intended to run over to the College to meet the famous Bill Pickle, but was prevented by circumstances. So I induced Frank to tell me the whole story in his own inimitable way with the fullest details, for it is something of a spiritual classic. A rollicking story, it captivates all sorts -- Pagans as well as Christians. Frank started and established the Group in Oxford by telling a series of stories such as this and inspiring others to do the same. Frank is a born raconteur. His aim is to inculcate principle while keeping his narrative as bright and as human as possible. Principle with interest.

One of the forces in the religious world, John R. Mott, invited Frank to take charge of the religious education in Penn State at the time when there was a difference between the staff and the students, who did not seem to understand each other. The atmosphere was antagonistic, suggestive of those student strikes which have since developed in many parts of the world -- Bucharest, Santiago, Germany, China, America. The life of the students reflected the godlessness of the place. There was a great deal of drinking. There were nineteen drinking-parties in progress on the night of Frank's arrival; so much drink was consumed that the proverbial battleship might have been floated on it.

The man who supplied the drink is the hero of the story, boasting the priceless name of Bill Pickle, a bootlegger, employed by a local doctor by day and by the students by night. Frank used to see Bill's stealthy figure sneaking about the spiral staircases leading to the students' rooms at all hours of dark nights -- a Deadwood Dick in University life. These times, of course, all the faculty was in bed; only Bill and the students were awake and merry.

Bill is the son of a Colonel. He has a strong, stocky figure, a terrible walrus mustache, and looks like a roaring pirate. Bill soon knew of Frank's arrival, and expressed immediate dislike of him.

He published abroad his desire to knife Frank, that usually darted into a side-alley when there was a chance of an encounter.

Frank surveyed his difficult new job. To turn this College God-wards -- there was the problem. The solution, if he could find it, would be a miracle.

His sought direction, and the names of three men came to him. Later these three proved to be the strategic points in changing that. They were:

(1) Bill Pickle the bootlegger.

(2) A cultured and popular graduate student possessing every physical grace and charm.

(3) The College Dean, a frank agnostic, whose wife was an earnest Christian.

The graduate student brought a letter of introduction to Frank which disclosed that he was the son of a Supreme Court Judge and grandson of a State Governor. He seemed to be clever, but dissatisfied. Frank felt that this handsome and influential youth should be approached with intelligent restraint and nonchalant reserve.

They became friendly. The student frequently visited Frank's house, and showed his fondness for the Southern cooking, including the inevitable fried chicken and "beaten" biscuits for breakfast.

Often they would ride together, but for a long time Frank said nothing about the things that meant most to him. Meanwhile the student was getting more interested and pleased with the atmosphere that Frank radiated. One sleety day, when the streets were slippery with ice, and the rain was frozen on the telephone wires, the student came into his room and said, "Let's ride."

Frank said, "All Right," although concerned for the horses' legs, feeling they could not possibly venture out.

For fifteen miles they walked their horses in the cold, biting wind, and then settle down into a hostelry for a good dinner, followed by much hot coffee over the fire. The driving wind had made them drowsy; they retired and would soon have been asleep, had the coffee not begun to act. Frank heard the clock strike eleven,

Twelve, one, two, when his friend said:

"Are you asleep?"

"No."

"Would you like to talk?"

"Yes. What about?"

"Will you tell me what Christ means to you?"

At last Frank's chance had come. He had played his cards right.

They talked on and on for several hours, and finally the student said: "I'm not going to be a Christian."

"Who asked you?" rejoined Frank.

"You didn't. I know you are much too prudent to push religion down anyone's throat."

Then Frank asked him what he believed.

"Confucius," came the unusual answer.

"Wonderful!" said Frank, deciding to humor him. "Tell me about Confucius."

Frank says his friend did not seem to know much on that subject. But Frank had been in China and India and knew that Confucius said he could tell people how to be righteous, but he hadn't the power to make them righteous. Moreover, he had been to Confucius' grave, and been entertained at tea by the seventy-sixth descendant of the Chinese sage and seen the seventy-seventh descendant on the day when he had to wear four coats because of the cold. But Frank's principle is "Argument is not profitable, but possession is."

"So I said to him: 'Try your Confucianism on a chicken-thief, who is a friend of mine, his wife and five children, and see how it works.'"

The student agreed. He gave money to the chicken-thief's wife, who washed herself thin over the wash-tub; more money to keep the eldest daughter off the streets; paid for picnics for Elizabeth, Robert and Danny the dwarf, a town delivery boy. (Recently Frank was at Danny's grave. "He died a beautiful Christian.")

The student spoke to the chicken-thief himself, but to no purpose. This worthy soon found himself in jail for catching chickens by the neat method of pressing a sponge soaked in chloroform under their beaks and whisking them noiselessly away when stupefied. He was accompanied by one of his sons, who worked with him. And for two months the student worked with the family, read to them, gave them money and treats, and tried to behave as their true Confucian friend.

At the end of that time he came to Frank in utter despair and said, "I give up. The more I give them the more they want."

"The reason being," says Frank, "that he was trying to solve the whole problem of social service without Christ, and treating the immediate surface conditions without touching the root cause."

And now the Confucian said he was willing to try Frank's plan.

"What is my plan?"

"I suppose you pray about it?"

So Frank suggested that since he had been unsuccessful with the chicken-thief, now in prison, they now try praying for Bill Pickle the bootlegger, who was free and very much alive.

The student readily agreed.

"Very well, you pray," said Frank, still believing in getting other people to do the praying whenever possible.

The student prayed: "Oh God, if there be a God, help us to change Bill Pickle, Mrs. Pickle, and all the little Pickles." An unorthodox prayer. But this unorthodox prayer soon brought an answer.

The next day was a holiday, and Bill went away to play baseball with a team which he managed. That evening the Confucian and Frank were on their way to dine with the Chinese Minister when, passing through town they saw Bill celebrating the victory of his team by challenging everybody to fight. He had consumed much liquor.

"There's Bill!" whispered the Confucian.

"I see him," said Frank, as though having no time to waste.

The student protested: "We've been praying for him. Now let's do something."

"All right. You do it."

"No chance! You do it."

Once Frank reached this point in the story he stoped and injected a little principle by asking, "What would you do in this situation?" Here was the problem of the wife and the drunken husband. He once asked this question of a Chinese friend, who said, "Approach him from the blind side."

Fearing that the muscular Bill would regard him as the Heaven-sent answer to his challenge to fight, and that possessing a good-sized nose, he might lose the round. Frank approached Bill from his blind side, putting a firm hand on his biceps as a measure of protection. What should he do next? The thoughts flashed: "Give him the deepest message you've got."

"I looked him straight in the eye," said Frank, "and whispered, 'Bill, we've been praying for you.'"

To his surprise, Bill melted. The fight went clean out of him. Tears came. He pointed to a church. "See that church over there?"

"Yes, Bill."

"I was there when the cornerstone was laid. And there's a penny of mine under it." There seemed to come before Bill at that instant a memory of his home and his early associations through the perspective of his ill-spent years. "Do you know, I had a good mother and used to be happy once?"

Frank was glad to hear it, followed up his advantage and introduced the Confucian.

"Here's my friend. He's praying for you too."

"That's decent of him. He's a gentleman." Whereupon Bill invited
them both to call on him at any time at his house on the hill,
which a student wag, adapting the name of a famous preserve,
had appropriately christened "Heinz Heights."

"Any time's no time, Bill," said Frank, pressing his advantage
further. "Make it some time."

"Then come next Thursday night at seven."

As no real duties in life conflict, according to Frank, the two went
on to their dinner with the Chinese Minister.

Thursday night came, and the two went up to see Bill in his un-
painted house on top of "Heinz Heights." Anticipating them, Bill
had also anticipated his customary Saturday shave by a few days.
When they arrived, all the neighbors (invisible themselves) were
out gazing at the visitors through their fences, assured they had
come to change the redoubtable Bill, who is now ill at ease, as
most people are when they think another has come to convert
them. But as they talked of little besides the weather, and said
nothing about religion, Bill lost his self-consciousness, and they
departed good friends. The bootlegger was able to go straight out
and boast to his neighbors that they hadn't changed him. Nevertheless, Bill's spiritual appetite was whetted. He developed a deep
hunger for fellowship with the two friends who were praying for
him.

Bill knew a good deal about many things beside liquor, and all
there was to be known about horses. One day the Confucian took
him to see a horse show on the college grounds. He spent all afternoon talking horses, and Bill voted it to be his best afternoon ever.
To think that a young gentleman should spend all the afternoon
with him talking about horses!

Meanwhile a remarkable change was being effected in the young
Confucian. Bill's new attitude suggested to him that God was really
answering prayer, and so when he prayed he left out the proviso "if
there be a God" from his invocation. The following Sunday a Bishop arrived at Penn State and nine hundred students turned up to
hear him. During the meeting he inquired of Frank if he should
ask the students to make a decision. Had the Bishop asked him
outside, he would have said, "Decidedly not, as a State School, it is
not a Christian institution." In those days Frank's idea of the Holy
Spirit was limited to a kind of five-by-eight picture, and he did not

expect Him to be very active at a meeting address so formally. Nevertheless, the Bishop went ahead, and the unexpected happened. After the usual tense silence, the first person on his feet to announce the surrender of his life to Christ was a young Confucian. As he was the most popular man in the College, this created a stir, and one could feel the whispered surprise circulating around the building as his example was followed by eighty others.

Frank's comment on this situation is that a great many people would feel this was the end of a successful meeting. That was where the old evangelism sometimes collapsed. The changed student came to Frank after the meeting and said he didn't know anything about the Bible, prayer or winning people. What suggestion had he to make?

"We will spend the summer together," replied Frank.

So they went riding through the great national parks of America, a peripatetic school of Christian development. On the way home they stopped at New York, where Frank bought a fine new beaver hat, usually expensive for him. He was wearing this magnificent hat on the night of his return when he met Bill Pickle, who immediately showed him that he liked the hat as much as its owner did. Instead of greeting Frank and inquiring as to how he had spent the summer holiday, Bill walked silently and admiringly round him.

"Where did you get that hat?" he demanded.

Smiling, Frank told him.

"How much did you pay for it?"

Ashamed, Frank told him.

Bill observed that he could keep his family for a week on the price of that hat, adding that he would do anything for one like it.

Frank was on the spot for the opportunity. "The hat is yours, Bill, on one condition."

"What's that?"

Bill waited, breathless.

"That you go with me and a few others to a student convention at Toronto."

Of course Bill was delighted to do that. He would go at once and get leave of absence.

"There you are, Bill," said Frank, handing him the prize.

Bill sprinted away with the coveted hat on his head.

Next morning Frank met Bill in his doorway.

"Can't go," said Bill dismally.

"Too bad! Why's that?"

"Nothing to put my clothes in," said Bill sheepishly. Evidently this was one of the no's that meant yes.

Frank offered Bill a bag, which he refused, saying the people on the hill would see to that.

Presently the Dean arrived and said, "I hear you are going to take Bill to Toronto?"

"Yes," said Frank, not knowing what frame of mind the Dean was in, and thinking he would be regarded as not a fool for Christ's sake, but merely foolish. But the Dean was in favor. Bill's daughter was a maid in his house, where, said the Dean, his wife did the praying for the family. This excursion of Bill's he believed to be an answer to his wife's prayers. He thought a miracle was impending. As he left, the Dean asked, "Who's going to pay for the journey?"

"I shall," said Frank.

But then the Dean insisted on paying. "Do you think the other fellows will object to Bill on the team?"

Frank thought not, and the next morning the party of nineteen (including Bill) left for Toronto. Bill's wife and most of his twelve children were at the station in full war-paint to see him off. The occasion was impressive. So was Bill's attire. He wore the beaver hat, leggings, and a stock-tie which made Frank think of a poodle's legs crossed. He carried a little cheap bag made of alligator skin containing a few articles he needed for the journey.

What were Bill's motives in going to Toronto? asked Frank. Of course, one motive was that he had heard that the liquor was good in Toronto. The trip was another attraction. And the good-fellowship. All natural reasons. There was a fifth reason which Frank discovered later. Bill was longing for a fur overcoat to match the beaver hat perhaps, and somehow expecting the calm on his way to Toronto.

Frank tried to make Bill feel at home on the first stage of the railway journey, and suggested that he must have something to eat. For some odd reason, Bill seemed against food, and told Frank not to be extravagant when he saw him taking a cup of coffee and a bun. Bill was planning how to get a drink when they arrived at the first junction. He was eager. I looked over the party of seventeen, at last alighting on one to whom Bill used to sell liquor.

"There's Bonehead," thought Bill. "I know he's thirsty."

When Bill saw Frank was busy with the tickets, he decided to follow Bonehead. The latter, true to Bill's surmise, made straight for the swinging doors. He saw there was a bar only and no diningroom, the place he really sought.

"This is no place for us," said Bonehead.

Bill thought exactly the opposite, and said so. But Bonehead resisted and through that resistance, said Bill later, he laid the foundation-stone of Bill's Christian life. For if Bill had taken one drink, he would have required many others to quiet that particular train thirst he had developed. He consumed a heavy lunch, and the party started safely on their way again, the bootlegger now firmly convinced that it was no use planning for himself, because everybody had their eyes on him. Here Frank comments that "Bill's awakened conscience was at work."

The evening meal was served in the dining car, and one of the party, a former agnostic, suggested to Frank that he thank God for the food.

"All right. Go on ahead," said Frank.

Here Bill suddenly intervened.

"What's the matter this time, Bill?"

"That fellow" -- pointing to the former agnostic -- "has spoiled my dinner."

At first Frank thought he meant the colored waiter, but Bill insisted that it was the man who had said grace. He didn't bargain for that sort of thing in a College party. He recalled his early home and it took away his appetite.

Bill jibbed again later when they reached Niagara Falls and he found they were going to spend the night in a temperance hotel! Of all places! The bootlegger was told that it would be less expensive, but he shrewdly doubted. How could a hotel-keeper make his place pay without a bar? He must get his expenses somehow.

Besides, what would his fellow-bootleggers say if they heard he had slept in a temperance hotel?

Frank good-humored him, took him up to his room and showed him how to operate a folding-bed, of which he was also chary at first.

"Now, do you want to take a bath?"

The bootlegger's walrus mustache supported the glare in his eyes.

"What, in the winter time. What for?"

"Why not?"

"Do you want me to catch my death of cold?"

"No, Bill."

"Don't you know we sew up down our way in November and don't unsew again until March?"

Still a little suspicious of the folding bed, Bill tucked himself in for the night. Then Frank, coming in again, told him he had forgotten something. Bill searched under his pillow for his watch and money and then demanded, "What?"

"Prayers."

"I can't do them things."

"You come out and I'll help you."

Weak in this form of exercise through long disuse, and suffering from temporary ague, the bootlegger came out of his folding-bed and knelt down in his nightshirt.

"You begin," said Bill.

"Our Father," began Frank.

"Our Father," followed Bill.

"Who art in Heaven," continued Frank.

"Who art in Heaven," continued Bill, and then stopped his mentor with, "I used to know that."

"Alright. Go ahead."

"No, you go ahead. I'll follow after."

And so they went through the Lord's Prayer, after which Bill re-entered his folding bed sighing hugely as though to say, "It's hard work living with these Christians."

Next morning they started again for Toronto. The Porter was carrying the luggage for them. Frank saw the bags of the ex-Confucian plastered with labels of the Niagara Falls Temperance Hotel. There were at least five of them on the handle, and crowds everywhere. The student had been one of Bill's best customers; he turned to Frank and asked if he had done that. Frank said, "No," and smiled. Bill was playing 'possum grandly. Presently Bill owned up. They had reached a point of contact when Bill felt so much at ease that he could play with them. The first wall which separated Bill from the classes was breaking down.

They had settled themselves in a Toronto hotel when the time came for the first meeting of the convention, but Bill didn't think he would go.

"What are you going to do?"

Bill thought he'd like to go and look at the fur shops. Perhaps he could find something to match the hat. The additional motive that had brought Bill to Toronto was now clearly revealed. Frank said Bill must go to the meeting, cajoling him with the news that the Governor General and six thousand people would be present. Bill replied that the Governor came sometimes to Pennsylvania State College, and he wasn't any more interested in him now as then. Presently he agreed, on condition they sat in the rear seats. Arriving in the hall, Bill showed no signs of interest in the meeting save to count the number of people present. Not unlike a great many churchgoers, who prefer to figure out the profits of the week while waiting for this service to end, says Frank.

But Bill's attention was quickly arrested when the second speaker came along, a colored man, who, according to Bill, was so black that charcoal would make a white mark on him! All the time he was speaking, Bill was nodding in agreement or registering violent disagreement, to the amusement of everyone around him. But Bill was blissfully unmindful of anyone save the colored man, who was hitting him between the eyes with every shot. Afterwards he accused Frank of taking him there specially to hear the colored man, and of telling the speaker about him. Nevertheless, he rather liked that sort of speaker. A Group meeting held later in their hotel added to Bill's reviving interest in religion, especially the story told by a football player of how a foster-child had disowned his foster-parents, which somehow greatly moved the bootlegger. When this man had finished, Bill jumped up like a shot from a gun, as Frank puts it, and announced that he wanted to say something.

"Go ahead, Bill. It's a free country," observed Frank, not knowing what on earth Bill would do next. Speaking with great solemnity, Bill announced:

"I'm an old man of sixty-two, and I've decided to change my life. I have grandchildren, and I can't bear to think of them turning on their grandfather like that foster-child I've just been hearing about, because all my life I've been disobedient to my Heavenly Father."

After that outburst Bill went out of the room, beckoning Frank to follow him. "For what?" asked Frank. Bill desired his help in writing a letter to his wife and son, as he wanted them to know at once of his determination to change his life.

From that time onwards Bill developed amazingly. He became one of the great figures of the Convention: one of those miracles which make conventions occasionally interesting and memorable.

After a strenuous week they returned to the College, but when we reached the junction we were met by a liquor missionary supported by a pair of Bill's old-time friends, two quart bottles of liquor. Bill's old associates, finding it impossible to believe that he had changed his way of life (for the news had flared through the town), had brought two bottles of the choicest for his benefit. As Frank saw the tempter surreptitiously handing Bill a bottle, his heart wobbled. As Bill let it slip through his fingers, he gave a great sigh of relief. It smashed on the pavement. The next attempt was more subtle. The liquor missionary unstopped the second bottle and held it under Bill's nose so that he could savour the old familiar boquet. This time Bill gave a swift tap on the missionary's wrist, and again the bottle of the best was smashed to smithereens.

Bill's change and Bill's resistance to the tempter were the talk of the town for a long time to come. Would this astonishing miracle last? Even the clergy weren't enthusiastic in believing that it would. One told Frank that he did not want Bill in his church.

"Don't worry," said Frank. "He likes a church where he can take part and talk back if necessary and say an occasional Amen or Hallelujah."

On the next Monday, when Bill was to stand with Frank, he came in looking very aggrieved.

"Heard what's happened?" he growled.

Frank tried to waive the question aside, for gossip had already brought a whisper of trouble.

"They won't have me in church," stormed Bill.

Frank felt he had been stabbed. Now surely Bill would not be able to hold out.

"Don't worry, Bill," he soothed, thinking hard.

"I'm not," said Bill, and then suddenly announced: "We've got a church of our own all planned. We want you to take charge of it."

Here Bill produced a list of nineteen men, mostly his old bootlegger friends, whom he had already collected under his new Christian banner. They were to be the nucleus of a new church to meet in the old porter's lodge. Frank is still in possession of that treasured list. Before consenting to be the minister, Frank said that Bill must find out from the others what they wanted him to speak about.

"Don't worry," said Bill. "We've thought of that!"

"Well, what is it?"

"The Apostles' Creed."

Of all subjects for a bootlegger to choose!

And so, Saturday night after Saturday night, Frank met with Bill the bootlegger and his old associates, one of whom was once so accomplished at swearing that one could almost smell the sulfur. Saturday night was chosen to avoid conflict with church services. Everything went well with the Apostles' Creed talks until Frank came to the part about Christ going down into Hell, at which Bill jumped up and suddenly interposed:

"I believe everything so far, but that's too much."

Apparently the preacher had overstepped himself. For a time

Frank and Bill cogitated on a way out, until at last Frank said:

"Well, how do you explain it?"

"I don't know," said Bill, "I guess He went down there to clean things up."

That answer satisfied everybody. Peace again. They proceeded. But the upshot of those Saturday nights was that all attending eventually became forces in the Church life of the district, including Bill, who grew into a good Wesleyan Methodist, and occasionally turns up at one of Frank's house-parties to confirm all the details as Frank narrates the true story of the change in Bill Pickle the Bootlegger.

The miracle of Bill's changed life, and the changed lives of his family and friends which followed, become a standing witness to the Professors and the graduates who were in the habit of returning yearly to celebrate the liquor they once received in college from the hands of Bill. But Bill now refused to grace their parties if they had liquor. As they preferred an interesting character, even to the exclusion of the liquor, they fell in with Bill's new ideas, and so Bill appeared and told his old-time stories with a new zest and a new restraint, on a new plane.

Bill still treasures the hat which he earned by going to Toronto, and though he has retired from work -- he is over eighty -- he still remembers the mighty movement of the Spirit of God which spread throughout the college and other colleges that season when he was changed.

Not only was Bill Pickle and the Confucian and the Dean, the three strategic points of that College, transformed through personal evangelism, but before Frank left there were over twelve hundred men in voluntary Bible-study. Thus, after three years' work, it was no longer good form to have drinking-parties. Athletics improved and there were winning teams. The scholarship, too, improved, and a new relation between Faculty and students changed the old-time factional spirit of the campus.

The change in Bill's family life was equally marvelous.

"What a dinner Bill's wife used to cook for the reformed bootlegger and their children!" exclaimed Frank.

The most significant factor of all was the improvement in the college discipline. So radical was the change that the salary of an extra disciplinary Dean was saved, and Bill, the ex-bootlegger who knew everybody, was given a seat on certain disciplinary committees --*for maintaining order!*

Chapter Fourteen

THE CALVARY MIRACLE

I had heard from Garrett Stearly and read so much about Calvary Church and its dynamic Rector (the Rev. Samuel M. Shoemaker, Jr.) that I was eager to see what both were like. I knew that Sam Shoemaker was one of Frank's early captures in China, and that after he had come to Calvary he had begun to make things hum in the middle of Manhattan. I knew that he had started a running spiritual fire in the lives of an ever-increasing number of people drawn from all parts of New York and environs, who had discovered that a workable religion was being preached in practical sincerity in Calvary; that God did not always stand aside and watch, but really entered churches and human beings, and guided and helped all those who had the wisdom and courage to fulfill His conditions: that in the first two years of Sam's ministry the congregation had increased by about two hundred percent, although the Rector protests that he is not out to fill churches, but to fill people.

My attention was first directed to the old brownstone church of Calvary at the inter-section of Fourth Avenue and 21st Street by a smallish cross hanging low over the pavement, illuminated by white bulbs. The church is large and darkening with age, perfectly merging in the faded grandeur of Gramercy Park, once the fashionable quarter, but now flanked by smart apartment-houses.

As in all Gothic churches, there are high pillars. The pews are a deep brown, and comfortably crowded on Sunday mornings when the Rector is preaching. I have seen over three hundred at Holy Communion after Matins.

In the stained-glass windows there are a few figures, and more are coming from Cardinal Newmen's old church at Littlemore near Oxford. The chancel is smallish and friendly, flanked on the north by a tiny chapel and on the south by a baptismal font of white marble. The man who designed the organ had a fine eye for symmetry, as the array of gilded pipes over the chapel and the font is exceptionally pleasing. The altar is small and plain; there is a life-size statue of Christ in white shepherd's robe, hands outstretched, as though beckoning all to come onto Him.

A ruby-red cross in the stained window above the white figure of Christ gives the chancel a picturesque dignity. As the fine old organ peals, the mixed choir emerges from the vestry, led by the women choristers, wearing becoming skullcaps of black velvet and white surplices. Black cassocks are worn under their surplices by the men. The choir moves in procession towards the entrance and then up the central aisle to the choir-stalls, with the clergy following in investments and Princeton hoods of black and orange. Although the church is mellow and darkening with age, save at the altar, the congregation is invariably bright and friendly, always ready to be helpful.

Some great sermons, preached in the pulpit of Calvary Church, have circulated throughout the world. Sam is one of those powerful and convincing preachers who doesn't know it. He is still mystified as to what constitutes a successful preacher in New York. He names some who have come to the city with great reputations, but the congregations have faded away. Others have sprung up and preached the usual discourses with nothing remarkable about them, and their churches have been crowded.

The Rector of Calvary prepares his sermon carefully, and then spends a couple of hours on Sunday morning finally familiarizing himself with it. He knows that the pulpit is not the only place of inspiration. I have heard him preach many good sermons on striking themes. The one on "Ye serve the Lord Christ" was particularly notable, and so was the one on "The Modern Prophet" and a third on "The Surrender of Saul." The sermon that made the deepest impression when I was around Calvary was entitled "The Romance of Real Religion." That sermon is still discussed, especially by the young Oxonian who was inspired to a changed life while listening.

It was some weeks before I met Sam Shoemaker, for he was on holiday when I arrived. It was longer before I saw Sam full face. Whenever I looked at him squarely my gaze was irresistibly drawn straight to those magnetic eyes of his, those eyes that are always bright and twinkling merrily, one or other closing over and anon in fact and impish wink one comes to love and respect.

Sam very definitely gives the lie to the saying about distance lending enchantment. From a distance he is just another curly-haired Southerner: medium-height, fair-haired, getting on towards middle age and pleasingly plump. In other words, not particularly uncommon. In the pulpit, omitting for the moment his sermons, there is nothing remarkably magnetic about him to whet one's curiosity. His delivery, though convincing, is not dramatic, and he rattled out his words clearly, like silver bullets from a machine gun. Get near to Sam and you at once feel his magnetic personality. His happy faith and contentedness so permeate the atmosphere that you feel it unnecessary for Hoover to declare the depression visually at an end.

So cheery is he that you might be tempted to take liberties with his time and convictions were you unaware that he works about fourteen hours a day, most days, although he occasionally takes a gallop in the country or plays a game of deck tennis on the roof of Calvary House for town exercise.

Sam calls all those around him by their Christian names -- the Calvary custom -- and everybody calls him Sam, with one exception, another Frank, who is butler and general factotum of Calvary House. Frank supervises the workers who wait on the rest of the staff. He is a happy product of Calvary Mission, an Irishman who has lost much of his hair and none of his humor. For five days and nights he was unconscious in a speak-easy after a bout of drinking, and came to the end of the things. The speak-easy attendant when he ultimately woke up suggested Calvary Mission. Calvary Mission reclaimed Frank, who is now a leader there. Frank keeps his Quiet Times regularly in the mornings, reclaims down-and-outs at night, and attends to multitudinous duties at Calvary House both day and night.

Frank is one of the happiest men I know and is a Calvary miracle. He dotes on Sam Shoemaker, his employer, but somehow cannot bring himself to practice the Group customs of calling everybody by their Christian names. He addresses his chief as "Mr. Shoemaker."

Sam pulls him up. "Don't call me Mr. Shoemaker, Frank. Call me Sam."

"Yes, Mr. Shoemaker," says Frank politely, and incurably disobedient.

Good natured and kindly though Sam is, he has a strong presence and a force of personality which is suggested by a powerful jaw. It was that jaw which figuratively slipped out of joint on the occasion of Sam's first meeting with the real Frank. Sam was born in the Chesapeake country, and once, sitting in his great family pew, listened to the stories of great heroism, of violent men changed and restored, told by an evangelist working among the iron mountaineers of the far South, and vowed one day himself to become a pioneer of Christ.

Later, after studying at a well-known University, he went to Europe during the War, but was confident he had been unable to touch one man all that summer.

On to China to the important centre there maintained by his University, where he was impressed by the wonderful machinery, but depressed by the feeble output of changed men. All the workers assured him that he was doing wonderful things, but he did not believe them, although the school, the library, the classes, and the gymnasium were crowded with young Chinese.

About this time Frank arrived, accompanied by his tonic band committed to changing lives. Frank was indicated to Sam as the man who was doing what Christian workers were talking about. Sam looked at Frank and disliked his associations. But stories of Frank's startling achievements with men were continually recounted to Sam, who began to speak to Frank, finding him a person worth knowing. One day he drew Frank aside and made the dangerous suggestion that he tackle a young Chinese in whom Sam was interested, giving Frank the opening for his habitual reply:

"Why don't you do that?"

He added, "And if you haven't got anything to give him what's the matter?"

Sam was not merely offhanded, he was infuriated. He went away in a towering rage. When he cooled down he realized that Frank had merely spoken the truth.

Sam brooded over the talk. What use was he? Must he go on in this life as a powerless worker with nothing to give forever? So he went back to the man who had challenged him and had the matter out. He told Frank both his temptations and his sins. Once these came startlingly into the open, the position was quite clear to him. He had no overflow of power, because there was no flow, as sin was damning him off from God. Sam's attempt to introduce intellectuals to the difficulties had no more influence with Frank than similar attempts by a long line of changed predecessors. Sam says that might have seemed a source of weakness to some but the fact remains that Frank was right.

Frank asked Sam a bold question. What good was he? He was selfishly allowing sin to exclude him from the vital consciousness of God and to make him spiritual. The challenge was irresistible. Sam knew that if he took the plunge of absolute surrender it would mean a very different life for him than he intended. Instead of continuing to take a decorative and patronizing interest in religion, the association of a cultured young man with a University scheme for social welfare, it meant the real mission-field everywhere for life.

"That night," said Sam afterwards, "my sins rose straight before me like tombstones. They must all be cleared away. I saw that was a matter for my will rather than my intellect. I asked myself if I was willing, and then I thought how ridiculous it was ever to think of opposing my pygmy will to the will of God."

Frank had won Sam. He surrendered, experiencing no loss of nervous energy, but sensible only of a great calm, that he had jumped a fence which for a long time he had refused to take. That night as he lay in bed there came to him a distinct voice that said, *There is no work of Mine for him who is not wholly Mine.*

"Those luminous words," says Sam, "were different from all other words I had ever heard. And they revealed to me what I believed to be the central truth of religion."

Which really meant that in some supernatural way there had been repeated in Sam the discovery made by Frank years before, that the demand of both God and Satan is identical -- the whole heart. From then onwards Sam became one of the men who swung around Frank, and whom he describes as "The gayest I know -- fellows who have found something worth finding. We never meet but we have a good time. This is far from the professional mirth of some religious people: it is the laughter of men who really know there is a way out for the world and are doing their best to show it to others."

I heard that laughter ripple forth as Sam and I recently encountered three of those young men outside Calvary House. Sam made a jolly, provocative remark. They made a jolly, mutinous reply. I told him his remark would have demoralized any regiment of soldiers. But it merely increased the good feeling among them.

Sam's favorite Biblical quotation is "If any man will to do His will he shall know of the doctrine." Those in the Group who have experienced this mighty change claim to speak not of what they think or hope, but of what they know. They have a unified personality transcending all difficulties, giving miraculous assurance.

That Calvary Church is deeply interested in helping and changing the individual is witnessed by the amazingly friendly gatherings after service at the church door, where Sam and his staff greet everybody, and where there is an interchange of friendly greetings among the congregation rarely seen in these modern days of formal worship.

Sam's congregation and staff are taught that aloofness may sometimes be sinfulness, especially when other people are in need, as they mostly are of spiritual help. Sam and his staff teach that everyone should have a real experience, a maximum experience of God, which means we are to have the same transformation as sent the Apostles out after Pentecost to turn the world upside down.

With the arrival of Sam, Calvary soon became the most cheerful and perhaps the most spiritual church in New York -- a congregation of earnest, happy people who had found the meaning of life.

It was from Frank, who taught him so much about real religion, that Sam learned never to mistake sympathy with the teaching for a genuine experience of Christ -- a common error with many; and that he should be all the time emphasizing the need for change or conversion, for full surrender issuing in guidance, and for every grown child of God to found an ever-widening family of his own spiritual children. From the same source he learned how to uncover the real facts in people's lives, so helping them to peace and serenity and to becoming workers of moral miracles in others. Sam teaches his staff and congregation this essential art, in his sermons, in the Group meetings, and in the special conference held annually, known as the School of Life.

At the start he found the going not so easy. One wealthy old lady, having listened disapprovingly to a sermon by Sam on personal evangelism, stumped down the aisle saying she did not want to hear any more about changed men; she wanted the Gospel. She expressed her indignation at this "new" doctrine, and declared that nobody should drive her from her family church. For a time she stayed away, and then she came back beaming, ready to carry out the "new" teaching. She had been talking the matter over with a ministerial relative who was on Sam's side and had persuaded her to change her view. Which goes to show how disturbing can be the doctrine to those who love to sit at ease in Zion.

The charming wife of the choir-master, Mrs. Bland, was one of the earliest to adopt the new basis of Christian living as taught by the new Rector. She had held out for some time, and her husband had held out longer. He remonstrated strongly, objecting to "this Church Army business." It was over-doing religion and losing them all their Pagan friends. But he, too, capitulated.

One Sunday evening, soon after my arrival in New York, I heard the choir-master (Mr. John Bland) make an announcement from the chancel to the congregation, which the Rector described as the best sermon ever preached in Calvary. He was speaking on his twenty-fifth anniversary as choir-master, and speaking from his heart. He recalled the days when he first came to the church, when one of the near-by hotels was known as the "Church Inn" because the choir was so frequently to be seen inside drinking. Then came changes, in pulpit, congregation and choir.

"My greatest ambition," said the choir-master, "was to be at the top of my profession, and in my effort I developed a lot of the envy and intolerance for many musicians. I envied them because they had much more money for their choirs and were better paid than I. Intolerant, I felt they were teaching singing without the necessary groundwork and study. When my friend, the present Rector came to Calvary I was restless and uneasy. Always being devoted to the Church in a conservative way, I felt that I was a good Christian. However, I soon came to see, from his life and the way he was helping men and women to a vital experience with Christ, that my Christian life was more or less dead. I was not helping a soul except by my music. When I fully realized my weakness, I went to my Rector and told him my many shortcomings and sins. I made up my mind, by the help of God, to overcome my envy, intolerance, drinking, and gambling; and ever since that time I have had freedom, radiance, and am learning the joy of living."

I have never heard such a remarkable statement as that from the choir-master of a parish church. But many another Rectors will agree that his own choir-master would be all the better for such a performance.

One evening at Calvary I saw an astonishing site for an Episcopalian church. Calvary has a rescue mission run by a remarkable Superintendent named Harry Hadley. That evening Harry had brought up with him a hundred or two men rescued by the mission from the streets of New York. Instead of a sermon these men were invited to stand in their pews and tell what contact with Christ had meant to them. If ever one was conscious of the Holy Spirit in a church service it was at that extraordinary Evensong.

There was no waiting. Men popped up one after the other from all points of the front rows of pews and rattled out their life-stories. The pathetic tales they told of broken homes mended, of drunkenness cured, of victory over vice, of the new reign of love in lives and homes previously disordered, divided, discordant, would have melted the heart of the most complacent modern Pharisee.

And at the end the invitation was given to others to come forward to the altar and dedicate their lives to the service of Christ, the Mender of men. Most unique of all -- there were responses. In an

Episcopalian church! They walked boldly to the altar, and kneeling there dedicated their lives to God as though they were at Holy Communion. All done in simple reverence.

One of the men changed at the service was known as "The Spider." He had served a number of terms in prison, but is now an ardent life-changer.

I spent an interesting evening exploring Chinatown and the Bowery under his genial guidance. He showed me many reminders of the old saloon days, including a hostelry that was once known as "The Bucket of Blood," because its patrons, before starting their quarrels, would knock off the edge of their glasses to make them sharper for the fray.

As we passed, "The Spider" pointed out to me the undertaker who specialized in free funerals for gangsters.

The story of every live church is the story of a continuous war for spirituality. There has been no compromise in Calvary.

No one pretends that the devil never enters Calvary, though the combined effort to exclude him seems to be maintained at the highest intensity humanly possible. Some of Sam's captures hold well for a few years and then drift away. Christ had the same experience. So did Paul -- "Demas hath forsaken me." They are good sprinters, but unwilling to stay the course. Why do they go?

Meanwhile, the commendations continue to be large and fresh faces are constantly seen at Calvary Church, which is becoming a power-house, spirituality spreading through other churches in America and Europe. The number of Englishmen seen in Calvary Church is a perpetual surprise.

Sam traces the fruitage of his ministry back to that night fourteen years ago when, following a heart-to-heart talk with the man he once avoided, but who read him off like a page of print, he decided to "let go" of self and allow God to run his life.

"How long from that conversation until you began to get results?" I asked Sam.

He slapped his knee enthusiastically. "Bless my soul, I started immediately. I saw Frank on Saturday, and my first convert, the one I had spoken to Frank about, came along on the Sunday afternoon. After that I was busy with one or two fellows almost every day, and frequently there were changes."

Sam smiled reminiscently as he recalled how much the work of Frank and his Group had meant to foreign and Chinese leadership during that fruitful period.

"But those were great days in China," he said. "Real converts were being made because we were out to obey God rather than men who had made the commandment of no effect through their tradition. About this time I read William James' *Varieties of Religious Experience*, and saw what he was arguing being actually fulfilled in the lives of Chinese turning to Christianity."

"What is the greatest mistake made by evangelists?" I asked Sam.

The Director of Calvary Church was very emphatic: "The neglect to intrigue the man's imagination before moving in on his will." Sam said the same thing again with more American snap: "Lure is more effective than logic. I am never worried about a man who seems interested, who cannot leave us alone although he does not announce his decision. That is where some of the old-timers fell down. They started to cudgel their wits and prove their theology before they had caught the interest of their own type of life or by stories of those who were living the life."

"You ever get the modern Nicodemus calling on you by night?"

"That we do."

It occurred to me that sometimes people were driven away in anger by the bold challenge put up by the Group. I asked Sam about it. He saw I was expecting a story of muscular Christianity in action, and he roared.

No, I don't remember any untoward incident of that kind," he said. "We never offend you. Besides, people understand that when we talk about men's sins we are being impersonal, just as a doctor is impersonal who puts his finger on the spot that produces the pain.

"But wait a minute! I did see one man go off in a temper -- in a worse temper than I was in when I had my first talk with Frank. He was an elderly crewman. He went white and then red as I suggested his trouble, and refused to stay longer. But came back ten days later, said he was in a terrible mess, admitted that my diagnosis had been right, and asked me to help him."

"Have you ever known anyone let down who was trying to live on faith and prayer?"

I was thinking of the stories Sir Philip Gibbs had told me of children he saw dying from hunger in Russia, and a missionary tells of men dropping dead in China from the same cause.

"Never!" exclaimed Sam. "What I have noticed is that God comes in just in the nick of time. I have seen Him try a man's faith right up to the last minute, and then I have wanted to laugh when I saw the situation clear instantly just when most desperate. Strange indeed the effect on our room of faculties, seeing God silently at work, always providing while guiding."

"And now for the best piece of advice that Frank ever gave you?" The Rector of Calvary seemed to have his answer ready.

"Once I asked Frank what book I should read to prepare for special work. He told me to prepare myself, as I was the great problem. He simply meant that I must learn to discipline myself: to make sure that everything was right between myself, my neighbors and God."

Which is the same story that everyone has to tell who encounters Frank, a man who takes nobody for granted, be he parson or prodigal. And the measure of Frank's success with either can be tested by the shine on the countenance.

Sam's face shone.

Chapter Fifteen

GUIDANCE AT WORK

Was the Oxford Group right?

Is their teaching the teaching the world really needs? It was taking me much longer to make up my mind than it took me to discover that the movement contained a fine news story.

Unquestionably the Oxford Group aroused more initial interest than any other religious movement at work to-day in the world. Mention religion in the average drawing-room, and people freeze or else begin to talk airily on their own religious theories, which is usually miles away from the belief and practice of their fathers. But the discussion soon peters out, as it leads nowhere.

Yet introduce the subject of the Oxford Group, begin to tell some of the changes that have occurred in your own life through doing as they do, and you will assuredly get a hearing. Even if you have no story of your own to tell, you will find a ready-made audience listening eagerly to the principles of the Group if they are clearly propounded.

One night in New York I was taken to dine in a speak-easy. The last spare table was in the centre of the gay room. Waiters were stumbling about our table most of the evening in their efforts to meet the demands of the crowded restaurant. Seated as we were behind doors locked and barred against police raids, drink flowing freely, smartly dressed women and their escorts chattering gaily, there was an artificial freedom and even friendliness about the atmosphere not often sensed in public restaurants.

Our table settled down to enjoy itself when someone suddenly introduced the subject of the Oxford Group, told of how they had recaptured some of the lost radiance of the Christian religion, had learned the art of fellowship, of the living and working together, sharing their experiences and their troubles, losing their own aches through absolute and continued honesty, first with themselves and then with their associates. He spoke of a new spirit in their daily life, and their absolute surrender of everything, including their money, their fears, their sins, their time, to God. They even realized there was a difference between doing God's work and God's will, so asked God what was His will, and received an answer. He told stories which recreated in men's minds the fact of their own spiritual needs.

Our waiters continued their bustling, slowed down, then disappeared. A party at the table opposite rose and left. Others followed. But the talk at our centre table went merrily on, still entirely devoted to the Oxford Group and its insistence on Christianity proving itself to anyone who would try it whole-heartedly instead of half-heartedly.

Presently the tables not ours were vacated; the room swiftly emptied. And still the one last table in the centre of the speakeasy was debating the Oxford group and a return to first-century Christianity. And when the party rose, the last to leave the place, it was to be greeted with an extra charge per head, not for over-staying the time-limit in a speakeasy, but because *we had forgotten to order drinks!*

That is the kind of interest the Oxford Group invariably awakens at the start. When those who are first interested begin to realize what the teaching means in their own lives if they consent to its demand, then some opposition arises. Some hold back because of its teaching about confessing faults one to another, not realizing that, as Loudon Hamilton says, "There are few aches like the ache of working in a group of people who do not know each other, after working in a group of people who do. I believe that real fellowship in a group of people is the most challenging lack to-day in the whole realm of Christian living.

"We need to recapture the genius of fellowship. It is not enough to manage to get on together. We must learn the secret of living and working together. The price of that is absolute and continued honesty, first with ourselves and then with other people. We must be willing to share not only our time, our homes, our money, but to take down the mask and reveal our moral and spiritual struggles. There can be no enduring team-work unless the members of the team do know each other as well as possible. We must learn to weld the team at the centre so that there are no barriers between each other, nor any reservations about each other which have not been thoroughly aired."

That was the greatest stumbling-block to my understanding of the Oxford Group for nearly a year. At one time I had been in the habit of freely disclosing my thoughts on all subjects to anybody in social conversation. After a time I found that respected adversely on me. Then I went to the other extreme, and became intensely secretive, with occasional outbursts of garrulity over something that could not possibly injure me. And then I passed through a long, long period of worry and strain. Not perceiving that I was in the world for a purpose which may not have been for my immediate benefit. I resented the strain imposed, a strain which might have been lessened and I realized that the goal of life is not comfort and character, not pleasure but perfection; that we are here being perfected for a place in God's perfect state.

During this period I had a conversation with one of the Group leaders, who inquired if I had ever made a complete confession to another man. I resented the inquiry on the spot. I felt that if he were God-guided, as he claimed to be that was the last question he would ask of me. Had he not read the story of Job, who, passing through difficulties not of his own creation, had then to battle with blind, well-meaning friends who were doing their worst to prove to him how blameworthy he was? Furthermore, confession was dead against the practice of my own Church, except confession to God, and I had done that a number of times. I did not then fully realize that he was not interested in my past for his own curiosity, but for my benefit, because he knew there was seldom real release apart from confession. He argued that many persons had walled themselves off from God through an unwillingness to share their difficulties with their fellows. I told him that I had once been argued into believing that adult baptism was absolutely essential. Having once undergone that experience, I felt I was none the better after baptism than before. Concentration on one aspect of Christian teaching, whether it was baptism or Holy Communion or confession, threw the Christian life out of balance.

Already I had told Frank one or two regrettable things about my past, which were over, apologized for and forgiven. That was good enough. I felt no better for the performance, and I felt no encouragement to delve deeper into my past in the hope of getting this elusive radiance and peace they were so keen for. Besides, I had experienced some of that joy they claimed to possess on more than one occasion. Perhaps I had been vouchsafed a greater measure of God's Spirit than some in this Group.

"But are you winning people?"

Confound Cleve Hicks for his insistence! I wasn't. And I knew that it was by their fruits true Christians were known. One thought he had let his light shine a bit sometimes. Surely that was enough. Again that relentless query about winning people. Cleve said it was only when he had gone to a man he had offended -- made a deliberate sacrifice of time to do it -- that he made his first capture. Well, I had done that. But I still saw no necessity for full Sharing. I preferred to wait, to qualify. I had other reservations.

One by one these reservations disappeared, though the objection to Sharing persistly did. Instead of waning, I grew as my travels with the team and extended. But the Sharing went on all round me. It was a change from mixing with people who were always boasting of their achievement in business or in journalism or in advertising, of beating the other fellow with a good story, by an extra advertisement, or at the fifteenth hole; or hearing the bad qualities of a mutual friend thoroughly exposed, as so many good sportsmen are eager to do.

Furthermore, there was always the discomfort that I had a few more things up my own sleeve I could confess in a pinch. And always the consciousness that of late I had felt no certainty in my religion; none of the inner rapture which flows from the Holy Spirit. At one time, long before I met the Group, that was an oft-recurring experience, especially when things were most difficult.

These spiritual experiences were not always identical. Sometimes one felt as though a golden fountain were playing within. Before the white light flashed as I read the Gospel of St. John, I had been conscious of an intolerable ache which I thought no human joy could extinguish. Afterwards this sense of a golden fountain playing, extinguished the ache and gave marvelous assurance of the doctrine. Still it was a long time before I came to see a link between this physco-spiritual experience -- this apparent witness of the Spirit -- and the mystic words of Jesus to the woman at the well: "The water that I shall give shall be a well of water springing up unto everlasting life."

At other times the sense of a sweet fountain playing gave place to a mystic burning and glowing equally ecstatic, marking a step forward in the Christian path and making explicable those intimate words of the disciples after seeing the risen Christ on the road to Emmaus: "Did not our hearts burn within us as He talked with us on the way?"

Another spiritual experience which came to me I have not seen described in Scripture. Occasionally one seemed to feel a golden wire, of gossamer fineness, strung across one's body, which picked up a celestial melody. I had that experience when describing the principles of the Group in the Toronto drawing-room of a well-known Canadian minister, Dr. Powell, gifted with the grand manner. And once before I felt it when, throwing aside my many objections, I frankly shared some of the unhappiest defeats in my life with a friend in the Group. So, although I had experienced no noticeable quickening from baptism or Holy Communion, I did get almost immediately a renewed sense of the Holy Spirit's burning and glowing indwelling after I had frankly shared, even though there was still more to discuss and I was still pursuing a cautious Scottish policy of not putting all my sins into one basket. Not that anyone's experience can be exactly like another's, since we may have a different spiritual pitch, and those of my type evidently require far more encouragement to seek first and last the Kingdom of God.

Many receive the Spirit's witness at Confirmation, Conversion, Holy Communion, Baptism, and some, as I now know by experience, when Sharing.

"He who consistently refuses to share will never understand. But let such a mending come into share, and he will discover for himself a comradeship which manifests the power of Christ with compelling reality. . . . There is a hunger for fellowship with God and man, and there are many who have found that hunger satisfied in themselves and in others along this double road of confession and witness."

I had almost as much bother with the principle of Guidance. Once or twice I found the principle workout satisfactorily in practice; but for a time I could make little or no headway with it. Being in a Group of persons who were ready to sit down at any odd moment and write the thoughts which came as they prayed to God was disturbing and frequently embarrassing. One day a member of the Group asked me to lunch, and later announced that he had been guided to write me a check of ten pounds. Whereupon he produced his checkbook and was about to hand me the money. Here was a man living on faith and prayer, and maintaining a wife and two children from the same source, offering me some of the balance.

My friend returned the check to his pocket. Was his guidance right or wrong? The answer is that his overture gave me a chance of revealing something I was more in need of than money, which I could never have revealed but for what he did. It set up a chain of astonishing consequences which may be endless.

Before I met the Group I was walking down Whitehall when I was suddenly told by something inside to send money to two children in New Zealand. I obeyed, and the needed money arrived six weeks later, just before the death of their widowed mother, whose sudden illness I could not foresee.

Another experience of luminous Guidance came soon after I met Frank, when his insistence on setting his friends to work to build a spiritual family was still challenging me. Did he not know that religion was much too sacred a subject for talking about to everybody? One might be casting pearls before swine. Frank knew that, said we should be guided in our life-changing efforts, but we must remember that nothing was too sacred that helps men.

The name of a once-successful professional man had been on my mind often of late. It occurred to me that here was an excellent chance to help a difficult case. I determined to try Frank's advice and see this man, though uncertain where he was to be found. Our last meeting was in Lincoln's Inn, not far from High Holborn. Some months before, I had met him in another part of the town. I prayed about him, listened for guidance, half-expecting to get another such luminous thought as came to me at Oxford. The word that was pressed into my mind at that moment was "Temple," but there was not much luminosity about it.

Strolling up Fleet Street, I waited at the top of Middle Temple Lane, wondering if I should encounter the man I had in mind, convinced that I had no earthly chance of seeing him there at that haphazard moment. It was about one o'clock in the afternoon. For half an hour I watched Londoners pass and repass me while I was apostrophizing myself as: "You great big stiff to stand here in the middle of London expecting to meet someone with whom you have no appointment, who does not work here, and whom you have only seen at this spot once in your life."

But reassuring to me, he came. "If there is anything in this guidance business of Frank's and his human engineering, as there seemed to be once before, it is surely up to Providence to make this test work, since I am honestly endeavoring to find out the truth while assisting someone probably in great need."

I waited another ten minutes. And in normal circumstances I should then have strolled into Lincoln's Inn Fields for exercise or gone somewhere to lunch, as there was no need for my return to the office for some time. Just as I was about to move away, there came to me a sudden flash, distinctly luminous, identical in shape and feeling with the Oxford flash, and entirely different from my ordinary human thoughts. The message of this sudden luminous thought was commanding and urgent.

"Now go straight back to your office."

But why? I had no wish or need to go back just then. Yet I turned

and went down the street, and as I swung into the side road leading to my office *the man I had been seeking simultaneously turned
in with me.* Side by side we walked up the outing together.

I was surprised, and yet not really surprised. I felt that just had
to happen. To say the least, it was an amazing coincidence. Feeling rather excited, I asked my friend if he was looking for me or
thinking about me. Perhaps telepathy had something to do with
our meeting. He said, "No." He had been trying to keep an appointment with a man outside the Temple -- the word I had got in guidance -- at the opposite entrance to where I stood waiting for him.
I had met with him before in Fleet Street, and so my encounter
may have been coincidence. Nevertheless, it was most remarkable
that I met him at a time and place revealed to me by a luminous
thought while trying out the new theory.

But for that sudden flash I should have been somewhere else
and should not have met him that day. Again I felt that Frank's
"guidance" was not altogether eye-wash.

I saw a good deal of my friend during the next week, but I'm
afraid my further efforts with him must have been singularly unguided, for I detected no evidence of a great transformation in his
life. Nor, probably, did he in mine.

Was that guidance or coincidence? Apart from the conviction it
gave me, I can trace beneficial results. I described this incident
to one of the men in the Group, who reminded me that the art of
changing men's lives was not necessarily an art to be practiced
at the same speed as getting a good news story. With the former
there was need of infinite tact and patience, a willingness to lay
yourself alongside another man, regarding him not as a duty, but
lovingly as an opportunity; to be ready to devote an hour, a day, a
year, a lifetime, to his redemption, if so guided. The rush methods
of journalism might be applied to the Kingdom of God, sometimes
with satisfactory results, but not always; and it was probable I
was more in a hurry for results than God. I must regard every
failure as an opportunity for success; every punch I received must
be negotiated as spiritual jujitsu. Every blow, every failure, every
misadventure must be a lesson for a further advance. As Christ
accepted the wrath of the world in Gethsemane, we must be prepared to receive everything that came our way and re-direct the
impact for the good of the Kingdom and our self-development.

After that, guidance became a desultory sort of affair with me.
Occasionally, I would try to keep a regular morning for direction,
and sometimes I would receive clear ideas as to what ought to be

done. But the main idea that I needed, the next big thing to take in hand, persistently evaded me in organized guidance. I watched the Group listening to God. At first I felt the women seemed more susceptible to clear leading than the men; some of the experienced ladies in the Group seemed to take almost every action on the guided principle. One night in Calvary I asked a newcomer to make herself known to another lady, Mrs. Lee Vrooman (wife of the Dean of International College, Smyrna), on the other side of the room, while I carried on a conversation. She arrived just as Mrs. Lee Vrooman was quietly listening for special guidance on what to do. That contact brought remarkable results. But still no special guidance for me. I seemed to have slipped into a lonely rut.

At one Calvary meeting I encountered Dr. Philip Marshall Brown, Professor of International Law at Princeton University. I reminded him of how I had stormed his cab when he was leaving Oxford and shared his compartment on the journey to London.

Inspired by the Group teaching about reconciliation, he had called on his neighbor and settled a difference which had kept them apart for a year. But what was the Professor's experience of guidance? I wanted to know. The Professor is a commanding figure physically and intellectually. He has a fine head and a clear, powerful brain. No, he was not accustomed to receiving specially luminous thoughts distinguished from other thoughts, but he was quite confident he received guided thoughts. In fact, he had settled into the Quiet Time habit at any time as well as every morning. Only the other day someone had called on him for help over a problem, and together they had listened to God for guidance. Afterwards he read over those thoughts received in that consecrated half-hour and he was quite confident his thoughts had been guided.

I was waiting for special guidance in my next big step. Still none came. I grew restive and a little skeptical of the guidance theory, which I criticized to Cleve Hicks. Cleve said he understood my view. When first he saw people at Quiet Time he thought they were "crazy."

"Let's try a Quiet Time now," said the imperturbable Cleve. We tried. It was the same result. He read out to me his own guidance, and he gave me his paper. He will be surprised to discover it in a book "For Sinners Only." Here is what he wrote:

They went everyone of them with their faces straight forward, as the spirit was to go with them, they turned not as they went. (Ezekiel 1:12)   .

Trust the living God and He will give thee thy Heart's desire.

God does guide one even to the picking of texts. Trust Him in all things.

Tell Mother you are starting for your remarks about . . . (Cleve's mother died shortly after).

Commit thy ways unto the Lord and He will direct thy path.

Talk to Ray Purdy about this feeling of the defeatism and things being snarled up. God will direct it. Beware of cheap optimism.

Take a college by storm.

Be more generous towards those who differ from you.

A. J.'s future is in God's hands -- the good is soon lost when the best is not aimed at.

Get to the bottom of the sin and the way God delivers from all the lures of the evil one. Be of good cheer. I have overcome the world. Pray that you be not disturbed.

Constant prayer. A much deeper prayer life. A new trip south is right. Pray for money for It.

Face and name your sins and commit them to God.

There is no urging and love. It is a free response to a measureless love, that meets every need.

A. J.'s time in America will be richly used. Learn to take burdens off one another. Let God do it. Where we deeply care there is no strain.

Whatever one may think of this piece of sample guidance, there can be known two opinions of the quality of life lived by the man who wrote it.

Nevertheless, I still had some doubts about the guidance question and the possibility of being able to turn on guidance at any time. Perhaps because I had not yet conquered all the sins that were defeating me. As I waited I began to grow careless, and before I realized what was happening I had slipped a long way from the Source of guidance. Feeling remorseful, highly self-critical and definitely repentant, I asked for leading again, not feeling very confident as to getting more guidance, since its coming had been so desultory and unsatisfactory, and the quality of my spiritual life was so low.

Then, suddenly a flash came to show me how this book was to be written, followed by another giving me the title. The real purpose of my visit to America now came out with great clearness. "That checks. It rings a bell," was the opinion expressed. Immediately I began to tell others what was in my mind. The urge had come not as a strong luminous thought or a soundless whisper in the atmosphere, but as sudden pressure on the spirit.

And now I had one day left to decide which of three beckoning finger-posts to obey. My investigations of the Oxford Group were practically complete, my story written. I was there to resume materialism once more. Should I follow one finger-post down to Florida, the second to new enterprise in the British Isles, or the third (the most enticing) into a promising field just miraculously opened in the middle of Manhattan? At last I gave up the attempt to solve the problem and through it back on the Group principle of guidance for one final day.

"Don't touch it. Don't touch it. Don't touch it."

There was nothing uncertain about the way those three warning words buzzed in my ear, like a field of grasshoppers. Loudly they whirred and definitely they warned -- warned me not to touch an enterprise which would have taken me back to England during the next few days. Following the guidance, I made investigations and found snags in the offer I was about to accept. That meant good-bye to England for a while. The choice now lay between a skyscraper in Manhattan and a sojourn in the Millionaires' Paradise around Palm Beach. Guidance again, but no shrill warnings. Yet guidance to leave both Florida and Manhattan severely alone.

But come, this was absurd! One couldn't throw away everything. Besides, this was now the last day of decision. Unless positive guidance came I was going to act without it. Slowly and meditatively back to the hotel. Hear a surprise: an urgent cable from London. Would I catch the next fast boat to Oxford? Signed "Frank."

So guidance had come again! Perhaps just the guidance I needed. It gave me the opportunity to make a few more inquiries which I had vaguely felt were necessary to complete my investigations of the Oxford Group.

A murky crossing in mid-March. Welcomed back in Brown's Hotel by Frank, whom I found entertaining newcomers to the Group brought in by the articles I had written in the summer.

With them was "Sherry" Day, whom I had come to regard as Frank's shadow and complement, sometimes following just behind or off-times going before and preparing the way for the house-party in some corner of the world where the Group was starting.

The Rev. Sherwood Day is now a Presbyterian minister. He was a divinity student when he first came to know Frank at Hartford Seminary Foundation, Connecticut, many years ago. Since then he has accompanied Frank on most of his world tours. Once I asked Sam Shoemaker to name the finest Christian in the Group.

Sam directed a merry eye at me.

"If you mean the saintliest, the answer must be Sherry Day. He's an amazingly saintly fellow. I'll give you an example. We were traveling in India and proposing to go out for the evening, but unable to find a servant. All our shoes were dirty. Presently we noticed that Sherry Day had silently disappeared. Later he returned -- just as silently. When we went to our rooms we all found our shoes clean -- seven pairs of them. I said to Frank: 'Who cleaned these shoes?'

"Frank grinned cryptically. 'Don't you know?'"

"That," said Sam, "is the type of man Frank has around him."

Sherry Day was imitating Christ, Who washed the feet of His disciples. Practical Christianity this.

On three of the five occasions I have seen Sherry Day, he was just in the act of catching a liner for England, for America, for somewhere; on the fourth and fifth occasions he was busy helping someone in need. He was always ready to do something for somebody, and something useful rather than spectacular, although willing to go to the ends of the world on faith and prayer.

"What a fellowship it is!" as Sherry is always saying.

Sherry knows instinctively what to do with a team in any emergency, for he is completely selfless and surrendered.

"The most trustworthy man I know," says Frank.

When Sherry first met Frank he was finding the control of evil thoughts a hard daily fight. The harder he fought the more he was conquered. Frank showed him that when the imagination and will are in conflict the imagination wins; that the imagination must be centered on God, goodness, and on helping other people, so that all the evil steam can be condensed into a happy, useful and satisfied life.

"Instead of getting tense in temptation nowadays," said Sherry to me, "I find myself able to make a long nose at the devil. It was not a trick I learned, but the simple truth that Christ, working through the absolutely surrendered soul, enables him to overcome his own weaknesses by helping others who are also struggling with temptations."

Sherry finds that Frank always jumps ahead of him in development, but he is the natural leader. But Sherry has a wonderful facility for enunciating the principles which Frank formulates. He explained to me how the principle of Sharing came to receive such a prominent place in the Group teaching.

"We were a traveling team in China, where we found that two of us would sometimes get together and secretly vent something we disliked about another. (It is notorious that some Christians cannot work together.) To end that kind of thing we decided that we should share with the person concerned rather than with another the dislike we felt. Then not only did we share our own faults whenever they stuck their heads up, but we sought guidance to end our quarrels and cement the team into the ideal fellowship. Although Frank had worked out all the principles of the Group before he left the Church of the Good Shepard, it required crises such as the these to put them into joint action. And they have worked splendidly."

Sherry says that ten years with Frank has made it possible to exchange his old divided will for a new and undivided way of life that has brought him far more pleasure than he believed possible. One of his typical prayers is, "Make me tired from intercession and service, and not from defensive fighting."

He has been present or near to Frank in all parts of the world when men have been in the act of making the great change from self to God. "There must be thousands of such captures," he says. "Of course some of these may later get spiritual colic, as Frank describes it, and slip away for a while, perhaps to return when they feel better -- just as a child might do. It is such difficult and patient work, changing men and keeping them changed. I have seen Frank shaking with the pain of it. Few people realize how serious and difficult is the task of creating apostles, which was the life-work of Christ. You are born without effort and much pain. There must always be a Peter who denies at first, and a James and John who want to sit on the right hand and the left-hand in the best seats in the Kingdom; and a Judas or two to come along only to betray."

When Sherry Day was a divinity student at Hartford, he was walking down the main street with Frank when they encountered two drunken men.

"You take one and I'll take the other," said Frank to Sherry, starting to collar his man and to take him home.

Sherry was unready and unwilling for the task. He thought the cure for a drunk was aspirin or coffee, a cold shower and bed.

"I watched Frank do what I felt I couldn't do," he told me. "He took his man's home, and next day, when he was in the midst of a meeting, Frank had one of his irresistible impulses to go out into the street, where he found his drunken man again, now perfectly sober. Frank has one guided habit of turning up unexpectedly just when he is wanted. He put his man on the right road that day while showing me how inefficient I was in my own job. I felt like a young man who had gone into medicine but was unable to do the simplest medical work in an emergency. Frank explained to me that it was because my religion was not in action that I felt so helpless in an emergency. That if I had real love for men I should be willing to share with them my temptations, my secret thoughts, to put myself alongside them, and work with them and for them. He said that every man could test the reality of his religion by finding out if he was ready to make sacrifices for others. He gave me an early chance to make the test, and I found I did not want to go to China when he invited me to go there with him. The truth is, I shrank from Frank's too effective methods, wanting to live a selfish life. I definitely do not want to get into the lives of others, for I knew it meant being out in the cold winds, among the strays; hard work and considerable pain."

"But you went?"

"Yes."

"And results followed?"

"Yes. The first vital talk we had was with a man tied up by the same problems I now know how to avoid. I shared my own experience with him. As a consequence there were now two men to help in changing sinners where previously there was one."

"And who is the most difficult person you have ever tried to change?"

Sherry's mind wandered back along the line of changed men who had fallen to Frank and himself, and presently he said: "The most difficult man is the one so encrusted with his sins that he has lost the sense of conviction."

It was late when Sherry and I had finished talking and he retired to bed. The next morning he was up at dawn, and once again off on an ocean liner to a guided destination -- a house-party at Briarcliff Lodge on the Hudson.

Chapter Sixteen

AN IDEAL HOME

A train journey with Frank to Oxford is just as exhilarating as any other experience with this vital personality. Watch him sailing to the booking-office, marshalling the port-manteaux, directing the porters (who take to him immediately), directing everybody, choosing his meal in a third-class dining-saloon the night after he has been living in a Royal Palace.

Spend a week with him at Oxford while he co-operates in running Ken Twitchell's ideal home; "God's house," Frank calls it. The establishment has been run on faith and prayer for some years, though not without many days when the future was not clear but waited with confident faith like a November fog. But the house goes believingly on. Money comes in, just enough to keep going. And always a stream of visitors to entertain as though there were a regular income or an overloaded banking account.

When Frank enters he seems to bring with him a breeze of the Spirit. He is religious quicksilver each day of a seven-day week. The shouts, the tempers, the pique, the postures, the vanity, the overdone censure and the overdone praise -- these concomitants of dictatorship are missing when Frank is on the job -- he gets his work done a little quicker, and sometimes a good deal more efficiently without any infirmities of the unsurrendered great.

Only by surrounding himself with men and women living the same kind of life could so much work be got through in so short a space of time. Every post brings mail gathered from the ends of the earth.

One would think The Group House at Oxford was the centre of an international religious correspondence course -- only there is no charge. News of the spiritual travail of much of the world pours in through the letter-box, and is faithfully dealt with in short, crisp answers, confidential and stimulating. Not answers tepidly charged with good advice, but dynamic messages inspiring the recipient to action in some reciprocally beneficial manner. Perhaps a message to a young man recently in the Group and suffering from one of those periods of colic or growing pains to which all of us are susceptible. Frank's reply may perhaps encourage a little more honest sharing at home, thus getting straight to the root of his probable trouble. Always the letter is a mixture of stiff challenge and good fellowship.

One of the stiffest letters Frank permitted himself to write was to some persons who were refusing to support him in a certain courageous action for the help of someone in need. Frank said their refusal to extend the help where greatly needed might involve them in a crop of cares they did not foresee at the moment. But it was a friendly warning, nevertheless, free from pique and resentment. Never does Frank mince matters where his correspondents compromise. If the man is living an undisciplined life, he tells him so in plain words. Fearless dealing with sin all the time. Honesty demands it. Spiritual growth is impossible without it.

Fifty or sixty letters a day are nothing to Frank. One night last year in Geneva, following a wearing evening meeting, he returned to his hotel and found the correspondence piling up from all quarters of the world. All through the night until 6:30 a.m. he dictated to Ken Twitchell. One of those letters brought about a change in the life of a nobleman, who subsequently opened up the Group work in Hungry. After such a strenuous day, Frank admits to his mind being tired, that he cannot think so quickly as at the start, but he is still a human dynamo.

All the time Frank is handling his correspondence he is listening for guidance as to the requirements of others in the house. His facility for anticipating a human need before the person concerned is aware of that need or before he can be approached or called to the spot is uncanny. I have been working alone in my room. Suddenly I have found myself stuck in an aspect of Group work I could not understand. I have looked up and found Frank just entering.

"I was guided to come up and see you," he says.

First you wonder if this is not just coincidence. But these coincidences continue to happen with me, and anybody who knows Frank says just the same thing. He hurried from a camp-fire meeting to a near-by tent where a man was in agony with appendicitis. Unknown to another human being, this attracted Ray Purdy to Frank. Sherry Day is never tired of telling that other story of Frank dashing into the street without warning to encounter the drunken man of the previous night. All his associates know so many examples of Frank's uncanny habit that they have ceased to be surprised. They know that he will always appear at the right time or else get in touch by telegram, telephone or cable.

Like the proverbial busy man, he is the person always to find time for extra work. Knowing that the real solution of his own problem demands as its natural sequence, the solving of other people's problems. His mind is always engaged on this altruistic duty. He might be in the kitchen thanking the servants for the way they have speeded up the work proceeding through the whole house, or be sending daffodils to some neglected person down the street; preparing Easter cards or Christmas cards, or saying just the right word to help his hostess put the self-conscious new arrival at ease the first evening. He thinks of everybody and everything. When he comes to stay, he comes not to be entertained, but to entertain. His wide figure, wide shoulders, wide forehead, wide smile, providing a training-post wide enough to support all comers.

Frank rarely acts alone, but always with the idea of training others. He is the natural pedagogue, often teaching without permitting others to know they are being taught. A visitor sat in his Group meetings for several days watching him in action, listening as he asked first one and then another how he would handle some new problem that arose. Though he may not always have gone around the circle, the visitor noticed with every query that one man's opinion was invariably asked. Presumably it was because his advice was so good. That was the visitor's first thought, but Frank did not defer to him more than to the rest. At the end of the second day the visitor sensed what was in Frank's mind -- this man was to be left in charge of the Group at Oxford when Ken Twitchell was away in America.

Frank's secretaries are all Group leaders; he feels this must be so considering the highly confidential nature of his work and the necessity of preparing others to carry on when he is taken away. It is also better so, for he does not necessarily give the final word after he has collected opinions. All through the day he is putting the important matters up to the guidance of the Group in their Quiet Times. When there is uncertainty, a further period of Quiet is called for, and then unanimity is inevitable.

Theoretically, if this guidance is really the Holy Spirit, there should be immediate unanimity. But there are obvious reasons why this cannot always be. Guidance must be thought of as not mechanical, but as becoming clear through reason, evidence, and luminous thinking. God speaks to us in all the ways of our human understanding. No man or group of men is infallible, but a group of people each individually seeking God's will and closely united together is most likely to receive the clearest consistent guidance. Often God reveals only one step at a time. Sometimes we have to go ahead on what seems probably right instead of acting on certainty. Guidance ultimately rests on a basis of faith, and if we ask sincerely on what God gives us He never lets us down, say the Group. "All things work together for good to them that love God," is the guiding slogan.

There is a constant coming and going at The Group House. I was writing in my room when a tall, blue-eyed youth from South Africa, and now a "fresher" at Cambridge, breezed in. This lad began to tell me his quaint experience with the Groups in his native country. His elder brother had come home one evening to urge parents to come down to Muzenburg and see what a Group meeting was like.

"I hadn't the slightest notion of what it was all about," said the undergraduate, as he lounged before my fire. "I didn't even know it was going to be a religious meeting. But I went down just to see what was going on. I was a college boy, and naturally interested in what my bigger brother was about. The Group crowd seemed rather happy, and gave me a welcome, which I thought was rather decent for University men. So I stayed on to their meeting, when they began to talk about something which I felt was right and really wanted. Hitherto I had thought religion was rather dull, but the Group seemed to have a new way of looking at things, which was not morbid, though very personal. But I wasn't quite prepared for this or what was about to follow.

"After several had told their stories, I was astounded to see my elder brother get up and begin to tell his own experience. To hear one who had always dominated his brothers and sisters stand up in a public meeting and talk so frankly about the change which had come into his life was to set my knees knocking together. I felt it meant I should have to do the same thing, unless I was careful.

"Well, I wasn't so careful. For I spoke to a happy-looking fellow after the meeting, who told me that Christ was the centre of his life. Nobody had talked like that to me before. It made me think. I could see he was thoroughly happy. After that I had a chat with my brother, and discussed pretty frankly some of the things in my life which I had not wanted to discuss before. That helped me tremendously. Then I saw Cleve Hicks, and with him I made my surrender to God. I saw that a new power came to me, accompanied by a great peace and joy; though there was nothing emotional about it."

"What about your parents?" I asked, knowing that the undergraduate's father was a prominent King's Counsel in Cape Town.

"Oh, they seemed quite pleased about it. Especially, Dad was. We all went home, and my elder brother and I had Quiet Times together, and also took part in the School Group at Diocesan College where we both were. Then my younger brother became interested, and next my younger sister -- all four of us. Made quite a difference in the home. There was much less scrapping than formerly, which so surprised my father that he decided to come in too. The thing which caused him the most astonishment was the sight of all four of us dashing off one evening to get his spectacles when he asked for them -- this, instead of our being asked several times to go, and each passing the buck to one of the others. So all four of us children, and father as well, now had Quiet Times together in the same house. Father is very enthusiastic. When the car hadn't arrived at the station on time to meet him, instead of losing his temper he spent the waiting period witnessing to a porter."

"What other changes occurred in your home-life?"

The undergraduate mused on the pleasant South African home thousands of miles away, for which he was slightly homesick.

"It was a different relationship for us all, of course. We found that most of us had to cut out some selfishness which we had nourished. That made life much happier for everybody. We had Group meetings every Sunday, and the fellows who came in about that time are still holding strongly."

News that this young man's father had associated himself with the Oxford Group speedily became known in the South African Bar. One day he was addressing a High Court Judge in Cape Town when he used the phrase, "Now, my lord, to be perfectly honest..." Whereupon the Judge jocularly interpolated, "Come, Sir, no Oxford Group here."

The Chaplain of Downing College, Cambridge, was another to arrive that day. He had been suddenly whisked up from Cornwall to rearrange plans for an April house-party in his University town, a party which he ran magnificently. A tall, slim, athletic figure with the lightest blue eyes, he had once distinguished himself as Captain of Boats at Wadham College, Oxford. The Reverend placed the invitations to the forthcoming house-party on my table, stretched his long legs before my fire and became ruminative. He had some very poignant recollections of his first meeting with Frank, which was as far back as 1922, when he was attending a house-party of Oxford men at Keswick. One evening Frank came in to supper and prayer. After supper twenty of us sat round in a circle to hear him, and two of us subsequently came into the Group -- the Rev. Howard Rose and myself."

"Tell A. J. that story of 'Rose, Rose, Rose,' and 'Wade, Wade, Wade,'" Frank had advised, when I was being introduced to the Chaplain.

Nick Wade (perfect name for an Ethel M. Dell) told me the yarn.

"I had listened to Frank's stories of changed lives -- typical stories of Frank's," said he, "and next morning awoke feeling rather rebellious. I felt there was something in religion and that I hadn't yet got it, and that perhaps Frank could explain. I went out and, oddly enough, found myself walking down a cul-de-sack, running parallel with the road I meant to take. Exactly how I got into that I don't remember. Just then Frank came unexpectedly out of a house and hailed me. It seemed rather queer when he said he was just coming to see me that I should have unconsciously, gone out of my way to see him. I told him this. Whereupon Frank opened his notebook and showed me the entry:

"'Wade, Wade, Wade; Rose, Rose, Rose.'

"I said: 'Why did you write that down?'

"Frank replied that in his early Quiet Time he had heard two names -- Wade and Rose.

"That," said the Chaplain, "was the first time I realized how an ordinary man could be in close touch with God. So we had a great talk, which opened to me a whole new vista of practical adventure and possibility which before had been just theoretical and theological. Not immediately, but very soon there came a new realization of the challenge of Christ. To live so close to Him that He could guide and control my life all the time and use me in the lives of others.

"A few years later I travelled around the world with Frank and a small-company, including Loudon Hamilton, Sherry Day, and Sam Shoemaker. I saw a cross-section of life in the Near, Middle and Far East. We mixed with missionaries, and people who had no use for missionaries. The discipline of that traveling team and my experiences during that year abroad with Frank, together with the vision it brought of the need of the modern world for Christ, led to my decision to prepare for ordination. That year with Frank was amazing. Barriers in my departmentalized life were broken down everywhere, and I was taught how to be willing to do anything that the Spirit of God wanted and how to do it. I found that Frank thinks of everything, always with the object of expanding God's

Kingdom. A whole new quality of life became possible through the principle of guidance. I found that if one is ready to pay the price, there really comes a power to diagnose the trouble and provide the cure in one's own life and in other lives all the time.

"More and more I came to understand how everything centers round an experience of Jesus Christ, so real, so vivid, so great, that it dominates the whole life. It is a dynamic relationship that issues in power. Since then I am continually finding that people, even conventional Christians, keep so many areas from Christ's control that they live merely a departmentalized life. My contact with Frank swept me to a higher level, where nothing now was either secular or religious, but everything spiritual and real. This life gets you more and more. I was asked to come up here from Cornwall quite suddenly, and I had no wish to come. But here I am. I know the only right thing to do is what God tells me to do."

Nick Wade is a popular Chaplain. He is priceless as the host at a big house-party; that he feels a sense of divine guidance and power in the details of his daily routine can be seen by anyone with half a blind eye who observes his earnest face and radiant manner. Lunching with the Chaplain of Downing means not a formal talk about generalities, but a heart-to-heart talk about the deepest needs of a man's life, those needs which the English gentleman is so expert in hiding from his closest friends.

Later on I had a chat with the Rev. Howard Rose, who is the Donald Hankey-Woodbine Willie type, and the well-worth detour to meet at his Vicarage in London, or to hear him preach in Christ Church in the same accessible thoroughfare.

Howard Rose is slight, tallish, with a wiry, athletic figure, ready to carry on alone without a curate for sometimes twenty hours a day. He has a domed head, a ruddy complexion, and the happiest of dispositions, with a completely disciplined character, which makes you ready to give him your confidence.

It was Howard's experiences during the War which decided him to enter the ministry. And in one instance, he was the recipient of special guidance which saved the lives of himself and the whole company.

Howard was leading his company out of the front-line trenches back through the dangerous terrain under a rain of shell-fire to rest billets when he approached a fork in the road. Both arms of the fork led to the billets, but the one to the right was better marching, further away from the enemy's guns, and in every obvious way the more desirable.

Howard wavered between the two roads -- he knew nothing of the Group in those days -- and asked God to guide him, trusting for an immediate answer. The answer flashed back clearly:

"Take the left."

The Sergeant Major was astounded to see the commander taking the worst road, and protested. The men, too, began grousing, but followed. Everybody was sullenly convinced the captain was wrong, for the enemy shells were now falling nearer than before. Suddenly there came a fresh salvo of shelling, and then the other road to their right, at the exact spot where they would have been marching, was blown shapeless.

Seeing this, the men's feelings changed instantly, as was shown later when Howard addressed them before the dismiss. He said he felt they should know the real reason why he marched left instead of right against everybody's better judgment, including his own. Ten of his company (including some of the N.C.O.'s) afterwards wanted to know more about religion, and, thinking they would catch it by being confirmed, approached the Brigade Padre for this purpose. Says Howard:

"The Brigade Padre was one of the very best, and had already won a Military Cross and Bar for conspicuous bravery. Knowing what I stood for, he put up to me that I should prepare my own men for Confirmation. At first I was taken aback, and told him I was not a padre, but just a soldier. 'True,' he said. 'But you are also a soldier of Jesus Christ. Tell them simply what He means to you.' Accordingly, at my next opportunity, when the battalion was out at rest, my Confirmation class was begun. It was comprised of a sergeant, a lance-corporal, and eight privates. We met some dozen times, and these talks have since formed the basis of my Confirmation talks as an ordained parson. They had been practical and real to meet the circumstances and needs of active service, and so probably got across better than the classes I had myself attended as a boy. My candidates were duly confirmed by Bishop Gwynne, Assistant Chaplain-General, and one now deeply interested in the Groups, and it did seem to make a very real difference, not only to them, but to the whole battalion."

These incidents and innumerable talks with officers and men finally led Howard into the ministry.

"It was just after my ordination," he says, "that I met Frank for the first time and was deeply impressed not only with his quality of life, but with his emphasis on the need of unhurried quiet in the early morning. Twice Frank visited me in my parish in Sussex, leaving an unmistakable influence on my life, and after the second occasion I determined at whatever cost to keep an unhurried quiet time daily. The change in one's effectiveness was instantaneous, and shortly afterwards I was called to Oxford as a chaplain on the Pastorate ministering to undergraduates. It was here that I found no way so effective as that advocated by the Group in dealing with students.

"In my six years in Oxford over one thousand students, both men and women, came of their own accord for personal talks. Many of them had deep needs which I knew I could not have met had I not had my own needs met by Frank or someone else. Each term several hundred men and women came into my home. It began the centre of the activity of the Group in Oxford, and in 1928 it was my privilege to lead the first team to South Africa, from which date I have been wholly identified with the work."

Howard's congregation has trebled during his first six months as Vicar.

During my stay at The Group House, Oxford, I had ample chances of observing Frank's love of festivities. His delight in making Easter Day happy for everybody was thoroughly infectious. Easter cards from him appeared on plates and desks, a fine Easter daily from somebody was ushered into the drawing-room, Easter eggs for the Twitchell Tots secreted in, behind and under the chairs. Frank can play with children and make them as thoroughly at ease as he makes the grown-ups. He waxed merry at my amazement in finding the number around the table for the special Easter Day lunch was -- thirteen! No such thing as superstition in the Oxford Group. I whispered to Garrett Stearly to sit in the middle of the train that afternoon, as he and Nan (his ideal wife) left for Wolverhampton -- just in case of accidents. The folks at the table were incredulous that anyone could be so sensitive to the figure thirteen. Then Marian (Mrs. Twitchell) unconcernedly announced that she was born on the thirteenth day of the month. One felt more certain that something would happen to that train to Wolverhampton. This was just tempting fate. The next day the Group came together and fixed the date for a luncheon to Editors, calmly deciding on April 13th!

Presumably, the reason why there was no accident to the Wolverhampton train was because some worse fate was developing for these daring people who hurled their defiance at the skies of superstition. I had piquant memories of buying stocks on the morning of a certain November 13th, to see them crash on the afternoon of the same unlucky day. Later I called on the broker for tea at his private address. He lived at Number 13. On a subsequent February 13th I saw stocks I had just sold short go soaring to the clouds, leaving me more broke than usual. One Friday, December 13, I signed a lease for some new business premises. Three serious operations followed immediately afterwards, of a complexity of further misfortunes ending in the great depression. And while I was finishing this chapter the 13th President of France was assassinated. The Group of thirteen sitting around Mrs. Twitchell's table smiled complacently at superstition. I was not so confident. Telephone bell rang. A message came through from Europe inviting Frank to be the guest of a celebrity over the week-end. That was the answer to this Number 13 recklessness. He said the boat would go down like the White Ship. But Frank returned smiling the next week. And I have still to discover what ill-luck was brewing and went astray. A new moon peeped at us through the glass of the railway compartment on our way to Cambridge just after. Tragedy still held aloof.

Twitchell Tots -- Skippy and Baby Anne -- aged four and two, take their place with family and guests at the Group dining-table, which says a lot for "Modi," a young Swiss Quakeress, and whose charge they are. The Twitchell Tots have not yet begun their official Quiet Times, although they are unconsciously practicing them. Their shouts for Daddy and Mummy to come "say prayers with them" is evidence that religion will come naturally without the coercive methods which did so much harm in a past generation. Skip is a tall, serious boy, with a fair complexion, fine dark lashes, a kindly nature and the promise of a poet. Baby Anne has a wide forehead, lots of brains behind it, much coquetry and a face full of mischief.

There is one point of exact similarity between all four -- Ken, Marion, Skippy, Baby Anne. Each has a pair of fine dark brown eyes. All appear to have been made from one model, a prize brown eye, multiplied eight times into a brown-eyed family octagon.

To see the family at work in The Group House, one would hardly suspect the discipline which underlies its happy freedom. All are in the world yet, not of it. Marian and Nan disprove the contention that two women in one house do not agree long. Sharing is again the explanation. I watched these two, used to the gay social round, imparting a rarer gaiety to the work of The Group House, so obviously enjoying their life of faith and prayer and surrender to God.

One morning at breakfast with Nan I read a letter from Miss Round, the Wrightman Cup tennis-player. I asked her what Miss Round was doing in the Group. Oh, Nan had met her at a house-party up in the Midlands, from which the tennis celebrity went home deeply impressed. As was well known, Miss Round had a strong religious background. Her mother asked her what the meeting was like -- "Goody-goody?" "No, the real thing!" So the tennis celebrity had become a witnessing enthusiast for the Group basis of life.

Donald MacKay blew in one day from South Africa. Donald is a merry fellow. Having once overstayed his leave as a soldier, he gave this cheeky explanation to his Colonel: "I've had a damn good time, and am ready to pay for it to." He paid -- lightly! He had done all sorts of he-man jobs on the veldt. Once he lived in a forest hut. The mice came and ate his food. One day they disappeared. Relief for a fortnight. Then he encountered a large cobra outside his hut and tried to kill it. The cobra ran into his hut and was killed as it entered a hole where it had lived -- inside the hut -- for a fortnight, protecting him from -- mice. One of his jobs was driving wild horses from Rhodesia down into the Transvaal to save the pound-a-head railway fare. He is the kind of man to do the right thing when the extraordinary happens, as he did in the middle of the night when his mob of wild horses were stampeded by a pair of undimmed headlights. He has a delightful fund of hunting stories. He told me a quaint incident connected with one of the Group meetings in South Africa. A young student had owned up to stealing money for cigarettes, whereupon the Negro servant promptly and unexpectedly confessed to having stolen the cigarettes his young master had bought with the stolen money!

But his best yarn is the tale of how he tried to dodge Loudon Hamilton in Pretoria back in 1929; how he went to his first house-party -- a camp on the veldt -- ostensibly to give his dog a swim, but really to find an answer to life's riddle; how he found it, and has since become a troubadour for God on three continents.

When the 1931 house-party at Oxford ended, we were all invited to the University Church of St. Mary to witness the pretty wedding of two experienced leaders -- Bill Browne and Polly Fox. There were ten bridesmaids. I described that ceremony under a banner headline----------

"FAITH AND PRAYER WEDDING AT OXFORD."

Frank had given an address, in which he said the wedding was a challenge to a world of materialism, for they would be trusting to God only for their sustenance while they sought to extend His Kingdom. Polly and Bill were known frequent callers at The Group House. I asked them how they fared in married life on faith and prayer. Amazingly well! Once they got down to just enough for the next breakfast. Then a little money had come in by post from a working girl in the North. A clergyman had heard of the incident, and had sent along a couple of pounds. From then onwards the faith and prayer life had continued to work out; always the cruse of oil, rarely an abundance. Subsequently Bill Browne took charge of a house-party at Matlock, which he ran with outstanding ability. Patrick is the name of their baby son.

Ray Purdy and Elsa Purdy were among those constantly coming and going to and from the Group House while I was staying there. Both radiant as ever, both ready to come forward and lead or efface themselves as usual, both doing good work which nobody heard anything about until perhaps a year or so after, when someone, telling the story of his or her life-change, would announce, "And when I met a Ray Purdy..."

It was like saying, "And then came the War." The inevitable had happened. They were now off to South Africa, where Ray was to take charge of a big church in Pretoria. They sailed on Friday the 13th!

Here in the Group House I met again a lady who has done so much for Calvary Church and the Group Movement in America and Europe. Olive Jones has silver hair, a clear brain, a sense of humor, a vein of sentiment, a voice in a thousand, and a heart of gold. Yet she has been a stern disciplinarian, and, as such, was given the charge of special schools in New York State, where she did more for delinquent boys than any person in America. At one time she was on sixty-four public committees, was elected President of the National Education Association, and is nationally regarded as an authority in her field.

One Saturday afternoon I drove Olive out from Oxford to Pangbourne -- a picturesque river-drive, to a tumbling weir (bubbles of a drowned past!), then on to Reading. Ken lent me his fifty-thousand-mile-old Morris for the drive. She went beautifully, but the engine had the knack of stopping when the car stopped at busy points *en route,* to the annoyance of everybody but Olive. Even when I took the wrong turning and the car stopped without power on the edge of the river. All gazed placidly on, careless of potential tragedy.

Adventures and misadventures, but the old Morris held out. I had one eye on the road, one eye on the Thames, one ear for the engine and one ear for the remarkable story that Olive had to tell. Though once a church member, Olive had long given up her belief in religion, and the Bible, in God, but still retained her faith in a future life. Her mother became stricken with paralysis, and just before she died was always calling Olive's name, though never able to make her understand. As her mother died, her paralyzed arms raised suddenly and a beautific expression came into her face, which convinced Olive that she had glimpsed the world beyond. Olive pondered over the mystery of what her dying mother had wished to tell her. And that time Olive's education theory was just ethical teaching, habit formation, and pre-vocational training, aided by social service. She believed that if a person was shown what was the right thing to do, he would do it, provided economic pressure did not prevent him. Her work flourished, but she was dissatisfied. A study of the after-career of her boys revealed seventy-nine percent. living useful, respected lives -- which meant great acclaim for her.

But twenty one percent were on the road to prison -- social menace is at best. Her dissatisfaction grew. A movement for week-day religious education of unchurched children had now started among New York teachers, Catholic and Protestant, working separately, but in absolute harmony. Olive began to think of this as a device to help her with that wayword twenty-one per cent. She agreed to help in the publicity side of the work, in which she specialized. This took her to see some of the class-work first hand. One day a small boy looked up into her face and asked, "What church do you go to?"

The unconscious emphasis on *you* made her feel a hypocrite. She could not say, None. As an evasive answer she gave the church in which she had been confirmed. To save her face (for she had always been honest with the children), she now decided to join a church. She saw an advertisement of Calvary in the street car, and went to hear Sam Shoemaker preach. Greatly attracted by the practical sincerity of the sermons and the cordiality of the people, she decided to join. She saw Sam, who urged her to attend the Thursday night Group meeting, but she evaded. A lady who knew Olive by reputation in women's organizations, a member of the Group, took her out to dinner and told her of her own changed life, which made Olive determined to find God for herself, as she was convinced she was hearing truth in spiritual things at last. So

Olive called on Ray and Mrs. Purdy at their apartment -- where, as frequently happens -- another definite surrender to God was made.

The capture of Olive was an important event in the life of Calvary Church. Here was a God-sent organizer arriving just at the time when a forward movement was in progress. Olive took over the direction of Calvary House, and ran the activities of that house on efficient labor-saving lines, efficiency she learned and developed during many years spent in powerful political organizations. The morning Quiet Time which she established in Calvary House became a period for gathering together the strings of the work and getting and giving general direction for the rest of the day. Then came the Geneva house-party, requiring Olive's attendance in Europe, and later presence in Oxford.

That drive with Olive to Pangbourne and then on to Reading was a spiritual feast. One always believed there were many women in the world who lived very near to God. A conversation with Olive proves she is one of them. As we were coming down the hill to Magdalen College in our return journey, Olive was telling me of a recent mystical experience. She was one of a party of fifteen (all in the Group) who were attending communion service. As all went to the altar rail, Olive found herself at the end of the line. Fourteen knelt, and then the Pastor's hand went out, and Olive had to wait. Just at that moment a separation from the rest she was vividly conscious of Christ's presence close beside her, kindly, sympathetic, and completely understanding.

A true mystical experience.

One last story from the dinner-table at the Group House deserves a place at the top of a news column. A woman had been divorced, and was living on a settlement paid regularly by her remarried husband under a Court order. The woman was changed through the Group, and she began to get guidance. This included the leading to write to her divorced husband and decline any more payments from him, as she had been just as guilty as he over the divorce. A courageous step, for it meant looking to God for her maintenance, for she had no other source of income.

Some other husbands would probably like their ex-wives to have an encounter the Group.

Chapter Seventeen

A MODERN WIFE'S ADVENTURE

Wives, like husbands, are sometimes fed up with the humdrum of domesticity and decide to cut away for a good time seeing the world.

At the dinner in a Southern home I picked up the first details of a priceless story of one of these wives' encounters with Frank, full of humor and practical evangelism. The heroine -- Lady W. -- was remarkably intelligent, a short-story writer, attractively but largely built. Had she been a size smaller she might have filled the bill as a film star. Despite her proportions, she had personality to make her a favorite in company and wit to retain that favoritism. She lived in the East Indies, but, wanting rest and change, decided to leave her husband for a six months' holiday.

As she went on the boat some wag warned her to beware of a religious fanatic who was on board. As the chief steward placed Frank and her next to each other at the mate's table, she was unaware who her neighbor was. Frank's other neighbor was an Admiral's wife, who stared with disapproval at Lady W., and was surprised that a man like Frank should talk with a person of her type. How could he help it when she was his neighbor at table, he asked. Frank told me the story complete. Here it is:

"Lady W. and I chatted together. She talked about her skiing experiences in the mountains, and I about some of my travels. I noticed that she always came in a little late for dinner, wearing some marvelous creation or other. She was a genial, happy companion and a great favorite with the men in the smoking-room. When we entered port, the Admiral's wife and party went ashore and left me to see the town by myself. As I was seated in the lobby of the hotel I saw Lady W. and a young man I had noticed on the boat arrive together. What should I do? Ask them to tea, or watch them wander into the Palm Room? Suppose the Admiral and his wife came in and saw me entertaining her *bete noir*? An intuitive prompting made me ask them to tea. The young man eagerly accepted, for, as I discovered later, he had no money, and regarded me as a merciful Providence.

"During tea I mentioned I was taking a drive, and invited them to join me in the back seat and see the sights. I sat with the driver, who was called Bunty. I told him all the interesting things I could think of, and he told me about the sites. I asked about his family, and Bunty mentioned his twins. And as I spoke I always heard an undertone behind repeating what I was saying:

"'Bunty has twins, and he's asking their names.'"

Frank decided to pass back more and more information as it came along. Each time he looked around, the couple seemed to be progressively more friendly. Before the tour ended the pair behind was receiving far more information (and interpretation) than they expected or desired.

Frank continues:

"We arrived back at the pier, and my passengers alighted, while I made some calls. As I returned to the pier I saw my friends, who overheard my farewell conversation with the driver. Bunty flatly refused to take any money for the drive, saying he had rarely been treated like a human being by his fares, and he was grateful for the ride with me. Lady W. and her friend looked on, more astonished at me than ever. I waved good-bye to Bunty, sent messages to the twins, and went abroad."

To Frank's surprise, Lady W. came aboard again, for she had intended to stay ashore for a long holiday. He now observed an under-current of worry about his table-mate, and discovered that she had not received her last monthly remittance from her husband, and no reply had come to her cable of inquiry. So she had quickly canceled her plans and decided to return home on the same ship.

Frank continues:

"As the steamer receded from the shore I found myself singing on a happy, moonlight evening. Lady W. asked me if I knew what I was singing. I said, 'No,' and she announced it was a hymn. She turned to her companion. 'Why, he doesn't even know he's singing to Him!' Soon Lady W. failed to appear at meals, so I thought I would now let her know something about myself and sent her down a book to read. Some days later we met on the companion-way. She looked at me startled.

"'My God! Are you that man?'

"'What man?'

"'That man in *Life-Changers*?'

"I said I was, and she said I was just the sort of man she had been looking for all her life. Her family had always taught her the

Bible, and lately she had reminders that one could not be happy without it. A friend of hers had jumped out of a window after a merry party in one of the night-clubs and killed herself. She wanted to talk more to me about the Bible, and proposed to get out a copy from her mother's old box in her trunk, which she had not read for a long time. Did I mind her getting some of her smoke-room friends along to listen? Of course I had no objection to that, and so we sat in one corner of the deck, and she volunteered to read the Bible to us, which she knew well enough to choose the fifty-first Psalm. Thus began aboard a little group of which Lady W. was the natural leader.

"Her sudden interest in the Bible introduced a good deal of excitement on the ship, as previously she had been none too careful what she said and did, and some women passed her by on the other side. A real battle came to her later, when she felt she must correct the wrong impression she had made and the things she had said. One day she came rushing up to me saying, 'I can't go and tell these people how wrong I was. What will they think of me?'

"I said she had told the original stories to raise a laugh, and that she was now big enough to risk their laughing again. Moreover, I thought they would be silenced and secretly challenged, though perhaps they would pass it off lightly. She said she could not do this without prayer.

"'All right,' I said. 'Let's have prayer, then.'"

"She made her decision during that prayer, and presently courageously did what she had declared was impossible.

"It brought an amazing response. Another woman writer with whom she shared asked if she could use the incident in her next magazine story. Lady W. readily agreed. The woman asked why she did that, and was told the power of Christ.

"'So that must be the power I need,' said the authoress, adding, 'I have not seen enough in Christianity before to inspire me to try to get that power.' She complimented Lady W. on her courage.

"And now, as an amazing result, the ship was almost turned into a religious house-party. It became quite easy and natural to talk about the things in life that mattered. Everybody began to be interested. The change from the average gossip on a liner was amazing. Lady W. easily became the centre of the talk; and her arresting and compelling personality and originality of expression of the great and the eternal truths sobered and challenged the ship's company.

"When we arrived at the port, everybody was interested to see if her husband would be at the dock to meet her. One of those most interested was the Admiral's wife, who had now become so devoted that she kissed Lady W. on both cheeks and expressed the hope that they would meet again, and meant it. So different from the average, 'Hope I see you again,' which secretly means, 'Hope I don't,'" says Frank, and continues:

"Lady W.'s husband was there ready for her. His reply to her cable had gone astray. Because of her new experience she was most grateful for that Providential mishap. Lady W. immediately witnessed to him, and told him of her new power in life, and he seemed quite glad to hear it, and sardonically hoped it would do her good, as a husband would say. She also witnessed to her friends at the night-club. Later she came to New York, and rang me up the first day, took tea with me and then went with me down to Calvary, where she registered a further decision to serve the Lord Christ.

"Early one morning I was called to the house of a well-known singer who was planning suicide as the easiest way out of her troubles. She was something like Lady W. in appearance, came from the same town, and in answer to my question, exclaimed that she had known her in school. I told her about Lady W.'s remarkable experience, and asked if she would care to talk with her. She asked:

"'Do you think she has the solution of my problem?'

"'I do,' I answered.

"I telephoned Lady W., and she gladly went down to see her with the good news that Jesus Christ still suits, saves (from suicide) and satisfies.

"Now what of Lady W.'s husband? Well, he came home from a long leave in the East to see his aged father, whom he had not met for seven years. Then Lady W. and he came to England for a house-party. The first evening I was walking up and down by the quad trying to tell her husband how natural it was to live with God, when a telegraph messenger came dashing up and handed him a wire.

"'My father's passed on!' he exclaimed, and then, as I tried to comfort him as we paced around the quad, he said, 'I'm in just the place where God has sent for the help I need at this time, for I can't stand alone face to face with the great eternal realities. I have no adequate solution for the problem.' Would I lead him to the source of power?

"Quite naturally, as we walked up and down, he expressed his gratitude to One who makes eternal plans for bringing men home. Under the stars that night he yielded his life to Christ, telling me how the silent influence of his helpmate, Lady W., had made a great impression on him. How he had tested her at every point, and her new life squared with the principles of her Master.

"They did not go home immediately, but stayed on, as he wished to be established in his faith. He told me later that the joy of his mother at hearing that he, too, was serving the One who had been the joy and guide of her loved one through the valley. The time came when husband and wife sailed for their Bar Eastern home, taking with them an orphaned child to bring up as their son, in another home re-made with Jesus Christ, the unseen Guest and silent Listener to every conversation."

Lady W.'s correspondence since that trip makes interesting reading. "My word! I'm learning such a lot," she writes to Frank. "I'm just beginning to get a glimpse of what you have had to face in your years of work. I'll say that I was an easy mark to a great many that you have come in contact with. A woman friend has just been staying with me, who, as women go down here, is one of the exceptions for the better. But many times while she is talking I hear myself speaking, as of yore, and want to cry out, 'It's all so useless to look at things in that way. Get the light of Christ on it'. I used to think that the personal Cross was a sort of illusion . . . . but I see there is an individual Cross for each, the true carrying of which is its own blessing."

She tells gaily of a return trip to a night-club: "I felt it all such a pity and waste of time. . . . The attitudes of some of the dancers and some of the clothes worn made me feel again my old wanton self, made out to be forced prettiness, with clothes far too extravagant, and the ego dominating every move. It was how *I* looked, *I* dressed, *I* danced; and my partner only came into the picture in the degree to which he was a complement to me. I must admit, too, that the Cabaret did amuse the flesh, while the spirit was grieved over the poor souls jigging and dancing their lives away.

"Don't think by this that I've got into a pessimistic mood or that I am always looking at things through blue glasses. Far from it, but I feel how small any monetary pleasure or amusement on this earth is compared to that which is waiting . . . and mass of souls blinded by the tinsel and hating to give it up simply appalls me. . . . We're so stupid, some of us. As for me, I've fought about every step of my surrender after I made it, and now I think it about time I gave in entirely . . . but to-morrow I may be fighting to hold out on some silly selfish point."

The old life peeps out again later: "When it came to hanging your picture, my husband was all for a prominent place, while I was for a bit of shadows. The shadows won, for as I have to live here daily, I said that I did not want Frank's picture to be always looking at me as though searching for hidden sins."

She tells of the discovery that she must give up telling lies. "Golly! Don't I remember that polite lie I told to the Purdys last summer. . . . Well, I'd rather have told all my shady past than confess that lie, but I had to, or cease to get guidance. . . . You know I do miss the house-parties, even here I feel the fellowship of the Groups. . . Really, I'm so happy I can't express it. . . . I'm hurting such a lot, in patience and much-needed discipline. My days are now mapped out like a time-table. But it's fun. . . . My hope is to teach my son to listen to God as soon as he can pray."

Another echo of the voyage:

"I'm trying to get in touch with the student in Australia who told me on the boat that you were a religious fanatic and to keep from religious topics when talking to you. A letter I had a short time ago from a friend there says he was in a fair way to commit suicide due to failing in an exam for the third time."

I have listened to many other bizarre life-stories told by women in the Groups.

"Kitty" was a picturesque figure as she road hatless and erect along the streets of Oxford, her bicycle in tow of her pet carrier, lively and vivacious as herself; a happy undergraduate at whom nearly every passing youth darted an admiring glance. "Kitty's" story is as vivacious as herself. It was not until her third year at Oxford that she came into touch with the Groups, in 1930.

"For nine terms," she says, "I had been free from thought restricting influence of a quiet home in the north of England, living merely from day to day, restlessly rushing from one pleasure to another, one trying everything once, one of spending my time with gangs with the care-free, idle undergraduates, in a ceaseless round of gay parties. I was drugging myself with continual cigarettes, drinking far too much, keeping far too late hours. My academic work was practically nil.

"I took no part in the social life of my college, where I was cordially detested, taking most of my meals out, and preferring the society of my men friends to that of the women students. And the men I chose to associate with were a tough crowd. Some of the cocktail parties to which they took me were pretty bad. Flattered by the attentions they paid me, I lived their pace, and rapidly became notorious. By the time I met the Groups I was well on the way to the dogs.

"What first attracted me about the Groups was the peace and happiness I saw in the faces of the people I met. Peace was unknown in my life at that time -- to me it stood for dullness and boredom. I got my happiness by living at top speed, with a maximum of movement, and it startled and fascinated me to find these people obviously enjoying peace. And when I was with them something of that peace seemed to enter me, and I had a foretaste of what the life in Christ could be.

"But the pull of the old ways was strong, and it was nine months after my first experience of the Group before I made a surrender to Jesus Christ. The change which followed was extraordinary. I was able to break with the old habits. I no longer had the restless craving for excitement which had dragged me from one thrill to another -- instead I had a peace which was anything but dull. It brought with it abundant life, a life packed with incident and glamour, a life given over to God for the fulfillment of His purpose.

"Since then I have been living in Oxford, among all my old haunts, with the old cronies within reach, but the new life God has given me so far surpasses the old, and the power of Christ has been so strong that nothing has availed to turn me back from the path in which He has set my feet."

At Oxford I ran into a remarkable lady from South Africa who has developed a wonderful flair for life-changing. Jesse Sheffield is the daughter of a pioneer South African statesman, Sir John Fraser. Brought up in the Orthodox manner -- Church, Sunday School, family prayers in plenty -- religion became a frightful bugbear to her. She had a horrible fear of God. Jesus Christ was a myth.

She started married life with tremendous illusions, only to discover that her husband and she were so much alike they could not hope to agree. She drank deeply the cup of pleasure. She controlled large tea-rooms in Johannesburg which became famed throughout south Africa. By her business ability they were raised from insignificance to great success. Her husband and she parted. When on a visit to England, she went to a church in St. John's Wood. The sermon convinced her she was losing the reality of life, and she began her search for God. She felt there was nobody with whom she could share need. She went home, and was a professional violin-player in a cinema when the Group arrived. At that time she was down and out physically, mentally, spiritually, completely disillusioned, thinking there was nothing in life. Then Garrett and Nan Stearly came to stay with her. She saw in their lives a quality she never thought to see on earth, and it occurred at her first house-party.

Jesse is now a modern miracle, and a modern miracle-worker.

One Group meeting I attended was at Mrs. Northcroft's in the fashionable medical quarter of London, where every house provides one or more distinguished specialists, with consulting-rooms. There have been many miracles of medicine in Harley Street, but apparently other miracles, nonetheless real and startling, have also been happening quietly in this street of professional respectability during the past eighteen months -- miracles in which doctors as well as other professional men and women have figured privately as patients instead of professionally as specialists.

Quite a sensation was caused at one of these meetings by a Jewess, who told a simple, straightforward story of her conversion to Christianity through the influence of the Oxford Group. There was good-humored laughter as she described some of her special weaknesses, including ungovernable temper. In her tantrums she would throw books about the room and be generally unpleasant to everyone. "A veritable whole-hogger," her friends declared. She naïvely admitted that her decision to attend a Group house-party, on the invitation of a college friend whose room she shared, was only taken because she wished to demonstrate her ability to drive a new car. At this remarkable house-party -- it was in South Africa -- she heard educated Christians sharing their experiences, and began to feel very uncomfortable about her own life, though she still refused to follow their example during the next six months.

Pride was her chief trouble, and fear of friends' opinions. Ultimately, she yielded pride and fear and herself, and next day obtained great joy through a definite experience of the Holy Spirit. Her Pentecost!

A woman artist then told an interesting story of a miraculous life-change which she had experienced. She described her unsatisfactory search for lasting enjoyment in studios, in literature, in art galleries, in sport. Sometimes she enjoyed herself very much. Yet always, at the end, a terrible aching feeling of "What is it all for?" and the old longing of something eternally elusive which she later discovered to be just peace through freedom from sin and the indwelling presence of the Holy Spirit.

The visit to an Oxford Group house-party was undertaken partly as a joke; certainly she did not put peas in her shoes and go there with the mentality of the old-time pilgrim. She was embarrassed to hear talks on sin at the house-party. She felt very annoyed about this, while very miserable. Anyway, what business had they to talk about her sins? What about their own? Furthermore, she was an artist. To be a good artist she must see all sides of life -- live life as everybody lived it. Otherwise how could she express herself through her art? The principles of the Group were all very well for other people; but not for her special case. Then light came. She saw she must be honest with herself, willing to make her life conform to the pattern of the New Testament, and discovered Christ's Spirit could help her express herself through art, while sin no longer had dominion over her.

Many other simple convincing life-stories by educated, unemotional though happy people; most of them young, all of them ready to testify to an attitude of Christian experience through readiness to surrender their own wills to God's Will. And all told openly in a Harley Street drawing-room in an age of frank materialism and cynical unbelief.

Each week more miracles. New testimonies by new visitors to changed lives. Young men and young women, middle-aged men and women, the last word in modern culture, some bearing well-known names, country folk, professional men, stenographers, students, foreigners, all meeting together in perfect fellowship with no class distinctions, because all sought to live, and be led, by the Holy Spirit of God.

Chapter Eighteen

THAT KNOTTY MARRIAGE PROBLEM

The genius of the Oxford Group movement is that it seems to get at the fundamental problem in every life and offers the real cure. It does not profess to cure human bodies, although human bodies have been cured through the Group message. But it gets at the root cause of the disordered life, removes it and then joyfully observes that life straightening out into happy contentment irrespective of the size or character of the problem.

Of course, the real solution to the marriage problem is the guided engagement. The Group believes that falling in love is not one of man's rights, but one of God's privileges, that where He allows, it spells happiness. Where He does not approve, it is a fatal mistake. God has his choice for a man. To marry another is to look for trouble. But most people to-day marry on any and every other basis than God's will -- affinity, proximity, femininity, personality, affability, sociability, financial ability, and almost every other ability on God's earth. And they find trouble waiting just around the corner.

I asked one happily married man in the Group: "How did you happen to marry Anne?"

"Guidance," was the answer.

This was a new one for me. I knew we had gotten beyond the stage where parents decided the question for their offspring. But my idea of pre-nuptial bliss was catch-as-catch-can.

"You mean you fell in love, and then God told you to go ahead?"

"No, there was more to it than that. I had known Anne for some time," he explained. "I knew she was the kind of person I wanted to marry. But one day during a Quiet Time on a railway these thoughts came to me: 'Would you like to marry Anne?' 'Yes,' I answered, 'if you think it's all right.' 'Well, then, why don't you go ahead and try?' came the clear but whimsical answer. I made up my mind I would. But before I committed myself I checked with my friends, as people in the Group are wisely accustomed to do. Their guidance confirmed my own. Take the chance, and see what comes of it. I did . . . We were engaged before the week was out, and it has been glorious ever since."

That is the Group secret of marriage, where romance never fades.

One of the most tragic problems the Group encountered, and one now being smoothed out, is that of a woman graduate who fell in love with her future husband when he was studying for the Church. It was a love-match, but something happened during their married life to produce what became an insoluble problem. The woman accepted his offer of marriage while he was studying for the Church on condition that she continue her profession as a doctor, for which she had a great natural aptitude and love.

It was several years before she agreed to marry, fearing that children and the duties of a clergyman's wife would prevent her carrying on. He silenced her fears by saying he would engage a housekeeper.

They married and the husband made no attempt to interfere with her work until he became a clergyman. By now she had successfully developed a flair for children's diseases, and then established herself as *the* specialist in the city where she practiced. Her husband was appointed to a church in the same city and, being an eloquent preacher, became as well known and successful in his own sphere as she was in hers. Then trouble began. Undoubtedly the preacher became jealous of his wife's professional fame, as some husbands are apt to be, as some wives are apt sometimes to be jealous of their husband's success. The congregation grew, and the clergyman wished his wife to do some entertaining and to take over the usual duties of a clergyman's wife, which she did to prevent a scandal in the Church.

He failed to fulfill the promise of providing the help of a housekeeper. Naturally the wife began to fret over the situation. She tried to carry on, though the work was becoming too much; but as there were no children for some years, she did manage.

During the next seven years four children arrived, rather too close together for the comfort of her home. Their coming definitely ended her practice as a doctor. She thought over her situation, and decided to face her duty as a wife and mother and put it before her opportunity as the best children's specialist in the city. Then she tried to talk over her great renunciation with her husband, not so much for help, but for sympathy and a loving understanding of her situation. Here he failed her utterly, jumping to the conclusion that she preferred her career and wanted to break away from him. About this time a girl was born.

Her husband's inability to give her the sympathy she needed in her most crucial moment preyed on her mind. She did her duty for another sixteen years, striving not to think of the sacrifice she had made, but brooding on his failure to supply the sympathy she craved. Those around her had not the faintest idea of the struggle that was going on in her own mind, though she had been such a great loss to her profession. Her husband had now developed into a power in the city. She supported him in every way, for the two were very much sought after. Then he died -- suddenly!

After the funeral it was discovered that he had made investments not only of his savings, but also of her money, which, under the law at that time, he had a perfect right to do, though there was no moral sanction. So she held no resentment about that. At the time her eldest child was just about finishing law school and the youngest was in kindergarten. She had to do something to maintain them. Her mind flew back to her old work. She began to make inquiries, and discovered that medicine had progressed so far that she was now hopelessly behind the times, and inadequate for the work, although her degree still held good.

She did what she could, taking any opening that was offered. She was at one time a nurse in a doctor's office, a medical assistant in a nursery; she took in borders; she had a wonderful voice and sang in public. Though resourceful and energetic, she was increasingly unhappy. She became an automatic worker, always doing something in her own house; and all the time there was the remembrance -- her husband had blocked her own career, refused her sympathy, and wasted her talents on common jobs. A very natural frame of mind for the best of persons to be in after such an experience of matrimonial joys. But these thoughts, traveling ceaselessly along one line of nerve energy, were making a fissure in the track which could only be repaired when the thoughts were excluded.

Then, through the Group, God loomed as a reality. She had many talks with one of the women leaders -- Olive Jones. She said that before her husband died she had lost all her faith and was going through the forms of religion with no conviction. She began to pray and ask God's help. She was afraid of going insane through all her troubles. It took the kindly Group leader a long time to get her to the place where she was prepared to surrender her terrible and natural resentment against her husband, which was eating into her brain and destroying the working of her mental processes through too long concentration on one subject. Finally she made the complete surrender of that old resentment. She told the whole story to her son, who joined her in the new life of release that came.

After she had realized that her great sin was un-forgiveness, she began to think of restitution, which was now impossible. There was now danger of this, too, getting on her mind, for she felt at first that she had committed an unpardonable sin. Perhaps her attitude of mind had caused her husband's death. But the Group leader, quoting help previously obtained from Frank, said that since she would have been willing to make restitution if she could, then to continue in remorse was hopelessly wrong and itself a sin. Her brain is now becoming normal again, through the release from her old resentment.

In the foregoing story God's will was only sought, and so the solution was only reached, after the husband's death. In the story that follows it was reached much earlier. Here the woman was only a law student when she gave up her studies to marry a professional man. She was extraordinarily ignorant of the facts of marriage. She developed an overwhelming hatred of everything to do with sex. Yet she gave birth to nearly a dozen children.

There was no respite. Two years was the longest space dividing one from the next. Before the youngest child was born, her husband began to be called to duties away from home, and she naturally found herself praying for more periods of such loneliness. Her experiences reacted on her nerves, her temper and her character, and she became well-known as a disagreeable person. But everybody was sorry for him. She hated her life and had thoughts of suicide. Two or three times her health broke down and she was in a nursing-home for nervous prostration. Several times she tried to talk to her husband, but only succeeded in hurting him, for he was very much in love with her.

As the children grew older, she realized she could not bring them up in that atmosphere. She joined women's organizations and became interested in welfare work. Then she met someone who knew her as a girl interested in law, who advised her to study again. She did so for several years without her husband's knowledge. All her old thirst and hunger for professional work came back. Presently she told her husband that she had decided to be a lawyer. He said she must be insane and unfit to be a mother. If she continued with such a purpose he would take her children away from her. . . . So she gave up the idea for a while, and the home life became worse. The husband continued his own professional work.

Trouble came in adolescence with some of the children. The

mother had another breakdown. The doctors told her husband the wife must be allowed to go ahead with anything that would give her relief from her mental troubles, or she would become insane. He grudgingly consented. Then the Group leader came into a gloomy picture. Her husband received an invitation to a house-party and was intrigued, but rather scornful at first. He thought it was a new and possibly competitive form of religion.

He told his wife about the house-party, and she became curious and went. She asked one of the speakers to talk with her, and he introduced her to a leader, who had already had a similar experience. They had a long Quiet Time together, and it came to the wife that she must just share the whole story with her husband . . .a terrible painful performance and a great shock to the man who had not understood until then. It ended in both offering their lives to God, and they are rebuilding their home on understanding lines of simple Sharing. The wife has become a lawyer, and is practicing law with the whole-hearted assistance of her husband.

But what of people who marry when madly in love and fall out of it, developing more and more incompatibility as their lives unfold? Here is the example and the answer in her own words:

"My husband was an airman in France when we married. We saw each other at intervals during the War, and those intervals were naturally not spent in arguing and petty quarrels when death walked side by side with us. We each gave all our love to the other without criticism or blame, and each was everything to the other, and God was way in the background, existing for us as a benevolent Father Christmas who had to be constantly reminded of presents due and rushed to for assistance when we spilt the milk. Our real Gods were each other and ourselves.

After the War, with a husband reduced to 'C 3' with nerves and strain -- and a nervous baby girl and no houses obtainable -- there was more need for bravery and no glamour in being brave. It was very much harder to realize the illness of a person whose nerves have collapsed than it is to realize his bad temper, irritability, lack of control, and constant depression. Our Godless love did not stand the strain, and after two years studying farming, and an outdoor life in South Africa, my husband's nerves were strong again and mine had collapsed. Now I became resentful and self-loving, full of good purpose and bad thoughts, devoting myself to my family from pride in doing my duty. There was, however, little love for anyone but myself. I was full of self-pity for my illness and for the lack of what I considered the proper appreciation of my sterling qualities. I was ill, and in this state for the next seven years. I had an ungoverned temper with those under my authority, punishing the children severely for a small fault when the servant whom I could not afford to lose had angered me.

"My husband and I kept up a successful pretense of affection to the outside world, but we had no unity of soul or mind. To get away from this mental disharmony, we filled our free time with entertainment and visits to friends. If we had an evening together at home, I felt it was too good an opportunity to miss for telling my husband how unsuccessful I was, how misunderstood, and how badly he disappointed me, with well-illustrated instances and occasions. I grieved that our evenings at home were never happy. I always felt I kept a brave heart under my trials and never showed my real feelings. Of course, I could not smile much and usually wore an expression of disappointment. It was a great grief to me that I should be so ill-used and misunderstood when I was always doing things for others (and hating them) and when I was always in the right, too!

"Life was without future or hope, with no religion in our home. I could only feel I must carry on my brave fight and I should be appreciated in Heaven, and Jack would see how good I was. But I felt it was a losing fight, and told my husband that I should have to leave him when I was forty. I had decided that the rest of my life should be spent in the slums, working for the poor, where I might be appreciated.

"At a friend's suggestion, my husband and I went to hear the Oxford Group. We heard Frank and many others. We were frankly critical, and I got into 'low gear' to take it all in. Jack got into 'top,' and in three days had shared honestly his old life with one of the leaders of the Group and given his all to Christ. I was rather put out. With all my belief in God, I expected to get there first! But when my husband shared all his life with me, telling me all he had kept from me, I felt I must do the same, and I had more to tell than he and more to be forgiven. We left the old selves behind and surrendered all we possessed to Him who gave it to us. Our love for each other was renewed and deepened.

"We began to keep Quiet Times with God each morning on waking, and taught our two children to do the same. We asked God for Guidance and prayed for strength to carry out that Guidance.

"We began to treat our children with honesty and openness -- saying we were sorry for any unwarranted irritation and bad temper, and encouraging them to speak openly with us. The result was that when we shared sorrow for irritation, they shared sorrows for causing it.

"One morning my small son rushed into my room saying: 'I want to share; I've been reading instead of having my bath, and I'll have it now and be very quick -- I am sharing it with you now so you won't get cross and have to share that you are sorry.'

"I shared the difficulties I had experienced when I was a little girl with my small girl, and she shared things, told in an ugly way, that I had no idea she knew, and I was able to give her a new and happier picture of life. The result was that instead of her usual reserve, she showed an outpouring of love and affection to her Dad and to me that she had never shown before."

One of the happiest married men I know is Ken Twitchell. He gave me this recipe, which deserves to be in every home:

"The most disillusioned crowd is the younger married set. I believe their disillusionment is so great because they had hoped for so much from marriage, and found so little. Two people meet. They fall in love. They marry and look forward to blissful happiness. They believe their personal love is strong enough to bind them together in unity forever. But after a bit, sometimes even on the wedding trip, a mood of disappointment settles down. Nothing is said. Both make up their minds that it is just getting used to marriage. That 'married look' begins to appear.

"Many things lie behind it. Human love expects to give, but it expects to get as well. When it fails to get what it expects, it is hurt, and ceases to give with its first gracious glow. We have ideas and hopes for the other person which we have not yet surrendered to Christ. We rather cling on to them and demand them. We expect a certain sympathy, a lightness of touch, a marital tonic, a romantic quality. We expect a combination of Sir Galahad and Prince Charming. We are hurt that it is not forthcoming.

"Another difficulty turns up when we find that in marriage there is the problem of adjusting, conflicting human wills. 'I want this.' She wants that. Two difficulties often arise. One person superimposes his will on the other. He, or she, is a slightly more dominant person. And so he, or she, takes life and initiative out of the other persons hands. What happens? We all know the family where one person always must buy the tickets and arrange the plans, where father lays down the law, or voices a 'final opinion' at the dinnertable. The rest relapse into moody silence.

"But that is not the end. Tears, nerves, resentments, with their real cause unrealized, begin to appear. There is bred a sense of injustice, of rights being disregarded. It is the atmosphere that makes the children determined to leave home as soon as they are able. And not only that, but it isolates the dominating person and leaves him in a ghastly loneliness.

"For there is the other side of the picture -- the submerged personality. It is just as much a sin to give away to a dominating personality as it is to dominate. It is a sin to have a martyr complex, always to give in and let the other rule, excusing it by saying, 'But, you see, he's my husband.' Or, 'You see, she's my wife.' Usually it's done because it is easier. Yet not the other person's will, but God's Will must come first.

"The answer for this conflict of wills is to find a third will in which both can agree with enthusiasm. That third will is God's Will. Sin in marriage is often simply failure to find God's Will and to persist in a human giving or taking. Guided living is the answer.

"Another source of disaster is possessiveness in marriage: wanting the other person for what that person can mean to ourselves. Such possessiveness results in jealousy of outside interests, or other people, who may threaten to rob us of the undivided attention of the person we want for ourselves. We need to surrender our husband or our wife. The other person cannot be first. Jesus Christ must be first. On that basis jealousy and fear disappear, resentment of intruders in the guise of work or friends of either sex melts away.

"Human love fails because in the last resort we cannot really give ourselves to another human person. Where love burns strongly it passionately craves to pour itself out for the other, to mingle its own life with the other.

"But no matter how deep its yearning, it finds itself chained within the walls of individuality. God has so fashioned us. The only person we can give ourselves completely to is Himself. To Him body, soul and spirit can be yielded in glad abandon. And human love finds its passionate yearning each to be lost in the other fulfilled when each is lost in God, and in Him finds the other. Only in the divine love that is born from above does human love find its consummation and its utmost bliss.

"Vital Christianity has the real answer for marriage. It is Christ the Lord of the Household. He must enter into every relationship. On this basis the first romance and idealism of an engagement are retained. They are not an illusion of the past, but a reality maintained only on that high level of marriage as regarded as a team of two living for Christ. Marriage must always turn outwards into the lives of others, seeking to lead them to the same joy. It is a sacrament that must always be shared.

"This team-work for Christ demands an open transparency between husband and wife, with no hidden reservations about each other. Most people are lone wolves by nature, and they need a regular time of Sharing each day, when all the silly little irritations, the jealousies, the suspicions which skim away the cream from matrimony.

"In this kind of team-work the stronger develops the weaker, each holds the other to the highest. We make the other a leader. We don't decide for the other person: we let him or her decide. The stronger may be able to do the job better, but it may be God's Will to develop the weaker by giving him or her the opportunity. This requires a daily patience and self-sacrifice. It requires knowing when to be silent, when not to bring up problems, when to laugh the other person out of problems.

Of course, there is the physical relationship. Most divorce court cases begin in the failure to find a guided adjustment here. There is need for construction and preparation, for knowledge of the facts. We must explode the fallacy that marriage is the end of all physical problems. It is meant to be a spiritual unity of which the physical is the symbol. There is always the danger of the physical becoming paramount -- an end sought for its own sake. But the physical relationship is a sacrament. Someone once said that the acid test of love is that sacrament with unimpaired reverence for each other.

"God-control is the best birth-control. Here in God-control is found an over-ruling power that lifts human passion into its perfect consummation.

"So long as people marry for trivial reasons" (concludes Ken Twitchell) "they will be divorced for trivial reasons. But those whom God has joined are caught up in the divine love, where human love finds its glorious fulfillment."

Chapter Nineteen

AN OXFORD PSYCHOLOGIST SPEAKS

During my travels with the Oxford Group, weighing carefully and critically what was said, watching carefully and critically what was done, I was often wondering what was the real opinions of Senior Oxford (faculty and administration) on this remarkable movement spreading outwards from their midst. As a journalist I felt confident in my estimation of its news value. I felt, too, that I could appraise the movement spiritually with the spiritual; for I had sought and found God. But I was an amateur in the psychological and theological aspects of the message.

Therefore I decided to probe a well-known figure in Senior Oxford who is entitled to speak authoritatively on the Group Movement. He is Canon L. W. Grensted, one of the foremost scholars and psychologists in the Church of England, Oriel Professor of the Philosophy of the Christian Religion, the Bampton Lecturer of 1930, a member of the Archbishop's Committee on Doctrine and on Spiritual Healing, and Canon of Liverpool.

Canon Grensted has one of those flying, massive heads that we admire, while not eager for the burden of carrying it around. By-passed an enjoyable afternoon and evening catechizing him. It was a rich experience. The Professor has a fine, dry humour, a wry, sympathetic smile, a way of saying deep things with simple clearness, together with an engaging and boyish self-consciousness which takes occasional liberties with his great intellectuality. I asked some very pointed questions requiring a definite yea or nay, and he gave me the definite answers. Some of them he pondered over, but the Professor's mind is so large that it requires a lot of weighty evidence to incline it even slightly to one side.

I asked him why he had associated himself with the movement, and he replied that no Christian could stand aside and not be interested in it. At the start it was arousing unfair opposition, that irresistibly drew him towards it to see fair play.

"And what do you see in it?"

"An immense amount of hope for the whole spiritual life of the world. Without committing myself to any details -- only the principles -- I see plenty of the essential things that I need for my own spiritual life."

This was a very sweeping committal for a professor of philosophy.

"Are those in the Groups balanced and really sane?" I next asked him.

"The right answer to that," he said, "is that the leaders and those in responsible touch are undoubtedly balanced and sane. Moreover, some who have come into touch, who were obviously not so well balanced as they should have been, have become much better balanced. The people who move about in the teams do learn discretion and tact and trustworthiness. I suppose there are exceptions, as in the churches. But there are no more unbalanced persons in the movement than in the churches. In fact, not so many.

I had heard it suggested there were dangers in the movement. So I asked him bluntly: "*Is* the Oxford Group dangerous?"

"Oh, frightfully!" He spoke with irony. "It might upset the world, as Christianity did at first, for its possibilities are simply enormous. I find the greatest encouragement in its vitality. It shows a new and infinite power of adventure. It is a real inspiration to see this new creative work, suggesting to us once more those stirring stories in the Act's of the Apostles."

That was all very well. But rash things might be said at the meetings which would spoil the movement. When young folk of culture get up and witness, they know what to say and what to leave out. But when this movement becomes general and the unlettered begin to witness frankly in the Groups -- "Suppose they blurt out something shocking."

The massive head wagged humorously.

"And suppose they do? It wouldn't do much harm. For the fact is you can say anything you like that's true, provided you say it carefully and in the right way. And don't forget that human problems are being shared all the time in a great many places.

"A mother's welfare meeting would positively shock a Group meeting. So would much of the talk in modern drawing-rooms. A meeting of a Vigilance Committee is much more explicit. In the Press and in many public places problems are openly discussed *without the answers to them being supplied. There* is the danger. The Group touches lightly upon the problems and stresses the answers. It is always the answer that matters.

"Moreover, there is a Group check in team-work. As a rule, people don't share frequently in public until they have shared privately with the team. And in practice unlettered -- if there are any left -- are just as tactful as the highly educated in their public utterances. All classes have joined in the Sharing practiced by the Group. I know of homes where the maids are helping in Group leadership. In the factories of St. Helen's, Lancashire, there are Group meetings every day for Quiet and Sharing. And these are working with the same success that attends Groups run by University men."

I butted in:

"Yet things may be said which will be misunderstood. The scoffing mind is always alert."

The Professor was not sure that ridicule mattered very much at all, as it was based on misunderstanding. What mattered far more was the danger of not Sharing. The life shut in on itself fell into disaster. The danger of Sharing could never be so great as the danger of bottling up. This led to all kinds of tragedies -- including suicide and murder. As there were many recent examples.

"Sharing is a positive good," emphasized that Professor. "It is the real answer to so many problems. For it is almost impossible for a person to see his real problems straight unless he has an outside view on them, and he can only get that by Sharing. And weather done in a movement like this or elsewhere -- and Sharing is not confined to the Oxford Group -- it must be beneficial. Sharing has been neglected far too much by the modern Church. But," he broke off, "there is a long theological history behind that statement. And we are now in a phase which great reticence is general. That was not always so. There were times when so much effort was committed in the opposite direction that the regularization of the ministry became necessary. Though we haven't gotten anywhere near to that in the Group, and I don't think there is any possibility of our doing so."

"When might we reach that stage -- if ever?"

"Only when a wide range of people come to be unbalanced emotionally, as happened in revivals of a certain type whose basis was emotion, and not the new birth through a changed will. Of course, any sudden change must have an emotional effect, the consequence of a re-grouping of impulses. We explain it in this way. When the ego makes a response to anything to which it can respond, that response is the will -- the self in action. The emotion arises with a response. What takes place is really the formation of a new sentiment, of which the best example is the sentiment of love. There is then a whole new readjustment of impulses, now turned into the service of a new object. Changed sentiment around personal relations or the love of God cannot possibly happen without some emotion. The really serious thing is that people so seldom feel any emotion about the love of God, as they do about other mundane sentiments like their breakfast, fresh air, their dog, their car, their position in life, their being highly respectable -- which fits in with saying their prayers and church-going, but not necessarily with putting God first. Then when something like the Group comes along and suggests that God be put first, in the right place, and people find their disordered sentiments threatened -- God first -- they naturally begin to feel annoyed."

"But can the tenets of the Oxford Group be said to answer every human problem?"

The Professor weighed this sweeping question carefully. "I do think," he said, "that the general principles of the Group are generally applicable. There are certain persons who need specialized help, and there is serious danger if anybody thought this teaching could work by rule of thumb. And so the Group train leaders who can deal with difficult people, just as is done elsewhere. The Group can change men. They know that if you try to solve a conflict by effort from within, you never solve it. But if you try to solve it by a higher Power from without you always solve it, though the solution may not necessarily be what you or others expect."

"Then what is the real difference in movement?"

"It is positive and all essential," replied the Professor. "It has so many modern books which ventilate the difficulties of the times. Why should I write futile, emotional, impatient books unless you can offer a cure? In a local movement of this kind you see something being done, and if the Churches are not taking the lead, the duty of the movement is not to criticize, but to awaken them by action. As it is doing."

"What about the effect of the movement on scholarship?"

"There is always the danger that a certain type of man may become obsessed with religious work. Team-work is again the proper check. But, so far as I can see, the scholarship results are entirely to the good."

One of the points stressed by the Group, which often sends men sorrowfully away, is Restitution. I asked the Canon what he had to say on this prickly point.

"Restitution," he said with emphasis, "should only be made under guidance with a view to helping the people concerned. Don't make restitution for your own amusement. There are people in the world who are spiritual Pharisees, making restitution for the sake of working off an emotional complex. I have heard of men going around confessing they had committed murders which had never been committed. Which is absurd. In a Group a man may ask guidance from other members of the team, but in principle he must himself decide. The old books on casuistry are full on debatable cases of restitution. The man who through the Groups gave himself up recently to that Oxford police because he had committed a number of thefts, undoubtedly did the right thing. The rule in these matters of difficulty is to get at the real motive. And there must always be a willingness to make restitution; though some kinds of restitution cannot be made. Being hanged for murder isn't restitution. You don't restore the life. A Bishop has recently been perplexed, he tells me, because somebody has written to him from South Africa, following contact with the Groups, to restore something stolen. But the Bishop has not been able to estimate what was taken or to give the inquirer correct leading as to what he should restore. Nevertheless, the Bible teaches restitution. The Church teaches restitution. And restitution should be made whenever possible with a view to helping the persons concerned."

I knew that the Canon, like the Bishop of Leicester and the Bishop of Hankow, and the other Church dignitaries, His own guidance-book, a practice often criticized by those outside.

"Is note-book guidance an advance on memory-guidance?" I asked Canon, expecting him to be a little gun-shy.

But he was prepared stoutly to defend the practice.

"I find that carrying a guidance-book saves a tremendous amount of time, for it fixes a great many fugitive ideas, some of which may be genuine guidance and may be lost if they go unrecorded. Unless you take all means of securing what comes into your mind when trying to get guidance, all the resistances there are in human nature will rise up and block the most important things," he warned. "Behind that lies an important psychological principle. Forgetting is actually necessary to ordered thinking. We forget irrelevant or unwanted things so that all we know shall not crowd into our consciousness and interfere with the direct line of our thinking upon the matter in mind at the moment. Forgetting is a positive help to thinking clearly and acting straight. If we remembered everything, our lives would be just a muddle.

"When guidance comes, it may be distasteful or even dangerous to our self-esteem, and so would be thrust on one side by forgetfulness unless we take steps to prevent it. For a long time I had felt I should give up smoking, which was not good for me, but I shouldn't have done it unless I had written it down in guidance. Hitherto I had just forgotten it or shelved it. Smoking is a habit in itself neither good nor bad, but for my own life I found the discipline of not smoking carried with it a piece of God's grace large enough to give me victory over much more deeply ingrained habits of self-indulgence. And this I believe has been the experience of many men in the Groups. I'm not saying that everybody should give up smoking. Of course, also, it may be carried to excess and become physically injurious and wasteful of the money we hold in stewardship. Each person must do what he honestly feels God tells him."

The massive head inclined towards me as we probed deeper in the matter of guidance.

"Of course, nobody pretends that all of one's thoughts are guidance. There is no knack about it. Guidance often comes in the form of good impulses -- the work of the Holy Spirit in human life. I get strong and certain guidance about some things, and then some guidance which is not so clear. Often I get guidance on how best to handle people who come to me for advice who are in trouble. Yet the guidance that comes to one person is not very different from what comes to anyone else. It is simple and elemental. If one compared guidance-books, there would not be much difference, save that each contains things applicable to the person who wrote it for the time it was written.

Guidance is often getting a new sanction for what we know already. Once it came to me to take a certain text, 'Go into the City and it it shall be shown you what you must do' -- a text I had no wish to preach on, but I did, and three persons came to me afterwards to thank me for the special help which they had received. I often get guidance to speak on a subject that I have not prepared and I abandoned the prepared subject. I always follow such guidance. A great advantage of guidance is that with it you have to make only one decision on one subject, whereas otherwise you might make twenty. For a while guidance may differ in a group of several persons, but eventually it is clearly shown that no real duties in life conflict. Which shows that the leading is part of a plan of God."

The Canon continued: "I was once worrying as to which I should do: go on a long journey by car or by train. After a long time wasted in weighing the pros and cons, guidance came suddenly through with the message: 'Don't be a fool, go by car.' If I had trusted my guidance instead of my reasoning powers, I should have been told not to be a fool much earlier."

The Canon was convinced that willingness to do the Will of God was the measure of a man's true understanding of His Will, and that in team life could be found dependable confirmation or correction of individual guidance. A unified Group of surrendered people would be more sensitive to the Spirits full plan than would the individual.

I thought of those occasionally luminous flashes that had come to me in various parts of the world at various times.

"Do you get both guidance and super-guidance?" I asked him.

He shook his head. While not discrediting my experience of super-guidance, the Canon could not claim luminous flashes of outstanding intensity.

"You think everybody needs this guidance?"

"Unquestionably. Especially those who ascend in the world. As men climb to more important jobs, they find the difficulty of preserving a sense of proportion becomes far greater. By constantly referring their work back to God, it does put them into proportion for all sorts of situations, and helps them to add just the difficulties of others. One does not like to make claims for oneself, but in so far as I have been able to make spiritual progress, it has been largely through the insight which has come from these Quiet Times of listening to God. More marked, perhaps in my case has been the progress that has followed through little definite acts of decision for Christ. Some of these things have been very small, with not much meaning to them except that they have meant a personal loyalty. When those little impulses came, they knew they meant definite landmarks (what the Group calls driving in stakes)."

I was pressing the Bampton Lecturer to tell me more of what his association with the Group had meant to his own spiritual life when Frank observed that Canon Grensted was already a prepared instrument when they met. Their association had heightened and deepened the spiritual experience of both. Without Canon Grensted's insight and knowledge, the Group might have encountered great misunderstandings, which would have seriously prejudiced progress when difficulties presented themselves. He was a sure guide, and brought a wealth of experience that matched what was the best in the Groups.

"It wouldn't be true for me to say," said the Canon, "that I owe anything like my whole religious experience to the Oxford Group, for most of it was lived before I came into touch with them. But I have seen the help and power that has come into other people's lives through the Group and the great possibilities which may come from Sharing, although I have not progressed very far myself in that direction.

"But the things relevant are these. I came to know the movement here seven years ago. In those days the difficulty of knowing men and of doing real work as a College Chaplain, as opposed to my office job, were the things that worried me. I knew that people needed help, but I could rarely get near them, for I didn't know how it was to be done. My contact with the Group has multiplied many times over my contacts with individuals whom I had been seeing through the Group on things that matter to them. Until then they had not come to me, because I wasn't getting that note in my preaching which made them want to talk to me. Of course, I had gotten a certain amount of interest before, but that has been a great deal heightened and deepened by these past seven years.

"What I have now come to see is that the keynote of preaching is in something personally felt and experienced, and that the moment it becomes official it is dead. This does not mean that theology is untrue, but that it has no life unless it is related to personal experience. This new impulse of personal experience in preaching came to me from contact with the Group. My sermons may not be so good as before, but they seem to produce more results.

"I remember preaching one under guidance at the last house-party in Mansfield College of which this distich was the theme:

Watching God's terrible and fiery finger, Shrivel a falsehood from the Souls of Men.

In that sermon I was thinking of the tremendous majesty of God at work not only in the Group, but everywhere."

Wondering how many more words of wisdom I should be able to extract, I urged him on, and the Canon continued:

"More and more I am coming to realize the impossibility of there being any finality in one's religious development. The idea that at any one point in life one knows the whole gospel and is ready to preach it seems pitifully inadequate. Trying to work with the Group, I find myself continually being brought back to simple religious experience -- often to the simple religious experience I was missing because I was getting too sophisticated. In my early Group experience I missed a lot because I was too much the Court of Appeal. When I ceased to be that and worked with a small team I found quite a new experience. It brought home the importance of ordinary and simple things. I found that I was getting friendship and fellowship with a degree of naturalness and sincerity I had seldom found elsewhere."

One of the other Group leaders told me that he had seen a meeting of ministers dissolving into a meeting of men just because the Canon had shared his own true experiences. In actual fact, crows *are* black the whole world over.

"Again and again," the Canon went on, "I have seen the intense need of the clergy for that real freedom which Sharing can produce. The clergy is often very lonely, and a great many disastrous things occur in life because of loneliness."

The Oxford Group is enthusiastic over the new zest in life which the fellowship produces. With all barriers broken down there follows a naturalness, a trust, a freedom, an abandonement, which is neither offensive nor presumptuous. I asked the Canon about this. He, too, was enthusiastic:

"The fellowship provided by the team helps you to face the world and bear the world," he said. Nothing but God can help you to read and understand the Oxford Group at St. Helens, where I observed a real world -- not the unreal world of the newspapers -- placed before the people. Only Christ can enable one to see the real world. Only Christ can produce this kind of fellowship which is part of it. As Canon of Liverpool I invited eight vitalized youngsters to come up from Oxford to confer with some of the clergy as to the possibility of the work. The sample team we met with there was a little group that developed certain interesting contacts. We had with us John Watt of Edinburgh -- a highly converted Parson -- who was perfectly admirable. The others, with one exception, were about to be ordained in the Church of England. Preparatory work having been done at Liverpool by Basil Yates, a recent convert, who once thought he was an agnostic, but was perhaps mistaken. While a lecturer in philosophy he had become an enthusiast for the Group. He and I (and some of the others) had had doubts of one another. At our first Quiet Time we said so, and our difference of outlook simply disappeared. The team was welded into unity in a matter of minutes. We had the guidance we wanted. Good work was done and good preparation was made for the St. Helens mission which successfully followed.

"It was at this time I first began to take down notes of my own guidance, and it was this consistent note-taking by everybody that helped to cement the work of the team. And it was in Liverpool where my first piece of written guidance came -- that about stopping smoking. I may get guidance to start smoking again someday.

But I doubt it. None has come so far.

"The important thing about that sample team was that a body of people of different ages and outlook found they could work within a common purpose, not muddled by their emotions. The great difficulty in life is that we are all mixed up with so many purposes, not all Christian, and owe a kind of loyalty to a variety of people. But it was shown in our team that there is a possibility of personal relationship of a high and rare quality of which most people are unaware.

"Of course we work together in our ordinary life, but on much too low a level. We accept the people we meet as decent folk. We work with them and like them, and leave it at that. But it is not satisfactory. And our production is not satisfactory. Some people are left outside, while the work of the world as a whole is pretty badly done. The Oxford Group takes all comers, shows them how to live the highest life, knits them together in an efficient unity, and elevates them into a fellowship resembling the pattern made by Christ with the Twelve Apostles."

Canon Grensted now holds a regular Tuesday afternoon service for the Oxford Group in the University Church of St. Mary. It is purposely a simple service of worship, and is not confused with other elements -- practically a service of meditation, rest and quiet. There is very little preaching. The institution is important, as, for a good many people, it means the realization of worship in a life resting completely on God. The service is meeting the needs of the Group, by whom it is gratefully accepted.

Canon Grensted goes to St. Mary's some time before the service is to begin, for a time of Quiet. Usually there are some forty or fifty worshipers. They began with a hymn and remained standing for a brief silence. Then a passage of Scripture is read, followed by a ten-minute talk. Then the congregation sits or kneels, as they choose, for five minutes or more of silence. There follows another hymn, and then an act of worship of some kind. During most of the service -- and this is an important point -- the Canon turns his back to the people, to stress the impression that the whole service is directed towards God. All who attended speak of the quiet, refreshing quality of the service, which builds and sustains them for the work in hand and inspires them for greater work ahead.

Chapter Twenty

SPIRITUALIZED SCHOLARSHIP

The number of persons ready to back a promising religious venture is scarcely less than the number ready to support a racing certainty. And the motive which inspires the big crowd may be the same in each case -- "What can I get out of it?"

When there is no inducement of earthly gain apparent or underlying a new movement Godwards, we usually find "Not many wise, not many mighty, but the weak things of this world are chosen to confound the wise."

The why often stands aside not because there is nothing to gain, but because there is a lot to lose by identification with a new untested religious movement. Like Gamaliel, they are unwilling to oppose what may be a work of God, but also like him are unwilling to espouse it openly until confident of no prejudice to themselves through public identification. Believe in associating without affiliating -- appropriating the kudos and avoiding the kicks. They circle about the fringes of the Oxford Group enjoying the company of the people within, whom they like and admire to a point just short of emulation, but persist in addressing them as "You" instead of "We." Timid souls these, both clerical and lay; vacillating souls some, who may have previously been identified with movements from which the Spirit of God was absent, and profess a reluctance to take the wrong step again; some are convinced, but just afraid, fearing to "let go" and trust themselves to God because to them God is too small or too feeble to compensate for the surrender of cherished self-interest, some point of pride, social popularity, ridicule, or even a little as delicately administered persecution, common properties of the Cross in all ages.

There are scholars in Oxford of this order -- hesitating, waiting for the very new to become the very correct. But the chief complaint against scholarship at Oxford, like the complaint against scholarship elsewhere, is of its aloofness, even divorcement from life. When the Oxford Group began to make its first stirrings in the University it was not a new philosophy, but a new life. What would the theological dons say to it? Would scholarship identify itself with the new abundance Holy-Spirit-directed life that it proclaimed? In the days of the Wesleyan Revival, a don at one Oxford College said rather querulously that all his younger colleagues were no sooner elected than they proclaimed themselves Methodists.

One Sunday evening not so long ago the Chaplain of Corpus Christie -- an intellectual College -- unexpectedly revived the old Magdalen College custom in his own chapel in regard to the newly-formed Group Movement. He quietly in interpolated a few phrases into his sermon which caused very little immediate comments and were unreported in any newspaper the next morning. Nevertheless, they were startlingly significant, since they were made openly in the presence of both senior and junior members of the College, and therefore amounted to a formal public espousal of the new religious movement by an Oxford Don in the performance of his official duties.

Pausing in the main thread of his sermon, the Chaplain announced that he had been convicted of not being quite honest with his colleagues. Through fear of what they might think of him, he had withheld the declaration of his complete identification with the Oxford Group movement. He then mentioned his friendship with Frank, through whom he had come to a deeper experience of the Christian life than previously, and learned the necessity of absolute surrender to God as the directing force of his entire life. Thence he had come to understand that to reach a state where guidance was all in all he must be obedient all the time, in spirit before guidance was given, and act when it was received and through the entire process of fulfillment.

The setting of this little scene, which may live in the history of the Oxford Group movement, is worth visualizing. Corpus Christie College Chapel, hiding itself and its alliterative name in the far corner of the Front Quadrangle, might be described as "The Concealed Chapel of Oxford." The building is smallish, sixteenth century, with much find dark paneling obscuring some of the windows and darkening the friendly Gothic interior. There is a pulpit, but that is obsolete. The Chaplain preaches from the steps which is no hindrance, for he is tall, and does not use those sermon notes so embarrassingly difficult to hide. Of the immediate results from the Chaplain's announcement was a new release in his own life, conscious of more power in his work through surrender of his unwillingness to identify, and an interesting conversation with one of his own undergraduates. Nevertheless, the step he had taken that day was a forerunner of other acts of identification by Oxford Dons.

His own act was particularly significant, because one of the youngest members of the Theological Faculty had come into the open and officially identified himself for life with a new evangelism, then and still exercising the minds of many of the University. For the Chaplain of Corpus Christie was the Rev. Julian P. Thornton-Duesbery, a scholar with Three Firsts to his credit in the Oxford examinations -- "Mods," "Greats," and "Theology."

His kindly eyes of deep blue, quiet dignity of personality, and his great intellectual powers are the first points you observe about him, points reproduced from two wonderful parents who provided him with the ideal home life and upbringing. His father was a bishop -- the Bishop of Sodor and Man -- and his mother a gifted mission-worker in Manchester at the time they met. Both parents were consecrated to the life of Christ, and they constantly maintained the true Christian atmosphere about him, although, as he says, "I did not always realize what it meant."

Before becoming the Bishop of Sodor and Man, Julian's father had labored in Barrow-in-Furness, Islington, Leyton (where his principal parish work was done), and then in a fashionable church in Marylebone, London.

Growing up in this inspirational environment, Julian did not wait until his first encounter with the Group to answer the Master's call. "What I look upon as the decisive moment in my own conversion," he told me, "came at Keswick through Bishop Taylor-Smith, before I knew anything of the Oxford Group movement. And it came through the concrete dealing with the known fact of sin as focused in one particular sin of my own life. From my own powerlessness to overcome that sin I was led on to seek power from the Powerful One whom I knew only in theory as Jesus Christ. Of the divine validity of that experience I have no doubt. This decisive moment was followed by some authentic works of the rebirth -- the discovery of the Bible as a new book, a new experience of prayer, and the beginnings of a message for my friends. Both then, and still more afterwards, I had considerable intellectual acquaintance with soteriology. But it was not until nearly eight years later, during a Group house-party in Scotland, that a major realization of sin as a betrayal of divine love and trust in my ministry led me to the personal apprehension of what Christ had done on Calvary for me. . . . From which it would seem that you cannot hasten an act of God."

In amplifying what he meant by the regeneration which was made possible for him through the running work of Christ, and his view of surrender of self and God, the Chaplain of Corpus Christie gave me this, as a favorite quotation from E. F. Scott's *Kingdom of God and the New Testament:* ". . . It belongs to the essence of the message that everything depends on one great decision. The one necessary act is to surrender oneself to the will of God, and all else will follow of its own accord. The will that has become one with God's will can henceforth be trusted to take the right path in all those moral complexities which had to be carefully mapped out under the old law."

The future Chaplain of Corpus Christi had now learned that the cost to God of forgiveness, "the Cross planted in time on Calvary, and the Cross set for all eternity in His Heart, may or may not be realized by the penitent, but in any case the cry of the prodigal is answered by the Father, and when the door has been opened the Lord comes in to sup. We must trust Him by His Spirit to guide the new disciple into all truth in His own time and way."

He is confident that guidance comes whenever necessary, and that it must be followed without compromise and irrespective of personal desires. Presently he came to see how Christian experience often gives back what we think it may take away. His real desire in life at this time was to be a Don and teach the classics. He went back to his school and began to teach Latin and Greek, preparing to become a schoolmaster, returning to Wycliffe Hall to be ordained. There he was to be tried out before going back to his old school, but instead was asked to join the staff at Wycliffe Hall to teach theology only, and not his favorite classics. For some time he was undecided what to do, to return or stay, his inclination being to return to his school to teach classics, his wish to do the right thing irrespective of his desires. Unable to settle down to his work until a decision was reached, he wandered down the Woodstock Road praying for guidance, until he came to St. Phillip's and St. James' Church. His speed for this walk was typical of scholastic progress -- a mile an hour. He rolled and cogitated. Returning to his school meant running into temptations which were better avoided. That pay offered at the school was higher, but that did not matter. Then definite guidance came with sudden clearness that he must stay where he was and surrender his desire to be a Don and teach the classics. Sometime after this there followed the offer of a Fellowship and the Chaplaincy of Corpus Christi with tutorial work -- an offer which would not have come to him had he returned to his school.

As a University Don he found that contact with Frank had shown him how to teach a new evangelism which would satisfy both intellectuals and non-intellectuals. While not shirking a genuine intellectual difficulty, he knew how to get down to the needs of all, whether really intellectual or merely masked under the cloak of intellectual problems. "When teaching men who are going to be parsons," he told me, "I find that my association with the Group gives me an increasingly clearer vision of the relationship to life of my subject. All the time I am conscious that it is not mere scholarship, but the only possible life I am teaching. Of course, lots of persons discovered this before I did, and lots failed to discover it. But it is a discovery which everyone must make before he can be of a real use. And that is not involved in any belittling of real painstaking and exact scholarship, for the genius of Oxford education is a wide grasp of general principle combined with the discipline of exact attention to precise detail. The one real temptation of the college tutor is to think of pupils in terms of the grading they will achieve. While just as keen as ever that they get Firsts, and so reflect credit on the college and my teaching, I am able to look beyond and feel more concerned that after they have taken schools (final examinations) -- which is only the means to an end -- they shall be physically, mentally, spiritually whole when they get into their life-work: in fact, the complete man. Any man who passes through Oxford should leave equipped to face any problem that may turn up in his life, irrespective of where he lives and how. But it is only during the last three or four years that I have seen how to teach this all-round knowledge, and have realized how everyone gets up against personal problems, with many of which he is unable to deal through lack of training for their coming. Not that the Group exclusivity helps in these matters, for the Principle of Wycliffe Hall and some others I know see the same need, and give wise preparation for meeting personal problems."

The Chaplain of Corpus Christi caused quiet a stir at one of the public Group meetings in Oxford at the end of the Easter Term in 1932. Suddenly called to speak at this meeting, he announced that he was a parson and a Don, one of the class apostrophized by Mr. Belloc as "remote an effectual." After quoting the old lady who was pleased with her new minister because the learned man was six days invisible and the seventh in-comprehensible, he startled the assembly by saying that if one were a Don and a parson of that type he was at the same time two distinct kinds of parasite -- a phrase which enlarged into newspaper headlines the next day. He also stressed the necessity for a Don and a parson to justify his existence by results just in the same way that the member of any other calling justified himself by results, and declared that if, as a parson, he did not know he had the answer in Christ to every human problem, including one in Oxford that he had encountered a few days ago for which there was no human solution whatsoever -- he would resign his Fellowship and leave the University.

Another startling view that the Chaplain of Corpus recently expressed is likely to be rehearsed a good many times in the future. He is not convinced that the days of persecution for Christ's sake -- perhaps martyrdom -- are yet ended, even in the more enlightened countries, possibly in England. He expressed to me his feeling that Oxford was now in for a time of open war (perhaps with pens only) more than the city had experienced for a considerable span. Never had the Gulf between secularism and Christianity stretched so wide as at present in the University, now experiencing the full effects of the change of sixty years ago, when it was decreed that the Fellows need no longer be in Holy Orders. Though he was not anxious to see the old order reinstituted, he felt disquieted to observe that nowadays the Fellow who was in Holy Orders was the exception. "All the same," he said, "we have still many earnest Christians among the lay heads of Colleges, and whatever conflicts may lie ahead of us, I am convinced that Christianity at Oxford is stronger and more vital to-day than at any time in the last eighty years."

The association of a true scholar in touch with life and not swamped with scholarship, who is prepared publicly to maintain the implications of his own spiritual experience, means much for the new evangelism in Oxford. A young man under thirty, his remarkable lectures on the Christian doctrine of God are woven out in deep experience as well as from theory through deep thinking. Even though not all of his pupils follow his precepts, his "God-guided" life is an inspiration in the age when modern scholarship knows so little of the Holy Spirit from personal experience.

Julian Thornton-Duesbery has an unruffled composure himself for every occasion. To see him conduct a meeting of Senior Oxford, reply to comments, the subtle catch, the straightforward disavowal, in quiet, scholarly accents, laughing with his critic against himself as readily as turning the laugh, and to hear his own laughter, midway between a roar and a growl, is an entertainment. He has a quick and cherry answer for everyone, unerringly locating the exact spot.

Julian's work on Tuesday afternoons in training leaders has enabled the movement to expand at greater speed, and his Bible-study classes at house-parties have been invaluable. It was largely through him (supplementing the work of pioneers already on the field), when traveling with a party of students from Wycliffe Hall last year, that the work opened in Egypt, Palestine, and the Near East.

"Fellowship with Group," he says, "has kept the highest steadily before my eyes, and when I have failed, I have been enabled to realize it pretty quickly. I am coming more and more to realize the worth of fellowship and the price of having It -- honest sharing -- also to realize that two are better than one, that it is the team and not the individual which has the better chance of success; and that is a good thing for a skeptical individualist like me to learn."

"There are plenty of scholars of Church History who know all that in the abstract (says Sam Shoemaker in *Twice-Born Ministers*), yet to concretely never get away from their own inveterate individualism or learn to merge their own experience and activity with others whose knowledge and experience will challenge and perhaps modify their own. It is much easier to study St. Francis' movement than it is to throw oneself into a contemporary movement which is in its initial stages, whose final outcome is not certain, and which tests the faith of its participants all the time. One need hardly say that self-identification with a modern movement which raises real issues and challenges so much in contemporary religious activity is harder for such a man . . . than for almost any type. The intellectual of all men finds it most distasteful to lose himself in a movement where the institutional emphasis is deep and to become one of a functioning group bent on definite evangelism."

The Chaplain of Corpus feels that the Group movement is making a real contribution to the Christian life of this generation, challenging all to a more vital witness for their Lord. It touches men whom ordinary pastoral methods do not reach, particularly the "hearty" type. The free and unconventional and intensely sincere atmosphere of the Groups finds acceptable to the modern mind, with its frank facing of every problem as opposed to the "Hush-hush" methods of the past.

He believes that the challenge to a full surrender to Jesus Christ, the insistence upon discipline, especially the "Morning Watch" or "Quiet Time," is in accord with all that is best in our ecclesiastical history and heritage, and that men and women to-day are hungry for the unification of life which acceptance of these standards always brings. Nothing can be more definite in its committal or stirring in its outspokenness than his recent challenge to a gathering of fellow-Churchmen:

"Whatever we may think of the Oxford Group, it has thrown a challenge to the Christian Church. Time and again, half humorously, half pathetically, clergy, both Anglo-Catholic and Evangelical, have said to me there must have been something very wrong with the Church if the Group had to arise. And I am afraid that is profoundly true. The Group has no new methods, no new theology; it calms with the old good news of Jesus mighty to save; and it flings the challenge to the Church that professes His name to experience that saving grace of fresh, individually and corporately, and so go out to battle with the world. We are moving forward from a long period of trench warfare out into an open war of movement. Christianity and Secularism stand face to face. The battle is being joined all along the line, even in placid, respectable, academic Oxford. There is no room for compromise. *The only vital people in the world to-day are those who are right out for God or right out against Him.*"

The voice of the new evangelism to-day in Oxford.

To find out everything about the Oxford Group when Frank knows your credentials is an easy matter, but try to get at the core of a changed life for unscrupulous evangelistic ends, and see how difficult things become. The Oxford Group knows how to protect their spiritual secrets just as well as the Christians in the Catacombs knew how to protect theirs. But once you've convinced Frank of your *bona-fides,* he becomes a kind of spiritual impresario ready to produce any information you may be in need of, or any interesting character whose experience seems to coincide with your requirements.

The door flew open and Frank's arms flew wide as he introduced one of his outstanding -- of Eton and New College -- a man who prefers to call himself the Introducer. He is another six-footer, for the University atmosphere is full of praying giants.

Here's a young man who will look well in your dental chair," laughs Frank, and another Oxford rowing-man takes the place just vacated. Some men are born saints, some die saints, some do neither. The first look of the newcomer told me he was born a saint. What on earth does a man with that pale, ascetic face, dark hair, rich voice and earnest manner want with the Group -- an institution that attracts sinners only? He is the kind of man whom you know at once will start life as the over-worked secretary of a missionary society and lose it in a Boxer or Bolshevist rebellion when he is the youngest missionary bishop in the Far East.

The Introducer was once, in fact, the Secretary to an influential religious organization, so I asked him why he of all persons wanted to come into the Group. His story was revealing.

"Just because my own personal life was wrong," he admitted.

You look at him and feel certain he is lying, only he is a born saint, and never does those things. He had been seeking to meet the intellectual requirements of people without meeting their need for redemption. There was a lack of power and a great absence of joy and peace in his own life.

"Before I met the Group," he confessed, "I did not know just how to put those things right. W. E. S. Holland, the well-known missionary, told me one day that Group was touching a type of person we were unable to get near. That annoyed me, for I knew our society was doing a good work. Then two things occurred which gave me a jolt. We had a committee of seven in our society, and one of the first persons to be changed was Francis Goulding, who seemed to radiate a wonderful new life. That made me wonder. About two weeks later, Julian, also a senior member of the committee, came to me transformed. Instead of being shy and negative, he had now a missionary love of men. He said he had been in touch with Group, and that made me wonder again. For I felt I had failed. Another incident occurred just after which seemed to prove my conviction. I went to Henley in a New College Eight. When I entered the bedroom at night with the other tough crowd I hadn't courage to kneel down and pray. That was the test of my Christianity which I failed to pass. Two nights went by before I produced the necessary courage. That was how far my preaching had taken me. When I should have been the happiest of witnessing Christians."

The saint in my chair paused:

"Then my father died suddenly, and I now realized I had been depending upon his faith more than my own. I was facing ordination in pursuance of my father's wish, and went to Oxford, where I came into touch with Ken Twitchell, who showed me I had not fully surrendered my life. All sorts of doors were still left open to the world. Fear was one of them. I had two sets of friends, a lot of worry, loved smoking, loved self-indulgence. These and other un-surrendered things I did surrender, asking for grace to give me power over my temptations, and joy of victory and ability to help with the lives of others. I started with the Group, and during the last two years passed from content to discontentment with self, feeding a constantly increasing need for God. Of course I have had wonderful times, especially in the campaigns in Edinburgh and St. Helens.

"I realize now only too clearly that self-satisfaction and content-ment are the gates to a religion of conventionality, to a religion which has no message for others, to a religion which lacks joy and which begets a worried, fretful mind. Only he whose will is contin-ually broken in the valley of humiliation can experience the joy of victory in Christ. 'We are so apt,' as somebody has written, to drift into 'the genteel inanity of a conventional religion which neither satisfies us, nor helps our friends, nor glorifies God.'

"Surely in all religious work of the future we must stress more heavily these two facts -- the necessity for a continual sense of need which can only find its answer in a fuller and more complete surrender to Jesus Christ, and secondly, the power and guidance of the Holy Spirit in the facts of life."

"Do you get guidance?" I asked him.

"Yes. During Quiet Times I have a sense of God being in my head and understanding, whereas previously I thought my own uncon-secrated thoughts. These have resulted in an utter dissatisfaction with the merely good and a passionate longing through discipline for the working of the best. And such love for God that I have a tremendous love for men, and never like to leave them in a state of spiritual mediocrity. Of course, I have slipped, but the Group never let me relapse. They hold me up. They give me a passion for winning souls -- which is one means for the sublimation of pas-sion."

"And have you made progress?"

"God alone knows that. All I know is that my vision has been clarified in certain directions. Once I used to take a man alone to Group meetings when I was bent on helping him. Now I try to turn him to Christ, which seems like progress. Anyway, that is now my real aim in life -- to bring my friends to Christ as St. Andrew brought his brother and the boy with the barley loaves. St. Andrew was the Introducer, and I wish to be the Introducer too."

Chapter Twenty-One

due to love THE STUNG CONSCIENCE

If the Bible contained a comprehensive list of Bewares as well as Beatitudes we should probably find in it "Beware of the Stung Conscience."

The thought was expressed in several parts of the Acts of the Apostles, though not in epigrammatic form. When they heard this they were pricked (or cut) to the heart. The first reference is followed by the news that three thousand souls were added to the Church. The second time Gamaliel stood up and warned the Assembly that if the movement was of God they might be found to be fighting against Him. On the third occasion, the crowd silenced their stung consciences by the stoning of Stephen.

There may be several motives animating the critic of the true Christian or of a deeply spiritual movement: fear, misunderstanding, deliberate wrong-headedness, hate or envy and other powerful elements that move humanity to action. But the stung conscience is usually the first cause. Humanity is so full of sensitive complexes that explode when touched by look, word or deed -- sometimes by the very presence of a pure character who is challenging life is taken as silent judgment on the critic.

I have seen more than one instance of this kind, especially when an earnest Christian encounters one who has back-slidden. An attempt is made to ease the stung conscience by fastening on the weak spots in the other, man or movement. Such persons often project their own failings to the other person, blindly believing the other is the sinner.

Canon Grensted told me the story of two temperate ladies who indulged in champagne for the first time. Presently one of them leaned over to the other and exclaimed:

"You're drunk! You've got two noses."

"That," said the Bampton Lecturer, "was just a clear case of projection. Drunk herself, she was accusing the other person. Another example of projection is the common one of a man losing his temper and then immediately blaming the other for losing his, while the crowd looks amusingly on.

"A prude is a person defending an inner conflict by being censorious of another's conduct. Christians are criticized more than sinners by Pagans because sinners did not sting consciences.

"Unfortunately, a Christian is so often pitifully trying to defend himself against this projection that he develops a censorious attitude himself. He should disregard such criticism remembering with Browning:

With me, faith means perpetual unbelief
Kept quiet like this snake 'neath Michael's foot
Who stands calm just because he feels it writhe.

"Not that all critics attack openly," says Canon Grensted. "Every psychologist knows the patient who agrees with everything he says so as to avoid trouble. But it is only superficial agreement. There are also many who talk about other persons' problems so often that they prove thereby they have similar unsolve problems of their own. The real key to the criticism made of the Group's uncompromising activities is in the emotions stimulated when attention is directed to any problem by particular words.

Some people try to solve the world's problems by silence, and by shutting their eyes to them. Then when something breaks through with sufficient emotional vigor they blow up. A man may threaten to do something drastic because sex has been mentioned at a Group meeting, though he rarely carries out his threat. Perhaps he has been living in a fantasy world where there is no sex, or is projecting some moral offence of his own in criticism of the Group. When the war broke out in Austria, some old ladies shut themselves in their house and declined to have anything further to do with the outside world. For them there was no war. But some of us know there was a little scrap in progress about that time."

The accuracy of Canon Grensted's diagnosis is indicated in the stories of attacks made on Christianity in the early centuries.

According to Tacitus, the early Christians were universally hated on account of "the abominable deeds of which they were guilty and their hatred of the human race. The execution of their leader gave a temporary check to the pestilent superstition. But it broke out afresh, and extended to Rome, where everything that is vile and scandalous accumulates."

Another complaint against the Christians was that they despised the temples as dead houses, scorned the gods and mocked sacred things. Gatherings of Christians for prayer and worship were looked upon as secret societies, and popular imagination ran riot in surmising what transpired . . . the practice of the kiss of peace suggested divers abominations to the impure mind of the masses. The celebration of the Lord's Supper and the holding of love feasts were capable of various interpretations.

Early Christians were said to be a people "who skulk and shun the light of day. It was a common charge against them that they separated themselves from the rest of mankind. . . . Many persecutions were popular outbreaks, and revealed the deep hatred which the people felt towards the Christians. We can see from the Act's that the preacher of the Gospel interfered with vested interests and provoked violent opposition. The fortune-tellers at Philippi and the silversmiths at Ephesus had no difficulty in creating riot, but they were careful to conceal their true motive. . . . But what roused the hatred of all classes most was the seemingly supercilious aloofness from the life of society of the followers of Christ."

And the chief opposition to the Oxford Group still comes not from people who are blind to sin, but from those whose consciences are stung. One day a man came to a house-party and opposed the work on psychological grounds. It was dangerous, he said. Two weeks later he was forced to leave the town because of his own misconduct. Of course, the teaching was dangerous to the life he lived.

An Oxford graduate stood up at one house-party and told the Group they were a psychological fraud, and sat down. Nobody took much notice, and the meeting proceeded on its own serene way. After the meeting he said he proposed to leave the house-party (such sometimes do). Garrett Stearly made what he thought was a guided contact, and in conversation the next afternoon the man faced for the first time a marriage problem in his life. Later he stood up and admitted he was the fraud, not the Group.

There are "letting-down parties" at some house-parties: people who get together and say things privately in criticism of the work. Usually there are several stung consciences among them. Before the house-party ends the letting-down parties usually become the "bucking-up" parties. Two children had attended an Oxford Group meeting and returned home different. They were behaving so magnificently that their father grew suspicious. What had they got hold of? He came to a house-party to see if everything was O.K. Silent at most of the meetings, he liked the getaway to one of these "letting-down" parties. But one day he got the better of his stung conscience and privately shared his real problems -- embezzlement and adultery.

How two sides of a person's nature will work on the question of honesty was shown at one house-party. Ken Twitchell tells of a girl attending a gathering who saw her own problems challenged by the Group, and attempted to turn the edge of the challenge by intellectual arguments. Some well-meaning but misguided of the pious attempted to answer her obstruse questions about the existence of God, but there were others who got nearer the trouble. She left the first day, and went away saying she was through with the Group. Arriving home, she enlarged on their stupidity, confessed all their sins, including some not there, and found all her family in agreement. Then she began to change. The more her family agreed and took the point of view she had just propounded, the more she excused the Group she had just derided. Finally, she found herself hotly defending. So she returned to the house-party and accepted the Group's basis of life.

One who came to a house-party was a middle-aged businessman, secretary of a Chamber of Commerce, proudly Orthodox, boastful of his Bible Class. A few of the boys in his class were changed through contact with the Group, which introduced a most disturbing element into the aggressively Orthodox life of their teacher. He stood up at one Group meeting, waved a Bible and dramatically announced: "I believe in this Book from cover to cover. I came to this house-party to see if the Group is orthodox, for I have a nose for orthodoxy. My life is based on it." The Group believed much more than he; they not only believed but they lived life.

With some difficulty he was it induced to stay. Though he wanted to nose out their orthodoxy, he required only one whiff. He found the honesty of the Group increasingly painful. But one night he sat up until morning with a Group-leader cogitating on this new honesty. In the Quiet Time next morning he openly confessed to his false piety, and that now his life had to be re-made. Most of all, he had been convinced that he was "just a big gas-bag." Though he could talk religion for hours, he had never been honest at home. He had superimposed his will on his son, who had left home, and on other people, asking them to do what he was not doing himself.

He called together the Chamber of Commerce and made restitution. He asked them to attend at his place of business to hear of certain matters of personal interest. He openly admitted his faults of aggressiveness and his garrulous piety. Some who came more impressed associated with the Group; but some criticized. This same man also toured the town making restitution to a number of people whom he had treated wrongly. His estranged son was seen, and a better relationship followed. A new unity came to his family through the children being allowed to develop their own initiative without parental browbeating.

A young critic, a Scot, who came to the meetings, opposed himself to the teaching, alleging that he was concerned about the unequal distribution of wealth, the truth of which statement he subsequently proved by admitting that he was in the habit of ringing up the wrong change on his employer's cash register.

When the Gospel is preached in the Holy Spirit it either convicts or enrages. A middle-aged professional man, forceful but suave, had been very successful in business, and was about to retire to a comfortable life of golf. He heard, when on holiday, of the Groups coming to his city, and being the son of a minister, he considered he knew all about that sort of thing. When he came back he found all the men in his club talking about that Oxford Group. He immediately telephoned his most Pagan friend and invited him to dinner. He packed off as soon after dinner as he conveniently could and went home disgusted. Soon afterwards he had a business appointment in a distant city, where he had a talk with one of the shrewdest magnets there. Thoroughly on his guard against this clever man of the world that he should not be cheated, he was taken aback to be thus addressed:

"Mr. Browne, I've been in touch with the Oxford group. And I want to own up to you I've over-reached you twice in a business deal."

This was a staggerer! But the minister's son held out manfully. A week later he went to another city, where he hoped to have a pleasant afternoon with a charming young lady, motoring in his car. To-day she was not so affable or responsive as usual. In the middle of their drive the girl produced a note from a friend who had just joined the Group and was urging her to do the same. This further blow coming so close to home completely punctured him for the day. His evening was spoiled, and not improved by the girl's suggestion that the Oxford Group was running a house-party near at hand. He determined to go and prove they were absolute charlatans; he would expose them thoroughly. He arrived barely managing to get a spare room among the cheery crowd. He was entertained by a bright young Englishwoman and sent to the first meeting mollified by her charm. He heard a sophisticated Scotsman, a typical man of the world, with close-cropped mustache and military bearing, stand up and witness in the semi-humorous, nonchalant manner that the world understands.

In the language of the smoking-room, Loudon Hamilton told how Christ had turned him from a waster into a worker for Himself. The visitor writhed under the honesty of this worldling who had become as wise as a serpent and as harmless as a dove in Christ. Disliking the man -- such is the phenomenon of conviction -- he was irresistibly drawn to the speaker. For hours they talked, and ultimately he found that same new life for himself. He now knew who was a real charlatan.

If you ask people to make radical changes in their lives and they don't obey, they must pick holes in you. As Canon Grensted has it: "When something like the Group comes along and suggests that God be put in the first place always, instead of the tenth, and people find their disordered sentiments as threatened, they naturally begin to feel annoyed."

The Gospel preached in the Holy Spirit either convicts or enrages. The Stung Conscience lyrics to Sting.

Chapter Twenty-Two

WHAT SIN IS

As this is a book for sinners, and as most sinners, myself included, are rather hazy about what sin is, it seems opportune to supply the answer in this chapter.

An Irish Rector told me that a famous preacher delivered a fine sermon on sin to a village flock, and was afterwards embarrassed to be told, "Sure, your riv'ence -- we didn't even know the manin' of sin until you came here."

After one of the meetings at the last Cambridge house-party Frank burst into my room, exclaiming: "You should have heard Loudon Hamilton's talk on Sin. Fine! Great! Never heard anything so revealing. That's what you should get for your book."

I inveigled Loudon into my room and induced him to go through his notes and give me the gist of his talk. He looked thoroughly at home with his subject, as his Highland figure lolled magnificently before my April fire. Loudoun has a fine head, dark brown hair, eyes and mustache, a strong voice and a witty, paradoxical turn of phrase. That day -- at a religious house-party in Selwyn College -- he wore a white sweater, a bright leather belt, navy blue shorts and (below bearing these) a pair of stockings that were "red like crimson" -- the sin color! A picturesquely powerful figure suggesting anything but his old role of the master at Eton. He told me they were the colors of the London Scottish Rugger Club, of which he had been a member.

Loudon began to give me this illuminating Group view of Sin:

Many people don't believe in sin, but they still live in it. We are indebted, it would seem, to Bertrand Russell, with some assistance from Mr. Huxley, for doing away with sin. Unfortunately, they have not been able to do away with temptation. I wish they had. But the fact is that men and women are still tempted, even intellectual people. And sin is what happens when we give way to temptation.

"If you were to write my epitaph," said a friend to Dr. Alexander Whyte of Edinburgh, "you would say: He had every virtue but a sense of sin."

A small sense of sin means a small Christ. It is, moreover necessary to be definite about sin and thoroughly honest with ourselves. Much of our efforts to deal with the wrong things in our lives is vitiated because we are too vague about them. We speak of forgiveness of sin in the abstract without getting deliverance from specific sins in the particular.

Sin is a force. It may be likened to a mathematician. It adds to a man's troubles, subtracts from his energies, multiplies his aches and pains, divides his mind, takes interest from his work, discounts his chances of success, and squares his conscience.

Sin does things to us. First of all, it blinds. While motoring in Switzerland we ran into mist. After some time the mist cleared, and to our surprise there appeared gigantic peaks in the sunshine almost overhead. We had thought we were high up. Actually we discovered we were on a very low level indeed. Similarly in a spiritual realm, we are befogged by sin and unaware of our real position in relation to Christ.

Secondly, sin binds. We are bound by fears, chiefly of other people -- of their opinions about us -- of the future, of our money and health, and a hundred other things.

Thirdly, sin multiplies. The lesson of the first chapter of James is that man is beguiled and lured by his own desire. Desire conceives and breeds sin while sin matures and gives birth to Death.

When we tell one lie we have to tell a number of lies as a rule to cover it up. Hence we have Christ's emphasis on being faithful in that which is least. And Alpine mountaineer knows that one false step is enough in certain places to precipitate an avalanche. Many of us have taken that false step, congratulating ourselves that the sin avalanche will not ensue; and when it has come we have made futile attempts to stop it half-way down the hill, with the inevitable result of disaster.

Fourthly, sin deadens and deafens. A hot cinder put on the heel of our hand may not hurt as much, but if put on our cheek would cause sharp pain. The temperature of the cinder has not changed, but only our sensitiveness to it. By repetition and habit many of us have lost the sense of sinfulness of certain things in our lives. We need to be made sensitive again. Sin has defeated us so that we cannot hear the voice of God. It is sometimes convenient to be deaf. Many of us have even become hardened to church services, and by repetition are dulled to the simplest truths.

The best definition of sin that we have is that sin is anything in my life which keeps me from God and from other people. Note that it is something in my life, and not in the other person's. Most of us like to confess other people's sins and not our own. But the first need is ourselves, and not the other person. We can't change others until we ourselves are changed.

Let us get rid of false distinctions right away. Most of us make an easy distinction between big sins and little ones. No such distinction exists in the Bible. Paul uncompromisingly states that all unrighteousness is sin. Sometimes we may excuse sin because it is occasional; we say, it is all right occasionally to get drunk. Then is it all right occasionally to commit a murder? The problem of most of us is not the open sin, but the secret; not the sin that makes us uncomfortable, but the comfortable sins. We must cease dealing with symptoms and get down to root causes and motives.

Christianity has a moral backbone. And let us take for convenience four of the simple moral standards that we see in Christ's own life -- honesty, purity, unselfishness and love. Those standards are absolute. No one has ever yet proved He compromised on any one of those four. Let us take them one by one and see how we measure up to His standard.

HONESTY

A child once gave a definition of an abstract noun as the name for anything which didn't exist, like truth or honesty. Take the matter of the tongue. Sins of the tongue are myriad. First is misstatement or misrepresentation, by exaggerating or minimizing or giving a false emphasis, usually to our own glory. Secondly come concealment and dishonest silences. Thirdly, we evade by the simple device of polite lying and false excuses. We call them by more comfortable names. We call sin failure, or amiable weakness, or ascribe it to temperament or our characteristics. We appeal to heredity and environment. We say it runs in the family, or tacitly excuse it on that score. Let the sin have an intellectual name and it becomes quite respectable. It is "so correct" to call a thing "inferiority complex," when it is really a very simple but deadly form of pride. Fourthly, there is criticism, of which we will have more to say, and negative discussion about people or their work. Fifthly, it is easy to slip into double-dealing: saying one thing to a person and another thing about him behind his back.

Then in the matter of stealing, some of us travel first-class on trains with a third-class ticket or travel further on the train than our ticket allows. I have myself entered a football ground by the cheap entrance and have gone out under the ropes to the more

expensive section. Shortly after meeting the Group I had to send
the money for the dance-ticket for which I had not paid. We sometimes borrow books and other things and somehow forget to give
them back. Will you go to your library shelves and look through
your books and see if you have any you ought to return? A friend
once said she could tell a lie, but she could not write one; so she
got her secretary to make out her income-tax return for her. When
the B.B.C. (British Broadcasting Company) announced they would
have an inspection to stop wireless pirates, over ten thousand new
licenses were taken out during the few days before the inspection
began.

There are sins of attitude -- often sins of pretense, pose and affectation. How common is the business of wearing a mask and
trying to make an impression on others, the anxiety to appear
better with the deliberate concealment of things that are unfavor-
able to ourselves. Indeed, we often defend the flaws in ourselves
by criticizing them most bitterly in others. Being socially inferior,
we may affect an Oxford or a Cambridge accent, though Heaven
knows why we should want to do that. Or we are like a chameleon
taking our color from the crowd we are with. We are one thing at
home. We can be religious if necessary with our pious relatives,
and we can be hard-boiled at a Rugger or rowing dinner. We can
be sentimental and romantic with our dancing-partners, anxious
to display what we fondly imagine to be the nice side of our na-
tures. We must be honest about our motives, which are always apt
to get mixed even in the best-regulated religions.

Another form of dishonest attitude is that of patronage of a movement like the Group movement. It amounts to this. We are approv-
ing of a thing we won't pay the price of doing ourselves. The Group
doesn't seek patronage, is not much concerned about approval,
and is not content with parallelism. ("We are running on similar
lines.") It is not that the Group is one method and the others have
other methods. Either we are living the maximum experience of
Christ or not.

PURITY

Feather-investors are not sufficient for purity, nor is it good
enough to squirt a little rose-water into the atmosphere and hope
for the best. There was once a negro preacher who wouldn't dare
preach about chicken-stealing because all his folk were doing it
most of the time and he did it himself occasionally. What we need
is a rotary street broom to clean things up. Equally bad is the

pharisaic sin of being comfortably blind or willfully ignorant or unhealthily inquisitive about these matters. Parents often live in a fool's paradise about the needs of their children. It is easier to live and deal superficially with people. But what would we think of a doctor who refused to make a drastic diagnosis of a disease from which we are suffering? What if he refused to deal with certain types of cases in his wards? Christ's standard of moral purity began with the eye and the thought. How would you feel if your thought-life at certain times were suddenly thrown upon a screen in the view of mixed assembly?

We may need to deal with the tongue and the touch. For many of us our history is this -- the look, the thought, the fascination of the thought and then the fall. And further, with regard to our relationships with the other sex there may be fellowship, but there must never be familiarity.

LOVE

Thomas Carlyle, after hearing a local minister preach on love, said that he had been like a flea in a tar-barrel. Love is a vast subject. The Bible tells us that hate is equivalent to murder. The one is as bad as the other. Is there anyone for whom you still cherish feelings of dislike, resentment and lack of forgiveness? The issue is fairly serious.

The sins against love are common with the tongue. Suppose we read the third chapter of James before our next tea-party. Let us deal with gossip. So live that you can sell your parrot to the town gossip with an easy mind. Most of us need to buy a padlock for our tongues and to throw away the key.

Criticism often hides much ill-will. Remember we criticize in others what's wrong in ourselves. The Pharisees condemned the woman taken in adultery and tried to get Christ to condemn her too. But He was free of the sin. They showed by their action they were not. Christ condemned this sin, but saved the sinner. "Neither do I condemn thee. Go and sin no more." Remember we reveal ourselves by our criticisms, our prejudices, our silences, and our nervousness. Criticism is the sin *par excellence* of Christian workers. *Only say about others what you say to them.* Is Christ the silent listener to all your conversation? We cannot help others if we laugh at them.

Jealousy is devastating to peace of mind and spiritual power. So are snobbery and superiority, whether social, intellectual or spiritual. Snobbery may take the form of liking to be known as one who goes a lot among the poor. We may thank God we are not as other men are, and so do they.

Intolerance of other people's points of view are their weakness as can be an equally devastating form of lovelessness.

And there is reserve. We say something was too sacred, when the real truth is we are too selfish. Most of us are in the grip of a false reserve. I used to pride myself on my reserve until I found my reserve was really pride. False reserve makes us rigid, separates us from others, gives them a false impression of what we really are, and, worst of all, prevents us from helping them or entering sympathetically or intelligently into their difficulties.

Temper cuts across love. Have you apologized for the last time you lost your temper to anyone, with a member of your own family, a bus conductor or a railway clerk?

The sin of Fear is a sin against love. Perfect love casteth out fear. Most of us are afraid of others and consequently don't help them.

UNSELFISHNESS

Finally, let us take the difference between ourselves and Christ as regards to our conduct, our attitudes, manner, judgments and feelings towards others.

Self -- Let us make a list of the different forms in which self operates in our lives. Archbishop Temple has said, "Your problems are mixed up with the things you love most and of which count most to you." Self-love shows itself in the love of praise and popularity and social success. Often we stand on what we are pleased to call our dignity. In fact, our dignity is so well stood on that there's really not much left. We dread almost more than anything to make a fool of ourselves. We develop what we are pleased to call sensitiveness, but which we can better call touchiness. Then self-pity creeps in. We feel inferior, we positively hug failure and point to previous defeats as evidence of our limitations. Or we may develop a martyr complex with all its false heroics. We say we "can stand anything." The truth is we may stand anything, but we don't change anything. Then self-importance often gives rise to jealousy and makes us run on our position and reputation, though inwardly feel defeated. We develop "self-respect." That usually means ninety per cent self and ten percent respect. We ask for special treatment like Naaman the Syrian, or we enjoy being interesting invalids. But times are so urgent that there is no place for the interesting invalid in the front-line trench. He ought to be shot at dawn.

Again, self-interest about money or possessions shows itself by being unwilling to lend them or give them, being fussy about them, but spending too much time thinking about them, suffering from an exaggerated carefulness about our own things. It makes us preoccupied and worried with our own affairs. We become penny wise and pound foolish. We painstakingly practice "the economy that leadeth to poverty." We only believe in Matthew 6:33 so long as the stock market is sound. This constant self-interest leaves to nerves and irritation. How often is the root cause of nerves just sin!

Another form of self-seeking is the ambition that disregards the interest of others and is not over scrupulous about its methods of obtaining its objects. The Prophet replies with direct simplicity, Seekest thou great things for thyself; seek them not.

Self-consciousness reveals a life and habits of mind that are still rotating around the axis ego. In most of us there is the instinct for self-display showing itself in love of attention and in the willingness to do our best as first string, but not being ready for the same effort when less credit will come our way. Such self-consciousness often appears in clothes and manners and in the subjects of our conversation.

One of the commonest forms of self is self-indulgence. There is self-indulgence in food and physical comforts. But we also indulged it when we are lazy, or we procrastinate, and we are unpunctual. We say we'll put off until tomorrow the thing we can do *the day after!* Some things we do in the sweet by-and-by which need to be done in the nasty now and now. We indulge ourselves by airing our prejudices about people, airing our likes and dislikes in matters of books, furniture, and furnishings generally; and we are tremendously taken up with whether a thing or a person appeals to us or not. We often regulate our behavior accordingly, and have no hesitation in even being rude to people we may not like or whom we consider socially inferior. Often we give way to moods when we become, as a lady said of her debutante daughter, expensive to keep and difficult to live with. Some of us are extravagant in money, sentimental about our friends, whether of the other sex or the same-sex, and vindictive when we are crossed.

Then, again, there is self-centeredness. Most of us are born rotating on the axis ego, and continue to do so until the end of our lives, often at an increasing rate. One result of that is that we are never able to keep friends for any length of time. It not only loses us friends, but often keeps us from bothering to make them. A girl once told me she had a private cinematograph tucked away in the back of her head, and that when her mind was not otherwise occupied she would set the film in motion and like to watch scene after scene, now romantic, now tragic, now pathetic, now sentimental, now heroic, in each and all of which she herself was the central figure. It finally culminated in the imaginary scene in which her own deepest desires were fully gratified with curtains and sofa covers of the right color and the husband with hair to match. All of us have our day-dreams in one form or another. Though not necessarily wrong in themselves, so far as they are centered in self-interest they are wrong.

And now for one of the biggest monsters of the self -- self-will. We simply want our own way, and will not yield. The results of it are as obvious as they are disastrous. It brings friction with others and tiredness for ourselves. It is one form of pride. We do no diagnosis, and are consequently useless to the people and the situations around us. With self-will unchecked we become precipitate in action, unguided in decisions, demanding in our efforts and impatient of restraint or advice. It is the most prolific source of quarrels in families. The objects obtained are always unsatisfying, and the result is that we crave more indulgence in the vain hope of more satisfaction. The final indictment against self-will is written by the prophet, "We have turned everyone to his own way." It is also, if we only knew it, incredibly stupid. We often mistake obstinacy for strength of mind.

It is extraordinary how prolific our minds are in finding reasons for our own failures which we endeavor to make satisfactory to ourselves and, if possible, to others. It is the well-known art, self-justification. When corrected, we seek to justify. And with that dislike of correction in ourselves goes a love of correcting others. Nothing alienates the hearts of people more quickly than that.

Then there is the very common business of being self-opinionated. We do love our own opinion about a thing.

We are very ready to assert it. We are confident it is right. We resent disagreement, even though we may know little about the subject. It makes us seek to impose our point of view, instead of sharing a quality of life. And there is the sin of the pet point of view. We allow ourselves to be so much absorbed by our own that we never see anyone's else. It is like Nero fiddling a little tune of his own while the horror of a burning Rome is all around him.

Again, there is self-sufficiency, which makes us feel no need of other help. This results from too small a conception of Christ and His demands, and too large a conception of our own capacities.

The last self we will deal with is the final atheism of self-effort. We do God's work, but not His will. It is our choice, in our way, on our strength. It leads immediately to a false objective, and self-chosen service. We do not God's best, but a good of our own. The results which ought to accompany the working of the Holy Spirit are manifestly absent. We are all the more eager, therefore, to achieve success in the false activity to cover up an inward sense of dissatisfaction, futility and frustration, which haunts all of us at times, when our lives are run on self-effort.

The same self-effort makes us "Divided Personalities." One Church-worker before she met the Group had two distinct sets of friends -- the officially religious people and her unofficial Pagan friends. There was no question in her mind which set appealed to her the more. We can run an organization on self-effort, but so can the devil. We don't change lives; the devil does. And an all full coldness may be the last for sandals on a church or any religious body when it is run as an organization. A minister told us that he felt each Sunday as if he were performing a solo on a spiritual ice-rink.

On the basis of self-effort we began to departmentalize. We say, "My job is so and so. It is somebody else's job to change lives." That distinction is thoroughly false. Either we have measles or we haven't! If we have measles, we give it away to everybody; if we haven't, nobody will get it.

Finally, self-effort makes us take refuge in a full-proof theology. We develop a point of view instead of living a quality of life. This draws us on to preach things which are beyond our experience, and are therefore unreal or even distasteful. We become wooden and rigid and falsely pious. I develop a false sense of duty, and live in the grip of secondary things, instead of being at the command of other people. We begin to run on principle and technique, and not on the Holy Spirit's guidance. Our prayer-life is spasmodic. We do the jobs within the reach of our capacity, and only think of asking God's help when the limit of our capacity has been reached. We use God like the Fire Brigade, and only call Him in a crisis. We ask Him to control only part of our lives, instead of being Lord and Master of all.

These are some of the world's alternatives to a Christ-centered and Christ-controlled life. Let us recognize in these sins what we really seek. We seek compensation for our defeat and for our lack of Christ. We take to substitutes for power. We need anodynes to stop the pain and discomfort, and to help us forget. We play with alternatives to facing Christ. We adopt camouflage to cover up our defeats and to hide from one another.

"Oh, wad some power the giftie gie us,
To see oursels as ithers see us!"

Chapter Twenty-Three

THE SPIRIT MOVES

Frank sees both sides of a subject, right through a man, and all round the earth.

Ten years ago he was thinking in terms of a spiritual awakening in many countries, which is now beginning to be manifest. When a man begins to think big like that, he naturally looks round for a big backer. Frank could have had a comfortable life-job that was offered him. He waved that away, and set out to initiate a world-awakening backed only by infinite faith and prayer.

Coupled with his world vision was the friendship of a handful of young men -- two English, two American -- University graduates who had been changed and with training might become pioneers of a world awakening. The traveling five were Sherry Day, Sam Shoemaker, Loudon Hamilton, Nick Wade, and -- Frank. They were away a year. He visited many distant lands, passing leisurely through Europe, Egypt, India (where Frank had done an amazing work some years before), China (where Frank's last visit was still talked about), Australia, America and home again.

When five friends travel together in close proximity for twelve months, their friendship may break under the strain before the tour is over; it would probably have broken on this tour had Frank not evolved the principle of Sharing. The tour ended, and the five parted better friends than when they started, and are still in the closest friendship after ten years.

The tour meant a stretching of vision and discipline that has since made them compelling leaders. Nick Wade returned and became Chaplain of Downing College, Cambridge, and leader of the work in the University. Sam Shoemaker went to New York and set Calvary Church alight. Loudon Hamilton went to Oxford, then to South Africa where he did an amazing national work for a whole year, and then to Edinburgh where he started the work moving strongly among the Scots. Frank and Sherry are here, there and everywhere, watching developments and opening new fields of Group work in all corners of the earth -- in Iceland, in South America, in Geneva, wherever the Spirit leads them.

The South African work of the Groups is one of the most amazing adventures, for which that world tour was a splendid preparation. It really began, says Garrett Stearly, when two Rhodes scholars, a Rugger enthusiast, probably the handsomest man in the Oxford Group, aiming at a brilliant medical career, and a boxing blue, both from South Africa, condescendingly attended one meeting.

No sack-cloth or ashes here, no pious psalm-singing. But a breeze and a gaiety and a sureness of direction outlived, outlaughed, out-loved their own crowd. They were fascinated, then nettled by its challenge, and finally went all out for this highest quality of life they had ever seen.

This new altitude of living was too good to keep to themselves. What of their University friends back home in South Africa? The two Rhodes men began to dream dreams of their homeland cap-tured to the same fascinating life.

Always men of action, they collected a team of six Oxford men, including Howard Rose, and one Hollander, like-minded with themselves; and the next long vacation set out for South Africa, trusting God for funds, and the power to capture a nation. Fool-hardy venture; but the foolishness of men is often the Wisdom of God.

They sought notably no large mass meetings. Their first move in Africa was a two week's camp with ten men from Rhodes Univer-sity College. A small beginning, but these ten were leaders in every walk of University life, and at the end of the two weeks each of those men had found a never-to-be-forgotten spiritual adventure. They brought this new life to the University. News of it spread up and down the land, opening for the team of seven men opportu-nities everywhere. They went to the capital, Pretoria. A leading minister was convicted and captivated by their uncompromising gospel. They went to Stellenbosch, center of Afrikaans culture and of anti-British sentiment. The Stellenbosch Rugger Team, hearti-est in the country, listened entranced to this news from Oxford. The president of Stellenbosch Club was convinced, and has since come into mission work for the black people.

But time was short. The team had to return from its long vaca-tion. Loudon alone stayed on to prepare the way for a larger team the following year.

In the summers of 1929-30 teams of first nineteen and then twenty-three Oxford Group people sailed from South Africa -- business and professional men and women, students, privileged and underprivileged. The House-parties were held in all the large cities throughout the Union. The seven Oxford men had lit a torch. By now the veldt was on fire. Their vision and their courage had not been foolishness. It was a modern romance of God's miracle-working power.

What happens in such a romance? In 1928 seven men sailed unknown and unheralded into the horseshoe bay of Cape Town, the Tavern of the Seas -- nestling at the foot of the awe-inspiring Table Mountain. Two years later the team of twenty-three, at a civic reception in the City Hall, was welcomed by the Mayor, who said, "I have long been thinking that our religion was in need of a bit of gingering -- I believe the ginger has arrived."

What caused this amazing awakening? Not oratory, not publicity, not organization, not dramatic appeals. The teams had nothing of this sort. They were plain men and women, but they had found in Christ a quality of life which enabled the ordinary man to do the extraordinary thing. Life-changing miracles in individual lives was their secret and their goal.

At Kimberley, the world's diamond centre, the Oxford Group team met in the sporting hotel in town. They came to it, thinking it was some new club, the city engineer, an acid atheist, notorious for his hard drinking and fast living. He found a charming company in evening dress. The engineer settled in for a top-hole evening of good stories, the latest from Oxford. A giant Scotsman, with clipped mustache, carefully tailored clothes, and the air of a man of the world, began to talk. He told how Christ had changed his life. The engineer was shocked beyond measure at this perfectly natural mention of Jesus Christ in a social gathering. "Horribly bad form," he whispered to the man next him. Later, soft drinks appeared. "A rotten show," he said to his friend as they went home late that night. But he could not forget that broad-shouldered Scotsman and the quiet challenge of his words. They met next day for a motor drive, and the engineer found a new life. His change startled the town. He made a habit of dropping in on the padre for what he called a "spot" of prayer. In his office, once blue with expletives, it was no longer bad form to talk of the issues that change men's lives.

The new leaven throughout the nation is not confined to any one class. While lunching at a well-known Cape Town hotel, a member of the team noticed that his waiter was extraordinarily happy and attentive, and remarked about it to him. "Well, you see, sir, I belong to the Oxford Group," was the reply; and between the courses the whole story came out. Gambling and drink had done their usual service in breaking up his home and propelling him out of a job into the gutter. Then a fellow-lounger had facetiously suggested to him, "Why don't you see So-and-so," mentioning a well-known and popular K.C. "He belongs to the Oxford Group; you ought to get a soft 'hand-out' from him." The barrister not only got him a waiter's job, but gave him an experience of Christ, on the basis of which this man was building a reunited and happy home. And at the end of the meal the waiter whispered with a wink -- "I'm out to win the headwaiter." That's the sequence. Across all social classes, into the most unexpected corners, goes the witness of Christ.

One of the most surprising places into which the Group found its way was a fire-brigade in the world's gold city of Johannesburg. Six years before, a fireman with a shock of red hair and a temper to match, had married a temperamental young woman, musician to her finger-tips. His passion was gambling, and hers was stage. Incompatible from the word "go," they had separated. The Group came along. The wife discovered its contagious quality, and she returned to her husband in Johannesburg. At her request he went to a Group, with much inward ridiculing. He came away convinced, and began to witness in his fire-station. The test came and they began to call him "softie," and say that he had lost his manhood; for his temper and his physique had made him the fear-inspiring leader of the brigade. One day an inferior in the firehouse dared to censure him for some mistakes. He felt a blaze of fury burn within. He prayed to Christ. The fury went. He realized that to serve Christ he must be willing to take criticism smiling, and replied, "You're right," and thanked him. The inferior was staggered. "I would rather he had knocked me flat," he was heard to murmur. And now that hot-headed fireman and his wife have a weekly Group in their home, which the fireman and their wives attend, always praying that the firebell will not ring during their meeting.

A new shaft of light was thrown on Africa's problem of Church unity when, at a house-party, people of all denominations and all shades of belief lived together for ten days in such perfect unity that a sister of an Anglo-Catholic Community, who attended throughout, wrote of it: "We lived on so high an altitude of Christian experience that we completely lost all sense of our differences." This spirit is in many quarters initiating a new working cooperation between the various denominations.

In the pressing problems of black and white antagonism it was significant that one of the best Negro minds in South Africa, Max

Yergan, once told Frank that South Africa had sufficient personal religion, and needed no more. Two years later he spoke enthusiastically to Sam Shoemaker of the astonishing racial results.

Still more striking is the fact that fast-living ranch-owners are being turned into life-changers working among their own native employees. No professional missionary appeal has so convincingly staggered the heathen black men as the simple about-face of their once-careless "big boss."

Not only a new spirit between black and white, but a new fellowship between English and Dutch is apparent. Because of the Groups many Dutch are learning English and many English learning Dutch voluntarily. This new cordiality of feeling was epitomized at a house-party in Bloemfontein, when three hundred Dutch and English stood up and took this vow inspired by the inscription on the Christ of the Andes: "Sooner shall this limitless veldt pass away, sooner shall this endless sunshine cease than we Afrikans and English-speaking South Africans shall break the peace which we swear here at the feet of Christ the Redeemer."

South Africa was an amazing romance, but I was more eager to discover what the Group would do in an anti-Christian country. Then I heard of another exploit which came about through contact with the remarkable Loudon Hamilton. Three Oxford undergraduates met him, committed their lives to Christ, and decided to invest their future in missionary work in Persia. They went out singly to Stuart Memorial College, Isfahan, and educational mission for Persians, Armenians and Jews. Each of these races by traditional custom regarded the other two as lowly. So here, if anywhere the group message had a chance to prove its potency.

The three Oxford men set to work quietly changing lives, finding that crows were the same glossy black as they were in Oxford. A Persian lad of such low character that all regarded him as hopeless was winning other students within the first six months, Armenians and Jews as well. Ancient hatreds began to melt. A team of four, an Anglo-Saxon, a Persian, a Jew, and an Irishman, set out to help a lonely missionary station. By honestly sharing and surrendering to Christ their race prejudices, they welded themselves into such a glowing unity of power that eight others were drawn in to form a modern Apostolic band. Their impact on the mission-station was so great that a group of Moslems was changed, and the days of isolated work were ended for the lonely missionary.

I asked one of these men on furlough in England just how he got his convictions across to a Persian. He told me the story of

The Three Tailors. A man at the College brought along a Persian neighbor to the Oxford man with the cryptic remark: "Hosham has a sense of sin. Help him to get over it."

This was a complaint rarely known in that corner of the world. But for Hosham it became the jumping-off place into a radiant life. Some months later Hosham's partner Mehdi turned up.

"Hosham has a new joy. I want it."

In the lands where Christianity is not good form, people may make most direct and disturbing demands.

"Very well, Christ meets you at the point of your greatest need," was the reply. "Let's begin with your sins."

"I haven't any," he said.

"Glad to hear that. But I found I had when I began with honesty. Are you always honest?"

Mehdi grinned and added confidently, "What do you expect? Don't you know, a tailor?"

"Yes, but Jesus Christ demands absolute honesty. Go away and think about it."

Six months later he returned. "I decided to try, but I can't do it," he announced, as though no interval had broken the conversation.

"Why not give the whole of your life to Christ? Then He will give you the power."

This he did, and his wife became his comrade instead of his chattel. His neighbors were astonished at him. Within the month a third partner in the same tailoring house, a Jew, joined in. They witnessed radiantly in the bazaar though they incurred thereby the risk of being stabbed to death.

But The Three Tailors are allied and witnessing intrepidly.

Wherever Frank and his friends traveled in their round-the-world tour ten years ago Groups have since sprung up. He passed through Egypt. Last year a Group house-party was held at the foot of the Pyramids on the edge of the desert. "From the house," says Ken Twitchell, "the desert appeared to be a huge wall of sand, with the Pyramids standing high above the valley. There was an afterglow of purple on the rolling hills of sand and stone, while above a full moon looked down on three thousand miles of a stretch of desert -- a stirring sight, heightened by the thought that so many of the great religious leaders had desert experiences."

The doctor of one of the most influential Cairo families witnessed at a large Group in a family drawing-room, where she told simply and naturally of the experience of Christ that had come to her Oxford house-party in the summer. She is now one of a group of several women who are beginning to change the rather worldly and bored upper strata of Cairo's society.

A young man, a University Don, came along and said he had been trying to help students under his charge, and was not able to do it. He needed help himself. He surrendered, and began to live under God's guidance. A week later, when going to luncheon with the Head of the University, the young Don said, "Last night so many of my students came up to my room to talk to me that I had to send some away and tell them to come back later. And I was able to give more help to those men that night than I had been able to offer any man in three years."

A dignitary of the Church told of a complete revolution in his life during the past few days. The head of a business said he had realized that for him surrender to God meant a restitution of wrongly-appropriated money -- fifty pounds had been unfairly added to an invoice -- and he wrote a letter explaining what he had done and included a cheque for the amount. This house-party also brought about a change in the life of his son, and the two are now working as a team.

There came to the house-party a leader of a great group of Egyptians who declared they must have this basis of life for their own work. A whole day was spent at Helwan with forty leaders of young Egypt, who showed the greatest interest in the new evangelism.

"You were used of God to do a world of good while here," writes a correspondent of the Cairo Groups, which have now come into vital being.

"Echoes of the day continue to come in. Stories of a real blessing in the lives of men. Three house-parties are being planned as a result of that wonderful day in the country. Two of us passed on your message to our Moslem Group, all of whom agreed to keep their Quiet Time each morning and evening and to report the results. . . I feel this is a way of approach to Moslems for us and a way of approach from Moslems to Christ that has great possibilities."

The direct approach to Christ is that experience is better than a human level of arguments.

The successful development of the work in Cairo was part of a spiritual pilgrimage from Constantinople right down through the Holy Land -- where an atheist was changed -- back to Egypt. The team comprised of Professor and Mrs. Alexander Smith, Ken Twitchell, his wife Marian, and his mother.

Ken told me a wonderful story of the work in Zürich, where two psychiatrists sent along a very difficult patient to a house-party, and one of the team was used to relate this person to Jesus Christ, so that his fundamental needs began to be met. A few days later he testified to his new experience in the house-party in the presence of the two astonished psychiatrists. As a result of his witness one of these two men became convicted of the need in his own life and later followed his patient's example.

When I heard that Group talk of South Africa and Egypt, I became restive. News that would sell a newspaper was usually news about England. When Mrs. Alexander Whyte proposed that the Group go to Geneva to introduce a challenging spiritual leaven into the Disarmament atmosphere, I was still more indifferent. Only a few old fogeys were interested in Geneva, I thought, but Frank's guidance was that the Group should go there, and Frank's guidance has a queer knack of being right.

The Oxford Group entered Geneva last January, and achieved definite results among individuals variously placed in Geneva society -- results that will become more apparent as the leaven begins to penetrate the fear, criticism and contempt which certain sections of the city seem to have for the others. The Group cut clean across the social life, the national differences and differences of language which are keeping the national representatives in water-tight compartments.

With the following debt duration of its principles, the Oxford Group announced its arrival in Geneva:

In this time of distress peoples and nations are eagerly awaiting, not more plans, but power; not machinery, but men.

The modern world -- disillusioned, chaotic, feverish -- demands a solution adequate to its disorder.

The international problems of to-day are, at bottom, personal problems.

Men must change if problems are to be solved.

Peace in the world can only spring from peace in the hearts of men.

A dynamic experience of God's free spirit is the answer to regional antagonism, economic depression, racial conflict, and international strife.

God-control is our primary need.

For years the Group had included in its life men and women of international affairs. To these it was a truth strikingly clear, that whoever held the secret of changing individuals, also held the secret of changing nations. It was a truism that the change of men's hearts wouldn't decide the direction of men's policy. And they looked ahead to the day when the wind of the Spirit would blow the Group to the great centre of international life.

Those whom viewed the fact, saw the need. Great as has been the ideal of the League of Nations, even its enthusiastic supporters deplored the failure to realize the ideal. With all the good work that Geneva had accomplished, idealism without God was not enough. Until two people joined together in marriage learned to care more about God than about themselves, or each other, there is no real solution to their problems. Until all the members of a family make this vital discovery, self-interest blocks the best unity of their home. And so it is with nations. Until the welfare of the whole family of nations comes to them more strongly than their own self-interest alone, until they learn that he who would save his life shall lose it, self-interest rides high in inter-national politics. And behind the veil of pious pronouncements and resolutions, the blind policy of self-interest pulls the reins in secret diplomacy.

Geneva leaves out God, and plugs along. But it is weary with its plugging. Many men came hoping to find a city of love, and they found a city of loneliness. They came to find in Geneva, at last, the peace where nations had fellowship together. They found instead the rivalry and jealousy they had left behind. They came, many of them at great personal sacrifice, to throw themselves into the work of building a new world. But they found that the issuing of reports did not rouse the world into great redemptive action. Men must be changed if problems are to be solved.

Into this city of disillusionment, of idealism and cynicism, the Group came with a simple, personal message. There was no organization to be set up, no conference to be held, no funds to be collected. There were no resolutions to be passed. Meetings of refreshing simplicity and friendliness were held in the midst of preparations for the Disarmament Conference. Personal problems were dealt with and the solution was indicated. Lives began to respond, and, turning to God, were changed.

Members of the Secretariat, heads of international organizations, Genevese business men, and their families, came into the release of the new life and the romance of the work. At a service in one of the churches of the city, the lady who had been chosen to represent the women's organizations before the Disarmament Conference spoke of the fresh experience of Christ which had come into her life, and told of her conviction that only as men and women were entirely surrendered to God could they bring positive results out of their work at Geneva. At the same service one of the heads of an international organization testified to the new honesty and joy that had come to him and to his family, and were now major characteristics of their family life. Others, of different ages and various groups, gave evidence of the new adventure begun.

The team for the house-party had been drawn from many countries. The Head of an Oxford college, in speaking of the Group, had described it as "a traveling League of Nations." To give their maximum message to the city a service was held in the historic Cathedral of St. Pierre, where, from the pulpit which still held the chair of John Calvin, that message was delivered. A Justice from Germany, an Admiral from England, a Doctor of Divinity from America, a Baron from Holland, a Prebendary of an English Cathedral, all gave what God had given them to say, to the hundreds gathered below them, Geneva and Oxford, the two great homes of religious life and learning, linked together by their common King.

Marvelous work was done among the women of Geneva. The message began to raise the feeling of depression and put new hope in place of despair, and God in place of an obstructed human will, and defeated intelligence.

One outstanding result was the case of a journalist well known in France, in the Far East and in America. She writes signed articles dealing with the politics being worked out in Geneva, and these are broadcast over France. The whole poem of her brilliant writings has been cynical, disclosing the general atmosphere found in Geneva, where so often the routine work is carried on all waiting for a roof to fall in.

This woman writer came to her first Group meeting with no belief in what the Group was doing, only to get copy for articles. Also to get material for what she thought was a new effort to sustain the Christ-myth by a group of English and Americans whose self-interest she strongly suspected. She meant definitely to discover the secret of that self-interest and expose it. Instead, she became convinced of its sincerity and reality. She began to attend regularly to get convincing evidence of what was offered, and soon showed that she, too, was personally as much in need as anybody. She talked to several people after the meeting, and next day saw Olive Jones. Following that talk there came an upheaval in her life. She called it a revolution.

Her life had been one long series of tragedies, including alienation from her own family and her husband's family as well. She lost her husband during the War. Gradually she resumed her writing, but with a strong tone of cynicism and despair. God was denied. A bitter sense of life's injustice was the chief motive governing her life. When she faced her sins the restitution to be made appalled her. But as one by one she put things right, each asked its own terrific struggle of surrender, and also, renewed peace and joy. Finally she faced the more difficult issue -- her feeling about her lost a husband and the causes which led to his death. She changed her attitude towards national relations and politics, the chief themes of her writing. This meant surrendering into God's hands all her work, for there was now the possibility that her new views would be unacceptable. Her influence in three countries was tremendous, and though she still continues her writing, it is in a totally different vein. She regularly attends meetings of the newly-formed women's group in Geneva.

As I reached the last page of this book there sat by me at dinner the vicar of a small English Village, who told me some of his experiences in putting Group principles into operation in his parish. He had gone back from a house-party and apologized to his choir for showing irritability toward them, and afterwards he had advised his congregation not to come to Easter Communion until they had first put things straight with their neighbors, as he had done with the choir. Consequently, Group principles are being freely discussed in the village public-house, while children in the church Sunday School listen-in to God during service. Anglo-Catholics and Evangelicals meet together in the Rector's drawing-room and share. And the bells in the belfry, the oldest six-bell set in the country, which have been ringing over the shire since Queen Elizabeth, are appealing to a new spirit of peace and goodwill in his parish.

So much for one English village. What of the towns and cities? Group house-parties and city campaigns are being held so frequently in various parts of Britain that as soon as one ends another is about to begin elsewhere. Men specially need changing, those men unable to conquer the drink habit, people with tangled matrimonial troubles, the man who is "broke," and the rich man suffering from ennui, enjoying the company of consecrated sinners, as well as an infinite variety of religious folk who seek a new fellowship of the Spirit.

The movement is growing rapidly in England. Within a year or two it may have spread throughout the country. It must grow, for it holds the answer to life's riddle, and makes Christianity intelligible to the man in the street.

"These little groups," writes James Douglas, "are spreading

all over the world. . . . They are proliferating cells. They have no churches, no organization. They are vitalizing all the creeds and all the sects.

"Nobody knows how many of these spiritual groups are in existence. There are no known statistics. . . . The process of permeation is going on under the surface of life. The Churches are aware of the silent religious revolution which is being wrought. They are sympathetic. . . . The great renewal of the human spirit for which the world is waiting gathering force secretly and silently. It may before long put new life into the dying forms of religion. It may do for the twentieth century what Wesley did for the eighteenth century. Who knows?"

All round the earth there are bursts of Holy Spirit flame. The new world revival is surely at hand, and coming to us in the same way that Christianity first burst on a Pagan world when Spirit-filled man, accused of being full of new wine, went everywhere witnessing to their experience of a risen Lord.

Chapter Twenty-Four

AS FOR ONE SINNER ONLY

This story of what I saw and did in the Oxford Group is finished. There only remains to be told what the Oxford Group did in me.

Unquestionably Frank and his friends showed me the secret of victory over certain personal problems by which I had been frequently defeated -- problems which were casting a shadow between myself and the God I thought I knew, and which I assumed were too difficult and deep-rooted to be conquered completely.

Had I not discussed those problems frankly with the Oxford Group, as I had never been encouraged to discuss them frankly before, I should know we never have realized the liberal truth of Wesley's line: "He breaks the power of sin."

The Oxford Group showed me in practice what I knew in precept: that "the heart must be at leisure from itself"; and that to share is better than to preach; to lose is really to find; to "let go" is to be held secure; to surrender all is to possess all things.

The Holy Spirit is still quick and powerful, and sharper than a two-edged sword. That God still owns this world and still controls it, although he has let it out to all children, not sometimes, but all times when they are surrendered to His guiding will. That it is safer to gamble on the unsearchable riches than to trust in bank balances.

By really living the life around me, the Oxford Group took me a great step forward in the secret of the living. By continuous daily demonstration they showed me that the only true social life is the Fellowship of the Spirit -- *the social life of eternity*. And that, since God often comes to us through His children, to be unfriendly to another is to recede from God.

Even when the Group irritated me by holding me up to my highest high ideals, I would find for them no worse expletives than those used by dear old Balaam:

"Thou shall l curse whom God hath not cursed? . . . Let me die the death of the righteous, and let my last end be like his."

THE END